S

THE ARGENTINE NOVEL IN THE NINETEENTH
CENTURY

THE ARGENTINE NOVEL IN THE NINETEENTH CENTURY

by

MYRON I. LICHTBLAU, 1925-

HISPANIC INSTITUTE
IN THE UNITED STATES
NEW YORK
1959

Printed in the U.S.A. by
Spanish-American Printing Co., Inc.
New York, N. Y.

I dedicate this work
to my wife Bernice and our son Mark,
to my mother and father,
and to my sister Jacqueline

PREFACE

The purpose of this work is to study the origin of the Argentine novel and its development in the nineteenth century. The starting point is about a decade prior to the middle of the past century, when the first writings of prose fiction appeared; the point of termination is a few years beyond 1900, when the novelistic manifestation of modernism took place in Argentina. In truth, the modernist current, rounding out as it does the nineteenth century, marks a suitable chronological limit for the study.

The scope is comprehensive. My aim is to examine the various stages through which the novel passed, to study both the major and minor novelists, and to consider the literary merit and significance of their works. I set forth the initial plan in New York and engaged in considerable research in that city, but it was obvious at the outset that a systematic and detailed study of the Argentine novel could be developed only by examining firsthand references found in Argentina itself. Through Professor De Onís' recommendation, the Comisión Nacional de Cultura of Argentina granted me a scholarship to pursue an investigation of the national novel. During my seven-month stay in Argentina, from July, 1952, to January, 1953, I gathered together essential information relative to the growth of the novel in the nineteenth century—in particular that information which could not be secured in this country. Accordingly, my work involved the scrutinizing of bibliographical and biographical references; the reading and analyzing of novels; the consulting of newspapers and magazines of the period; and the examining of books of literary criticism and works of social and political background. To acquire this information, I resorted in large measure to the Biblioteca Nacional in Buenos Aires, and in lesser degrees to the Biblioteca

9

del Congreso, the Biblioteca Popular del Municipio, the Biblioteca de la Facultad de Filosofía y Letras de la Universidad de Buenos Aires, the Biblioteca de la Universidad de La Plata, the Biblioteca de San Fernando, the Biblioteca del Museo Mitre, and the Biblioteca del Jockey Club.

I sincerely wish to express my thanks to Professor Federico de Onís, who as head of the Spanish Department of Columbia University guided me inspiringly in the preparation of this study; to Professor Germán Arciniegas, my immediate adviser, under whose direct supervision I obtained the necessary material and wrote the manuscript; to Professor James F. Shearer, whose courses in Spanish Literature provided me with indispensable knowledge and firm concepts; and to all the members of the Spanish Department, whose instruction and example served me well. Furthermore, I am indebted to many librarians of the Biblioteca Nacional and other institutions of Argentina, as well as to a number of book dealers and bibliographers, all of whom cheerfully offered their beneficial assistance during my stay in their country.

Indiana University

TABLE OF CONTENTS

I

THE LAND AND ITS HISTORY

To trace properly the development of the novel in Argentina, it is essential to understand the various elements which make up the particular civilization of that country. Geographical features, types of inhabitants and the history of the nation, with its political, economic and social conditions, are all factors which determined the course that the novel was to run. It is necessary, therefore, to examine briefly some important aspects of Argentine civilization and the environment in which the writers produced their works.

Argentina is the largest Spanish-speaking country in South America, occupying an area approximately one third of that of the United States and stretching 2300 miles from north to south. For such an immense territory the sparse population of about 18,500,000[1] is inadequate to secure maximum material progress. This disproportion between the geographical extension and the number of inhabitants has been and continues to be one of the major problems confronting the nation.

For purposes of classification we may divide the country into three sections—the mountain system, the Mesopotamian region, situated between the Paraná and the Uruguay Rivers, and the plains. Only the plains section necessitates further consideration in this study, since it gives Argentina its distinctive physiographical features.

The plains comprise four separate regions. The enormous central portion forms the pampas, an expanse of level, monotonous land, home of the gaucho. The excellent grasses which cover the surface of the pampas have always been advantageously used for pasture land, as the gaucho's mode of living

---

[1] It is worthwhile at this point to observe the growth of Argentina's population during the nineteenth century: in 1797 - 310,000 people; 1818 - 588,000; 1837 - 615,000; 1856 - 950,000; 1860 - 1,180,000; 1869 - first national census, 1,737,076; 1895 - second national census, 3,954,911; 1914 - third national census, 7,885,237.

strongly depended upon cattle and horses. The sturdy *ombú* is the only tree found on the pampas. Around its huge, shady branches the gaucho constructed his crude home and came to regard the *ombú* as having special significance in his life. Immense beyond comprehension and with nothing but emptiness on all sides, the pampas, nevertheless, provided the gaucho with an important element of unity and distinctiveness, so that as a cultural entity he could form the background of a vital literary production.

The northern part, commonly called the Chaco plains, has a warm climate and is generally characterized by thickly wooded areas which provide an abundance of good timber. Cotton growing and the cultivation of sugar cane are carried on widely in this region. Here also we find the important quebracho industry, which produces the highly valued tannin extract. The third region is the Saline plains, lying between the Chaco and the pampas, so designated because of its abundance of salt. Lastly, south of the Negro River the plains are usually referred to as Patagonia, which is composed largely of cold, arid land. Sheep farming is the principal activity of this region, that includes the territories of Río Negro, Chubut, Santa Cruz, and Tierra del Fuego.

Yet this vast extension of the plains, particularly the pampas, only partially represents what we may call the real Argentina. This designation is more properly applied to Buenos Aires, the political, economic, social, and cultural head of the nation. The modern, industrialized, and fashionable metropolis stands in sharp contrast to the relative backwardness and material insufficiency of the interior regions. The capital, it would seem, selfishly avails itself of the profits accumulated by the rest of the nation. This inequality between the capital and the interior was in part at the root of the struggle between "civilization and barbarism," and influenced the course of conflict between Federalists and Unitarians.

Owing to the favored economic position of Buenos Aires, the government has been confronted with the twofold problem of urging the *porteños* to populate and bring under cultivation the immense barren lands, and of discouraging the interior inhabitants from abandoning their rural homes in search of better opportunities in the overcrowded capital. In a similar vein, one of the major concerns of Argentina's immigration policy is to attract new arrivals to the rural provinces by pointing out to them the favorable aspects of settlement in those sections. The problem is a crucial one, and as long as the interior regions continue to play a secondary role to Buenos Aires, the solution is made doubly difficult.

Some historical considerations merit our brief attention. Until 1776 the land now called Argentina was subordinate to the Spanish government at Lima. In that year, to the Viceroyalties of Peru, Nueva España, and Nueva Granada, Spain added that of Río de la Plata, which was to last until 1810. The extension of the newly formed territory was considerable, for it comprised the areas of present-day Argentina, Uruguay, Paraguay, Bolivia, and small sections of Brazil and Chile. Buenos Aires, the capital, was only a small town, but of great commercial importance because it lay strategically near the mouth of a large river. However, Spain focused her attention upon other regions, such as Mexico and Peru, which by virtue of their abundant mineral resources could supply great material wealth. These lands she populated and developed to reap productive returns. On the other hand, Argentina proper, lacking gold, silver and other precious metals, was quite neglected, notwithstanding her pivotal position in the River Plate Viceroyalty; and for this reason the region remained sparsely settled during the colonial period, a condition which has persisted to the present day. Furthermore, with the absence of precious metals life centered around a basically agrarian economy.

In 1810, an Argentine patriotic movement overthrew the River Plate Viceroyalty and instituted as governing body a *junta* headed by Cornelio de Saavedra. Yet it was not until July 9, 1816, that an official declaration of independence was proclaimed. We need not enter into a narration of the numerous events that occurred during the early years of the Argentine nation. Broadly speaking, the period ranging from 1810 to Rosas' election as governor and captain-general of Buenos Aires in 1829 was one of political floundering, constant internal conflict, and struggles for power. In addition, during these years there were planted the seeds of dissension between Buenos Aires and the provinces, and between Federalism and Unitarianism. The provincial leaders, the *caudillos*, became virtual dictators in their respective regions and vied with one another for supremacy. One man, Juan Manuel de Rosas, stood out amid the welter of political intrigue and was able to impose his will on the nation. The history of Argentina from 1829 to 1852 is the sanguinary story of the rise and fall of this dreaded dictator.

The victory over Rosas in 1852 meant more than a mere military triumph and the termination of a reign of terror. It signified the conclusion of what we may call the era of Argentina in formation; it signified the end of an Argentina liberated from the bonds of Spanish rule, but not yet harmoniously joined as a nation. Despite the harshness and evil of the Dictator, it must be conceded that the Rosas regime did provide the necessary impetus to launch the country on the road to political unity. It is paradoxical that this despotic and restrictive rule should have set in motion the chain of events which culminated in a unified Argentina. Yet the struggle was an arduous one before that unity was achieved, as we shall note in the succeeding paragraphs.

After Rosas' defeat the nation's leaders were faced with the tremendous problem of the political reorganization of the country, and its economic, social, and cultural development. Agrentina was still a nation divided; the rivalry and mutual mistrust between the capital city and the interior provinces loomed more menacing and ruinous than ever. Very naturally was Buenos Aires reluctant to enter into any plan of government which might compel her to relinquish even a fraction of her coveted political advantage, or which might put an end to the virtual monopoly of foreign trade she had so zealously enjoyed under the Tyranny. At the same time the provinces, long suppressed in their political and economic activity, sought

to break the chains of their subordinated position by voicing
their demand for an equitable share in the affairs and prosperity of the nation.   One part of the developing country—
Buenos Aires—struggled doggedly to retain its enviable over-
all supremacy; while the other part—the interior regions—
contended proudly to assert itself and come into its own as a
vital and potent force.

In accordance with the San Nicolás pact of May, 1852,
Argentina was organized as a federation, and General Urquiza, who had just led the Unitarians to victory over Rosas
that past February, assumed the duties of provisional director.
Subsequently, a federal Constitution was drawn up at Santa
Fe and put into effect on May 25, 1853. Urquiza became the
first president of the Argentine Confederation, and the city of
Paraná was selected as the capital. Yet the stubborn province
of Buenos Aires, continuing to entertain the hope of forming
a Unitarian system of government, defiantly rejected the organization and set itself up as an independent State.

It was not until 1860, after its demands were met for suitable
changes in the Constitution, that Buenos Aires agreed to join
the Confederation. However, contention once again rose up
when the province of Buenos Aires insisted upon following
its own method of selecting representatives to Congress, instead of adhering to the national election laws. Civil war again
broke out in Argentina; and in the battle of Pavón on September 17, 1861, Bartolomé Mitre, in command of the forces of
Buenos Aires, ultimately won a victory over the national
troops. Santiago Derqui, elected president of the Confederation
in 1859, resigned his office, and on November 12, 1861, the
national government surrendered its authority. Mitre deemed
it far wiser for the welfare of the nation to continue to recognize the federal Constitution, than to reorganize the country
under a Unitarian form of government controlled by Buenos
Aires. Under the new Congress inaugurated on May 25, 1862,
Mitre was unanimously elected president of a united Argentine
Republic. At long last political unity came to the nation.

Argentina in the years immediately following the Rosas

era—the years of novitiate of the Argentine novel—may be duly characterized as a rutinary, mediocre nation, still half-colonial in its manner, and in truth a far cry from the modern and prosperous country that was to develop within a relatively short time. At his downfall the Dictator left a nation that had to be forged anew along beneficial economic, financial, and political lines. The Urquiza administration, inaugurated in 1853, put into effect a liberal commercial policy. Navigation on the Paraná and the Uruguay Rivers, vital interior arteries of communication, was declared open to ships of all foreign powers. Furthermore, duties on foreign merchandise were greatly reduced, a policy which brought considerably more revenue to the Treasury than that obtained under the restrictive commercial laws of the Tyranny.

Communication and transportation in the early 1850's were extremely limited, and in view of the immense territory over which the nation spread, normal intercourse between the interior provinces and the capital, or among these provinces themselves, was exceedingly difficult. The need to improve this condition was felt acutely, as Argentina embarked on a new, post-Rosas era; and by the late 1860's the country could show for its efforts at least a modicum of success in the construction and operation of railroads and tramways, in telegraph communication, in overseas maritime commerce, and in an efficient and centralized postal service.

Argentina in 1850 still maintained an essentially pastoral economy. Agriculture lagged in favor of the traditional cattle raising, to the extent that it was not before the 1880's that any marked development in this area could be recognized. Progress in agriculture necessitated a land free from the harassment of repeated attacks by bands of savage Indians. Accordingly, this wild indigenous element was gradually driven back to the more remote regions of the nation. The frontier receded with each furious battle, until the last real stronghold of Indian defense finally crumbled in 1879. Significant in the initial phases of the evolution of agriculture was the establishment of hardy colonies of hopeful immigrants, eager to transfer to their new home the industriousness and ability which they had demonstrated in the Old World. In the early 1850's the provinces of Buenos Aires, Córdoba, Entre Ríos, and Santa Fe welcomed to their soil ambitious groups of recently arrived French, Italian, Swiss, and German workers; and by 1870 acres upon acres of fertile Argentine land began to thrive under the careful cultivation of these agricultural communities. It is a significant commentary on the nation's history that the native gaucho, nomadic, carefree, and somewhat lacking in enterprise, should have witnessed how these sturdy and diligent immigrants contributed so vitally to the growth of agriculture.

In other important undertakings the native Argentine had to yield the initiative to foreign groups. To English capital, for example, the country had to turn for the construction of the nation's railroads; to the English again Argentina extended its hand for the establishment of the lucrative sheep-raising industry in the vast regions of Patagonia.

It is thus seen that the young Republic of the 1850's welcomed to its shores thousands of persons from across the Atlantic. The European, largely of Spanish, Italian, French, and German descent, came to constitute a numerically significant and economically vital group of the nation. Unlike such other Latin American States as Mexico, Peru, Colombia or Ecuador, where the Indian race in its many fusions distinctly prevails, Argentina presents a predominantly white population. Only in relatively small numbers are other racial strains found: the *mestizo* element is concentrated mostly in the central provinces; while the aboriginal stock and a very small Negro group remain almost wholly in the north. In essence, Argentina must be understood as a nation of primarily European background—a nation whose inhabitants have come principally from the mother soil of Spain and from several European countries, notably Italy.

We recognize, then, that the pioneers in the field of Argentine fiction—those artists who wrote novels in the years im-

mediately subsequent to Rosas' defeat in 1852—were witnesses
to the initial stages in the development of the Republic. They
started writing novels when Argentina, having just drawn up
a federal Constitution to govern the entire nation, endeavored
to seek out and define clearly its particular and readily discernible characteristics. The victory over Rosas brought forth a re-
vitalized Argentina, and signified the intellectual and emotional liberation of the inhabitants. Under the Dictator's sway
both Federalists and Unitarians lived in a state of constant
tension and misgiving. Their actions were hampered, their
emotions stifled; in short, their existence was one of repression
and insecurity. In such an atmosphere, creative, imaginative
expression was very much limited. After Rosas' defeat, however, Argentines enjoyed relative peace of mind and personal
assurance. Writers, whose desire for expression had been so
long pent up, felt free to cultivate their art and bend their
efforts toward the formation of a national literature.

Yet in these inchoate years of growth in the 1850's and 1860's,
Argentine society, lacking a strong national spirit, a sound
economy, and a stable government, did not present a very
suitable picture for novelistic portrayal. If the Republic in
these early years was without doubt raw and inexperienced,
so too were the pioneer artists upon essaying the field of
fiction. In most cases their novels contained very few original
features with respect to literary techinque, inasmuch as these
writers to a large degree followed the model of well-founded
French romanticists, notably Hugo, Dumas, Sue, and Ponson
du Terrail. Just as the young nation in the process of growth
strengthened its economy and culture with the assistance of
immigrant groups and foreign capital, so the early novelists'
felt the need of converting to their service the methods of
more firmly established literary masters.

Many years were to pass before Argentina could come into
its own as a country possessing either world-wide prestige or
an impressive national novel. Despite a meager start in the
1850's the ambitious Republic, blessed with a highly favorable

territory and endowed with the climatic and physical conditions conducive to growth and progress, achieved noteworthy social and economic advances by the year 1895. In the field of fiction, writers likewise began feebly in the 1850's, but by the turn of the century made recognizable strides by dint of their constant application and their genuine desire to portray Argentina in the course of its development. This process of fictional growth shall be our principal concern in the ensuing chapters.

II

THE BACKGROUND OF THE
ARGENTINE NOVEL

During the colonial period no true novels were written in
Hispanic America.[1] This failure to develop the novel may be
attributed to a variety of causes, among which are the following: 1) The repressive policies of the Inquisition. By legal
decree, the reading, writing, and importation of works of a
fictional nature were forbidden. Although many picaresque
novels and books of knight-errantry did clandestinely reach
the public despite this legislation, the influence of the Inquisition no doubt served to restrain many an imaginative mind
bent on fiction writing; 2) The decline of popular interest
in the Spanish novel by the second decade of the 17th century,
in favor of dramatic literature. In view of the fact that the
conquered territories reflected closely the customs and changing tastes of the mother country, colonial writers hesitated to
cultivate the novel when its vogue was in descent, but turned
their talents towards other literary forms, such as the theater
and poetry; 3) The unsympathetic and negative attitude of
many book dealers in the home land. Since Spanish editorial
houses and retail distributors reaped huge profits from the
sale of native fictional works, they felt no need to seek further
sources of revenue and did little to encourage colonial writers
to undertake the novel; 4) The lack of a deep-rooted social

---

[1] An interesting article on early forms of fiction writing in America is the
following: Pedro Henríquez-Ureña, "Apuntaciones sobre la novela en América," Humanidades, Publicación de la Facultad de Humanidades y Ciencias de
la Educación, Universidad Nacional de la Plata, XV, La Plata, 1927. A more
extended treatment of the entire subject of books in colonial America appears
in the following authoritative work: Irving A. Leonard, Books of the Brave,
Cambridge, Mass., Harvard University Press, 1949. For the considerations
mentioned here concerning the question of the colonial novel, I acknowledge
my indebtedness to Professor Leonard's book.

tradition. The novel, depending extensively upon the inter-play of setting and characters, could not easily be developed in the ill-formed and non-cohesive colonial society.

Although each of these reasons offered above to explain the absence of the colonial novel may be logical and valid, not one is conclusive. Perhaps all of them considered together may provide the most suitable answer. A definitive explanation remains to this day extremely difficult to set forth.[2]

A few works, such as *El carnero*, by the Colombian Juan Rodríguez Freile (1566-1638), *El cautiverio feliz*, by the Chilean Francisco Núñez de Pineda y Bascuñán (1607-1682), and *Los infortunios de Alonso Ramírez*, by the Mexican Carlos de Si-güenza y Góngora (1645-1700), contain many novelistic ele-ments, but cannot be classified as true novels. It was not until 1816, when Fernández de Lizardi published in Mexico *El Periquillo Sarniento*, that Hispanic America received its first real novel.[3] In Argentina, many years were to pass before the nation could acclaim its first genuine novel. We shall trace in this chapter the primary steps in the development of that genre.

1. Initial Prose Works of Imagination as Forerunners of the Novel

Some years before the appearance of the first full-fledged novel in Argentina, several prose works were published which re-vealed in embryonic form definite novelistic tendencies. These productions of an imaginative nature, ranging from a short story to a voyage narration, need to be considered in examining the progress of the novel.

[2] Arturo Torres-Ríoseco further adds in *La novela en la América Hispana,* University of California Publications in Modern Philology, Vol. 21, No. 2, Berkeley, California, 1941, p. 173: "También es posible..... que los pri-meros escritores coloniales, héroes del descubrimiento y la conquista todos ellos, sintieran cierto desdén por las hazañas ficticias de los personajes novelescos y creyeran de más valor los que ellos vivían."

[3] It is important to observe that Fernández de Lizardi furnished Hispanic America with its first three novels—*El Periquillo Sarniento,* 1816, *La Quijo-tita y su prima,* 1818, and *Vida y hechos del famoso caballero D. Catrín de la Fachenda,* 1832.

El matadero. The dark days of the Tyranny provided in-
centive for the first story in Argentine literature—*El matadero,*
by Esteban Echeverría (1805-1851). The work was written
about the year 1838, but political motives prevented its publication at that time, since the story, composed hastily by an
indignant patriot, was a bitter presentation of the bloodthirsti-
ness of the Rosas regime. Many years later, Juan María Gutiérrez found the rough draft of *El matadero* among Echeverría's papers and included the work in *La Revista del Río
de la Plata,* 1871.[4] In Gutiérrez' critical review he states:

> Estas pájinas no fueron escritas para darse a la
> prensa tal cual salieron de la pluma que las trazó,
> como lo prueban la precipitación y el desnudo
> realismo con que están redactadas.[5]

The story takes place in a slaughterhouse in Buenos Aires,
where an innocent Unitarian falls prey to the depravity of a
group of savage Federalists. They first mock, curse, and mal-
treat the youth, and then submit him to a simulated hanging.
Infuriated and convulsive with pain, he fails in a desperate
effort to loosen the ropes that bind him, and dies a horrible
death. The slaughterhouse, symbolic of the brutality of Rosas
and his henchmen, serves as the setting for starkly realistic
scenes that depict the slaying of cattle, the beastlike search for
food by hungry women, and the effrontery and ruthlessness
of the Federalists. The severe realism in *El matadero* stands
in sharp contrast to the highly romantic tone of Echeverría's
poetical works, such as *Elvira, Consuelos,* and *La cautiva.* In
the following account there is evident the descriptive vigor of
the narration:

> Hacia otra parte, entretanto, dos africanas lleva-
> ban arrastrando las entrañas de un animal; allí
> una mulata se alejaba con un ovillo de tripas y res-
> balando de repente sobre un charco de sangre, caía
> a plomo, cubriendo con su cuerpo la codiciada
> presa. Acullá se veían acurrucadas en hilera 400
> negras destegiendo sobre las faldas el ovillo y

⁴ Esteban Echeverría, *El matadero*, in *La Revista del Río de la Plata*, B.A.,
Imprenta de Mayo, 1871, I, 563-585.
⁵ *Ibid.,* p. 557, foreword.

arrancando uno a uno los sebitos que el avaro cu-
chillo del carnicero había dejado en la tripa como
rezagados, al paso que otras vaciaban panzas y ve-
gigas y las henchían de aire de sus pulmones para
depositar en ellas, luego de secas, la achura.[6]

Echeverría employs with pronounced effect certain popular
Argentine terms, such as *achuras, cajetilla, che, ño Juan, pialar,
tongorí,*[7] and others of more offensive tone. The use of this
familiar vernacular, at times daring in its rawness, is particularly suitable to the coarseness of the atmosphere and enhances
the vividness and force of the story.

For the harsh, realistic, undaunted narration, painful in its
candidness, noble in its sincerity, *El matadero* holds a merited
place as the first of many fictional prose writings which treat
of the Tyranny.

The Prose Fiction of Juan María Gutiérrez. The eminent
Argentine critic, Juan María Gutiérrez (1809-1878), published
in *El Iniciador de Montevideo,* June, 1838, *El hombre hormiga,
artículo sobre costumbres de Buenos Aires en 1838,*[8] a work
which attempts a rudimentary character analysis of a fictional
type. In its five pages the article reveals satirically the objectionable traits of that class of individual, the *hombre hormiga,*
whose habits and instincts resemble those of an ant. The hustle
and turmoil of a crowded street are compared to the incessant
activity of the ant community, while the constant desire of
the *hombre hormiga* to hoard money is similar to an ant's
storing of supplies for the winter. Even as a child this person
had a miserly preoccupation with money; meaningfully the
author states that at school he was successful in arithmetic, but

---

[6] *Ibid.,* p. 572.

[7] *achuras* - guts; *cajetilla* - a dandy; *che* - an interjection, commonly used to
call attention to a person; *ño Juan* - shortened form of *señor; pialar* - to bind
an animal by the feet; *tongorí* - guts.

[8] The work reappeared many years later in *La Revista del Río de la Plata,*
B.A., 1872, IV, 387-391. It was also published in Instituto de Literatura Argentina, Facultad de Filosofía y Letras de la Universidad de Buenos Aires, sección de documentos, serie 4, tomo I, No. 2, B.A., 1928. The publications of
the Instituto de Literatura Argentina were under the general direction of Ricardo Rojas. The series designated "Orígenes de la novela" represents the first
endeavor to classify and divulge those works which form the initial phases in
the development of the Argentine novel, and includes several titles which we
shall subsequently consider.

in nothing else. Thus, in his mature years he devised ingenious schemes to acquire his coveted wealth. Gutiérrez mentions other censurable qualities of the *hombre hormiga*—his unscrupulousness, hypocrisy, and indifference to everything not related to his personal satisfaction. Undeveloped and unsubstantial as the work may be, it is interesting as an early example of imaginative prose literature, where is manifested the desire to illustrate traits of a fictional character by means of appropriate description.

In 1843 Gutiérrez wrote *El capitán de Patricios,*[9] a long story of definite romantic tone, which appeared originally in serial form in *El Correo del Domingo* of Buenos Aires from April 3 to April 17, 1864.[10] The thinly developed story, set in the colonial Buenos Aires of 1811, centers around the idyllic romance of a proud girl and a courageous Argentine soldier. Gutiérrez, too academic and erudite, guided more by his intellect than by his emotions, could do no more than present a cold, artificial, insipid atmosphere peopled by characters lacking originality and vividness. The heroine plays the role of the beautiful maiden and the captain is the valiant hero, who remains nameless to add to the indefiniteness of the story. Despite its shortcomings, *El capitán de Patricios* possesses a tone of moral elevation and spiritual beauty in accord with the life of the author. Often mixed with rhetorical touches, the tender words of the heroine, her father, and the captain reveal a nobleness of heart and an honesty of living. On one occasion, the girl remarks to her meddling and intolerant uncle, who selfishly objects to her marrying a military man:

> Antes que a Vd. tuve por maestro al corazón,
> el cual siempre se sublevó dentro de mí en pre-

---

[9] During a trip to Europe in 1843 Gutiérrez spent some time in a country home in a valley of the Piedmont Alps. In the preface to the original publication of the story in *El Correo del Domingo,* 1864, it is stated that a distinguished lady of this house requested Gutiérrez to note in her album his impressions of the site. This album was exquisitely adorned with splendid paintings and poetry of illustrious Italian masters, and from sheer modesty Gutiérrez was reluctant to have his own verses appear in the same volume. Yet desiring somehow to satisfy the lady's wishes, he wrote in prose *El capitán de Patricios.*

[10] The same year the work was published in book form, B.A., 1864, with an autographical letter and dedication to Bartolomé Mitre. In 1874 the work appeared in *La Revista del Río de la Plata,* 1874, IX, 3-60. It was also published in Instituto de Literatura Argentina, *op. cit.,* 1928, serie 4, tomo I, No. 3.

sencia de las cosas vulgares y de los hombres ma-
terializados.[11]

Gutiérrez indicates his dedication to learning upon evoking
the memory of Fray Cayetano Rodríguez,[12] poet and theolo-
gian, and Pedro Fernández,[13] professor of rhetoric and Latin
at the Colegio de San Carlos. The author's fervent patriotism
is illustrated not only in the selection of a brave member of the
proud Patricios Regiment as hero of the story, but also in conversations held among the characters concerning the progress
of the Revolution.

El capitán de Patricios is the first prose work in Argentine
literature where the desire to tell a story is predominant, above
and beyond political and social considerations, and which exhibits an interplay of emotions and conflicts among several
characters. For the first time an author interweaves, although
in an extremely undeveloped form, a series of connected scenes
to produce a complete unit. *El matadero* likewise tells a story,
but intense and cogent as it is, it still remains a mere episode,
one incident in the life of an unfortunate Unitarian. In *El
capitán de Patricios* the succession of events occasions several
inner struggles. The heroine clashes with the opinions of her
dogmatic uncle over the selection of a mate, and has to choose
between letting the captain go off to battle or accepting him
as a husband without his having fulfilled his patriotic mission.
The captain, for his part, is torn between true love and sacred
duty, and makes his decision only after considering his sweetheart's wishes. Thus, two elements in *El capitán de Patricios*
—the beginning of a real plot and cross relationships among
characters—mark important steps in the progress of the Argentine novel and place the work beyond the category of a fragmentary novelistic attempt.

Cartas a Genuaria. There appeared in 1840 an interesting

[11] *El capitán de Patricios*, in *El Correo del Domingo*, op. cit., April 17, 1864,
p. 244.
[12] Cayetano Rodríguez (1761-1823), Franciscan, taught philosophy and
theology at the University of Córdoba, and then became the tutor of Mariano
Moreno. He took an active part in the struggle for Argentine independence
and achieved fame as a journalist and poet of patriotic verses.
[13] Pedro Fernández earned a notable reputation as an inspiring teacher.
Among his disciples were Vicente F. López, Bernardino Rivadavia and Esteban
de Luca.

work by Marcos Sastre (1809-1887) entitled *Cartas a Genua-ria.*[14] Born in Montevideo, Sastre played a prominent part in Argentine affairs. Bibliographer, book dealer, and journalist, he was one of the founders of the *Salón literario* (1835), which so greatly abetted the young literary generation. Also, he held many important positions in education. His literary fame rests largely with *El Tempe argentino* (1858), a geographical essay of notable descriptive merit.

In *Cartas a Genuaria,* composed entirely in epistolary form, an abject husband (the author himself) directs tender words to his absent wife Genuaria, speaking sorrowfully of his lone-liness and expressing views on such themes as morality, society, and immortality. For its presentation of states of emotion, couched at times in exalted language, the work contains the germ of subsequent sentimental novels which were popular in Argentine fiction during the 1850's and 1860's.

Tobías o la cárcel a la vela. The initial prose works of ima-gination assumed varied forms and treated the most diverse themes. A voyage narration in novelistic style, entitled *Tobías o la cárcel a la vela,* originated from the fertile mind of the famed legislator and political theorist, Juan Bautista Alberdi (1810-1884).[15] Written in 1844,[16] the work was not published until 1851, when it appeared as a serial for *El Mercurio,* a news-paper of Valparaiso.[17] Alberdi recounts a journey made by Bonnivard (representing the author himself) from Brazil, around Cape Horn, to Valparaiso. The ship on which he trav-els, the *Tobías,* operates under very poor conditions— the con-struction is faulty, the crew is inefficient, food and water are not fit for consumption, and living quarters are unbearable.

---

[14] The title page reads *Cartas a Genuaria,* B.A., 1840. The work appeared anonymously, but the authorship is clearly revealed by the content of the letters.

[15] The life of Alberdi will be treated in a later chapter, when we deal with his novel *Peregrinación de Luz del Día,* 1871.

[16] In the preface to the work, in the form of a letter to Admiral Manuel Blanco Encalada, dated Valparaiso, August, 1851, Alberdi states that the nar-ration was written on the high seas in April, 1844.

[17] Subsequently the work was published in *Obras completas de Juan Bau-tista Alberdi,* B.A., Imprenta de La Tribuna Nacional, 1886, II, 345-385. Many years later it appeared in *Obras selectas de Juan Bautista Alberdi,* ed. Joaquín V. González, B.A., Librería La Facultad de J. Roldán, 1920, I, 177-230. It also appears in Instituto de Literatura Argentina, *op. cit.,* 1930, serie 4, tomo I, No. 11.

During the voyage in the loathsome ship Bonnivard suffers all
sorts of inconveniences and deprivations, so that upon his
arrival at Valparaiso he exclaims:

> He pasado 70 días en este buque sepulcral, en
> este ataúd flotante, solo, sin hablar, sin comer, sin
> sentir, sin tener deseos, conciencia ni esperanza de
> nada; luego yo no debo estar vivo; y contra este
> raciocinio nadie podría persuadirse de que lo esté.[18]

Outraged by the sickening conditions on the *Tobías*, Alberdi
nicknames the ship *La cárcel a la vela*, and to one of her passengers he meaningfully gives the name of Bonnivard, a real
person who was once a prisoner in the Chillon castle in Switzerland. At the close of the work Alberdi relates his visit to
Bonnivard's cell in 1843, and expresses his consternation at the
living tomb:

> Seis minutos quedé en aquel lugar destemplado,
> y salí con escalofríos. ¡Cómo soportaría allí Bon-
> nivard seis años![19]

The slight story lacks sustained action and unity of thought.
Interspersed throughout the forty-odd pages are many details
concerning navigation, climate, racial groups, countries, and
customs, which although not entirely extraneous to the work,
tend to make the narration diffuse and the interest uneven.
Short but apt colorful descriptions of the Plata River, Patagonia, Cape Horn, and Chile indicate a rudimentary effort to
delineate the physical atmosphere in which a story progresses.

2. THE FIRST SHORT NOVEL: *La quena*

The development of fiction advanced a step further with the
appearance in 1845 of *La quena,* by Juana Manuela Gorriti
(1819-1892).[20] This work may be classified as the first short

---

[18] *Tobías o la cárcel a la vela,* 1886 edition, *op. cit.,* p. 380.
[19] *Loc. cit.*
[20] We have thought it advisable to treat of the life of Gorriti in a later chapter, when we consider in detail the totality of her novelistic production. For
the present, we have isolated *La quena* and dealt with it separately, owing to
its chronological importance and particular significance in the progress of the
Argentine novel.

novel written by an Argentine author. It was originally published in *La Revista de Lima* in 1845, and appeared again in 1865 in *Sueños y realidades*,[21] a collection of various fictional prose writings of Gorriti. Although the action is unfolded in colonial Peru and contains no Argentine elements, its proper place in the chronology of the novel should not be overlooked. *La quena* is of brief extension, but its ample conception, diversity of action, and treatment of characters are beyond the category of a short story, and place the work within the province of the novel.

The title of the work refers to a kind of small flute which emits a very mournful and somber sound. In the Quichuan language, *quena* signifies "remorse from love"; and the protagonist, disillusioned in love, enters the priesthood and eternally plays that instrument as a sign of his bereavement. The atmosphere of *La quena* is vague and unreal, as secrecy, darkness, and strange happenings veil the action of the work. Through her power of narration, Gorriti succeeds in creating a romantic mood of mystery and haziness. The plot lacks a well-knit construction and the characters are as indefinite and artificial as the setting in which they move.

That the first short novel written by an Argentine takes place in a foreign land, and not in Argentina, is significant. In 1845, when *La quena* was published in Lima, Argentina offered little material or opportunity for imaginative writing. The Tyranny was in full terror, and the people lacked not only a cultural heritage, but a sentiment of belonging and a consciousness of their nation as a unit. Gorriti, a writer with a fertile imagination and great narrative skill, sought an inspiring background to set her talents to work. She lived some years in Peru and grew to admire the beauty and dignity of the Inca tradition. The legends, customs, and beliefs of the Peruvians, and the associated elements of awe, mystery, and the unknown afforded suitable material for her vivid imagination. Thus, Gorriti wrote *La quena,* in which she reveres the glory of colonial Peru.

---

[21] Juana Manuela Gorriti, *La quena,* in *Sueños y realidades,* ed. Vicente G. Quesada, B.A., Imprenta de Mayo, 1865, I, 3-67.

3. THE NOVELS OF JUANA MANSO DE NORONHA

Many of the initial works of fiction written by Argentine writers remain quite unknown to this day. Such is the fate of the two novels of Juana Manso de Noronha (1820-1875), a notable educator and journalist. Her efforts may be examined in *Los misterios del Plata* (1846), a black portrayal of the Rosas epoch, and *La familia del comendador* (1854), a romantic work laid in Brazil.

Born in 1820 in Buenos Aires, at an early age Juana Manso emigrated with her parents to Río de Janeiro to escape the Tyranny. In that city she later married a Brazilian violinist named Noronha. After the defeat of the Dictator she returned to the Argentine capital, where she actively participated in many cultural affairs and earned a solid reputation as one of the outstanding women of her time. A close friend of Sarmiento, she dedicated herself assiduously to a career in teaching and held important positions in that profession. Manso was an indefatigable writer whose published works embrace many literary genres. Some of her verses composed in the early 1840's appear in an unpublished collection of American poetry gathered together by Juan María Gutiérrez.[22] In 1862 she published *Un compendio de historia de las Provincias Unidas del Río de la Plata*, a popular work which passed through many editions. Death came to Juana Manso in Buenos Aires on April 24, 1875.

The first novel of Juana Manso, *Los misterios del Plata*, was written in 1846, but there remain certain problems concerning the original publication of the book. The earliest edition that exists is that of 1899,[23] in which appear two interesting footnotes. One is by the author (she evidently appended it to the work many years after she had written it), in which she states that this historical romance was published before

---

[22] Juan María Gutiérrez, *Colección de poesías americanas, antiguas y modernas; impresas, manuscritas y autógrafas, por orden alfabético del apellido de los autores,* unpublished, n.d. This work is found in the Biblioteca del Congreso in Buenos Aires, in a special section containing the personal library of Gutiérrez.

[23] Juana Manso de Noronha, *Los misterios del Plata,* B.A., Imprenta de los Mellizos, 1899.

the fall of Rosas.[24] This edition has not been found, nor has
any reference been made to it, and we thus assume that the
novel never circulated among the people. The second note,
by the editor, states that the manuscript from which this
1899 edition was taken was not finished and had to be terminated by another writer.[25] Admitting that the work was
published before 1852 (but never reached the public and is
now lost), we have to conclude that this manuscript is not
the original, but one revised by Manso, wherein is contained
her note to which we referred. In 1924 another edition of the
novel appeared,[26] which, except for a few minor alterations
in language, follows that of 1899.

Juana Manso explains in the preface the selection of the
title _Los misterios del Plata,_ affirming that she intends to
imitate neither _Les mystères de Paris_ of Eugène Sue, nor the
Mysteries of London, an anonymous work,[27] but rather to
expose the contemporary political situation in Argentina, which
is so inadequately understood by the rest of the world. With
indignation she states:

> Mi país, sus costumbres, sus acontecimientos
> políticos y todos los dramas espantosos de que
> sirve de teatro ha ya tantos años, son un misterio
> para el mundo civilizado.
>
> Misterios negros como el abismo, casi increíbles
> en esta época y que es necesario que aparezcan a
> la luz de la verdad para que el crimen no pueda
> llevar por más tiempo la máscara de la virtud.[28]

[24] "El héroe de este romance histórico es don Valentín Alsina; como se pu-
blicase antes de la caída de Rosas, se hizo uso del seudónimo de Avellaneda
para perpetuar el mártir de Tucumán." _Ibid.,_ p. 21, note of Juana Manso.

[25] "Hasta aquí llegó en su manuscrito la autora. Quedando trunca la obra,
el editor la ha terminado, de acuerdo con las indicaciones de una persona com-
petente y conocedora de nuestra historia nacional, a fin de conservar, en lo posible, el carácter de novela histórica que tiene este trabajo. Se ha tratado, también, de conservar el estilo de la autora." _Ibid.,_ p. 203, note of the editor.
This edition of 1899 has 224 pages; thus, relatively few pages had to be added
to the manuscript.

[26] Juana Manso de Noronha, _Los misterios del Plata, episodios históricos de
la época de Rosas, escritos en 1846,_ ed. Ricardo Isidro López Muñiz, B.A.,
Casa editora de J. Menéndez e hijo, 1924.

[27] _The Mysteries of London,_ and _Stranger's Guide,_ publ. Cunningham, 1844.
This title appears cited in _The English Catalogue of Books Published from
January, 1835, to January, 1863,_ London, 1863, p. 547.

[28] _Los misterios del Plata,_ 1899 edition, _op. cit.,_ preface.

Manso chose a prominent citizen of the epoch, and around his constant conflicts with the Federalists constructed a loose plot, historical not only as regards major incidents, but also with respect to details and secondary characters. The central figure is a loyal Unitarian, Dr. Avellaneda, who is in reality the brave statesman Valentín Alsina. This self-sacrificing protagonist is consistently depicted as an upright, zealous defender of civil and political liberties, who struggles so that his compatriots may live free from oppression and persecution. Avellaneda is the incarnation of the loyalty and tenacity of the brave Unitarians who upheld their cause until victory was theirs.

The varied nature of Avellaneda's experiences—exile in Montevideo, return to Argentina, capture, plans of escape, and eventual freedom—lends itself to the introduction of many minor characters who add color and vividness to the story. Particularly significant is the portrayal of a primitive gaucho. Representative of the traditional nomad of the pampas, he prefers a simple, unaffected way of life. Bred in an atmosphere of crudeness and self-sufficiency, he cherishes his freedom above most things, and it is only for reasons of convenience that he becomes a follower of Rosas. Humbly, the gaucho says:

> Criado en el campo, viviendo siempre en el desierto, a nadie conozco y sirvo al gobernador porque es el único que me ha hecho algunos bienes, y a él le debo mi caballo, mi apero, y siempre me está haciendo regalitos.[29]

Nevertheless, his innate sense of justice and humanity causes him to betray the Dictator and give aid to Avellaneda.

In addition to the portraiture of fictitious persons, Manso presents, in a manner clearly revealing her detestation of everything connected with the Tyranny, many descriptions of influential members of the Rosas government, such as the odious Corbalán, the Dictator's aide-de-camp. The denunciation of Rosas' barbaric crimes is sustained at every step of the work. Manso attacks the *mazorca,* describes its insidious schemes, and

[29] *Ibid.,* pp. 79-80.

satirizes its officers; and by means of subjective remarks and carefully inserted details she makes the over-all tone of *Los misterios del Plata* one of bitter and unrelenting censure.

Juana Manso's residence in Brazil offered inspiration for her second novel, *La familia del comendador*,[30] published in Buenos Aires in 1854. The story, set in Río de Janeiro, treats in romantic fashion of an aristocratic Brazilian family dominated by an overbearing and self-centered elderly mother. Cruel, unsympathetic, and arbitrary, doña María virtually controls the affairs of the family, and her tyrannical rule is extended to the harsh treatment of the slaves on her land. The conflict reaches crucial proportions when doña María's granddaughter angrily rejects her proposal that she marry her deranged uncle, vowing to leave home rather than submit to such degradation.

Not relating directly to the story, but receiving incidental mention, is the lamentable plight of the Negro slaves in Brazil. Manso's acute awareness of the problem is cogently demonstrated by her sharp criticism of the uncivilized treatment of these shackled people. Most impassionately condemning slavery is the crazed uncle, who attempts to ameliorate the lot of the slaves on his estate, but encounters the censure of the less sympathetic members of his family. Manso is not entirely negative in her approach to the question, but introduces scenes of true understanding. On one occasion, when the heroine's Negro servant girl assists her in fleeing from home, the author remarks:

> . . . .llegadas a la puerta se arrojaron una en los
> brazos de otra; allí no había esclava ni ama, ni

[30] Juana Paula Manso de Noronha, *La familia del comendador*, B.A., Imprenta de J. A. Bernheim, 1854. Prior to the complete publication in book form, the first nine chapters (less than half of the work) appeared in weekly succession from January 1 to February 17, 1854, in *Album de Señoritas*, a literary magazine of Buenos Aires directed by the author herself. On February 17, 1854, she informed the public of the discontinuance of the magazine, owing to her son's death.

The wording and general sentence structure of the finished novel differ somewhat from that which originally appeared in serial form, tending toward a more simplified, direct construction and the suppression of some of the more overwrought and exaggerated romantic passages. For example, in *Album de Señoritas*, January 15, 1854, p. 20, appears the sentence "Al volver a Macacú no le fué ya difícil comprender los arcanos del lúgubre drama que presidiera a su existencia." This she changes to the more direct "De vuelta en Macacú, fácil le fué al mozo penetrar el secreto de su procedencia." (edition of 1854, *op. cit.*, p. 26).

blanca ni negra; había dos mugeres afligidas, cuyos corazones nivelaban el dolor y la amistad.[31]

One Argentine writer, in 1877, compared *La familia del comendador* with Harriet Beecher Stowe's novel, *Uncle Tom's Cabin* (1852), even asserting that it is an imitation of it.[32] Actually, the similarity between the two works is slight, for while *La familia del comendador* does treat the problem of Negro oppression, it does so only in an accessory fashion, without having Negro characters or their conflicts figure principally in the action of the novel. Juana Manso merely mentions the question of slavery; Harriet Beecher Stowe centers her entire novel on the theme.

If we consider *Los misterios del Plata* as a novel arising from the author's reprobation of political and civil injustices, we look upon *La familia del comendador* as a work reflecting her deeply felt ideas of social equality and sensible human values. With the first novel Juana Manso created a work genuinely Argentine, more historical than fictional and based upon incidents of an era through which she herself passed; in the second she employed a foreign setting and narrated a story of pure imagination, treated in the romantic manner of the epoch.

4. The Prose Fiction of Bartolomé Mitre

From the pen of the illustrious Bartolomé Mitre (1821-1906) came two works of fiction—*Soledad* (1847), a romantic novel laid in Bolivia, and *Memorias de un botón de rosa* (1848), an odd, poetic story of pure fantasy.[33] Both pieces were written and originally published outside Argentina, and present in-

---

[31] *La familia del comendador,* edition of 1854, *op. cit.,* p. 73.

[32] Cora Oliva, "Conversaciones literarias—la novela," *La Ondina del Plata,* B.A., July 8, 1877, pp. 311-314. This writer states, p. 313: *"La familia del comendador pasó por nuestro público como La choza de Tom,* saboreadas ambas por los inteligentes, y desconocidas del mayor número de lectores que por falta de discernimiento y buen gusto, sólo se apasionan de novelas corruptoras y detestables."

[33] Mitre's romanticism may also be noted in his dramas *Policarpa Salavarrieta* and *Cuatro épocas,* both written in 1840, as well as in his translation of Hugo's *Ruy Blas,* presented in Montevideo in 1838. It is significant to observe, besides, that four additional plays of Hugo were rapidly translated into Spanish and produced in Montevideo in 1838: *Marion Delorme,* 1831, *Le Roi s'amuse,* 1832, *Lucrèce Borgia,* 1833, and *Angelo,* 1835. With reference to this data on Victor Hugo, I am grateful to Professor Germán Arciniegas for permitting me to consult an unpublished essay of his entitled *Europa vista por Latinoamérica.*

teresting bibliographical material.[34] The first edition of *Soledad* was published in 1847 in La Paz,[35] during Mitre's exile in Bolivia. From July 18 to August 1, 1848, the novel appeared in serial form in *El Comercio de Valparaíso*; and in July of that same year, also in Valparaiso, the second edition was printed. The work was then forgotten until 1907, when Pedro Pablo Figueroa, a Chilean writer, offered it to the public in a volume which also included *Memorias de un botón de rosa*.[36] In later years *Soledad* was republished several times.[37]

One of the earliest commentaries by an Argentine on novel writing in America is that which appeared in the author's prologue to *Soledad*. In it Mitre laments the scarcity of original novelists in South America, advancing two fundamental explanations: first, that the novel, being one of the loftiest expressions of a civilization, cannot be highly developed in countries that are still (1848) in an incipient stage of their culture; secondly, that many critical minds still consider novelistic writing unworthy of literary esteem. Mitre understands the novel as an important instrument in revealing the social and political forces of a nation, and nourishes the hope that writers will soon make known to the world the history and contemporary situation of the South American countries.

> *Soledad* es un debilísimo ensayo que no tiene otro objeto sino estimular a los jóvenes capacitados a que exploten el rico minero de la novela americana. Su acción es muy sencilla, y sus personajes son copiados de la sociedad americana en general.
>
> Al colocar la escena en Bolivia, el autor ha querido hacer una manifestación pública de su gratitud por la agradable acogida que ha merecido en este país.[38]

Soledad is an early example of the romantic novel which was

[34] An informative article dealing with this bibliographical data is the following: Antonio Pagés Larraya, "Las ediciones de *Soledad*," *Logos*, Revista de la Facultad de Filosofía y Letras de la Universidad de Buenos Aires, año II, No. 3, B.A., 1943, pp. 110-114.

[35] Bartolomé Mitre, *Soledad*, La Paz, Imprenta de La Época, 1847.

[36] Bartolomé Mitre, *Memorias de un botón de rosa y Soledad*, ed. Pedro Pablo Figueroa, B.A., G. Kraft, 1907.

[37] The work appears in the following publications: La Novela del Día, B.A., 1921, Vols. 23 and 24; Instituto de Literatura Argentina, *op. cit.*, 1928, serie 4, tomo I, No. 4; Editorial Tor, n.d., Vol. XII.

[38] *Soledad*, 1847 edition, *op. cit.*, pp. iv-v.

to be cultivated fully in the 1850's and 1860's. From the incidents of the plot to the highly exaggerated passions of the characters, to the naïve and idealistic treatment of emotional conflicts, the romanticism is clearly discernible. One critic, Juan Millé y Giménez, states:

> Soledad delata su filiación romántica desde las primeras escenas; pero su romanticismo no corresponde al género histórico, iniciado por Walter Scott...., sino que se manifiesta más bien en una dirección moral y sentimental, con influencias bien manifestadas de Richardson y Rousseau.[39]

An angelic, impressionable, and imaginative girl of nineteen, Soledad is a typical romantic heroine. Successively, she endures an ill-planned marriage which makes her suffer untold mental torments, becomes the victim of a libertine, and finally finds happiness with her honorable cousin, who fights a duel for her honor.

Although the novel does not specifically preach, it is pervaded with a note of the importance of high moral values. The ultimate understanding between Soledad and her middle-aged husband, the sincere repentance and spiritual rebirth of a lascivious youth, the noble conduct of Soledad's cousin—these turns of plot are all indicative of the author's faith in human goodness. Moreover, the whole tone of the novel—revealed in the selection of events, in the dialogue, in the brief interpretation of emotions, and in the descriptions of nature—affirms Mitre's deep belief in the beauty, dignity, and spiritual consolation of good living.

Mitre's second work, *Memorias de un botón de rosa*, was completed in Valparaiso in August, 1848,[40] but the first edition has not been found. However, in a bibliographical study on Chilean literature the story is listed twice, as published in Valparaiso in 1848 and also in 1850.[41] The earliest available

---

[39] *Soledad,* edition of Instituto de Literatura Argentina, *op. cit.,* preface, pp. 91-92.

[40] At the end of the work these words appear: "Valparaíso, agosto de 1848."

[41] Ramón Briseño, *Estadística bibliográfica de la literatura chilena,* Santiago de Chile, Imprenta Chilena, 1862, 2 vols. In Vol. I, p. 237, there appears the following title: *Lenguaje de las flores i colores, con una novela orijinal titulada: Memorias de un botón de rosa,* Valparaíso, 1848. In Vol. II, p. 439, there appears this title: *Nuevo lenguaje de las flores i colores, con una novela orijinal titulada: Memorias de un botón de rosa,* Valparaíso, 1850.

publication is that which appeared in serial form in *La Mariposa*, a semi-monthly newspaper of Valparaiso, on February 5 and 20, 1864. As in the case of *Soledad*, the work was then forgotten until Pedro Pablo Figueroa edited it in Buenos Aires in 1907. Subsequently the Instituto de Literatura Argentina[42] published the story.

Memorias de un botón de rosa centers around the reminiscences of a once lovely rosebud, now dead and lying between pages of an album. In the introductory lines there is expressed the thought that beautiful things like the rosebud are most unfortunate, since so often they serve merely to flatter and adorn. Then as soon as their loveliness fades, they are forgotten forever.

What is most important in this fanciful work is the charming and tender manner of humanizing the rosebud, of endowing it with real emotions and sentiments, without producing a ludicrous effect. With a simplicity and lucidness of style, the author captures the perennial beauty of the rosebud and vivifies its imagined thoughts and feelings, its sufferings and torments. There is gentle compassion and warm sympathy for the misfortunes of this rosebud that assumes such lifelike qualities.

In *Memorias de un botón de rosa*, as in *Soledad*, Mitre reveals his interest in moral issues of life—truth, faith, beauty, and contentment. In a certain respect, the life of a rosebud may be compared to that of many individuals who see supreme happiness turn to infinite sadness, or to the grief of those who see themselves disregarded once their usefulness is passed. At the close of the work the rosebud, lying in a girl's album as a mere memory, comes upon her personal sentiments about flowers. She feels her existence closely identified with that of the rosebud, which in its mute way says so much and creates such unbounded happiness. Nature is beautiful, harmonious and inspiring, and its flowers lift our hearts and invigorate our spirits!

---

[42] Bartolomé Mitre, *Memorias de un botón de rosa,* in Instituto de Literatura Argentina, *op. cit.,* 1930, serie 4, tomo I, No. 9.

5. The Extensive Influence of *Facundo*

Although not classified as a novel, *Facundo,* one of the most widely read Argentine books of the nineteenth century, exerted an influence on every literary genre. Domingo Faustino Sarmiento (1811-1888), one of the most outstanding statesmen that Argentina has ever produced, wrote the work during his exile in Chile as a vehement protest against the Tyranny. The first edition of *Facundo* appeared in Santiago in July, 1845,[43] and since then has enjoyed an overwhelming success not only in Argentina, but throughout America and even Europe, being edited frequently and translated into several languages. Its appeal is far-reaching, for it is read not solely by the learned class, but by all who desire a penetrating interpretation of political and social forces in Argentina.

Owing to Sarmiento's impulsive and highly energetic personality, *Facundo* emerged as more than a limited biography of Juan Facundo Quiroga, and developed into a historical-sociological essay on Argentina from 1810 to 1845. The initial chapters of *Facundo* describe the physical features of the country, its inhabitants, the customs and modes of living around which the people shape their existence, and the ideas which form their philosophy. Sarmiento colorfully depicts the pampas, delineates various types, such as the *rastreador, baqueano, cantor,* and *gaucho malo,* and graphically portrays the typical place of reunion, the *pulpería.* There follows the life of Quiroga—his military career and rise to political prominence, his ruthlessness and lack of moral integrity in the execution of his office, the political and military events in which he figures, and his assassination. Interspersed throughout the biography and continued in subsequent chapters appears a comprehensive analysis of the contemporary Argentine scene, in which Sarmiento pens a venomous attack against Rosas. Historic personages are brought to the fore and their roles in molding the

[43] Domingo Faustino Sarmiento, *Civilización i barbarie—Vida de Juan Facundo Quiroga, i aspecto físico, costumbres, i ábitos de la república arjentina,* Santiago, Imprenta del Progreso, 1845. The work was introduced to the public for the first time as a serial of *El Progreso,* a Chilean newspaper, on May 2, 1845.

nation's destiny are explained. Vivid anecdotes and discerning observations are included, and numerous references to European and world affairs are made, especially as they affect Argentine conditions in this era. The concluding chapters of the work look toward the future, when it is hoped that Argentina, liberated from tyrannical government, will reconstruct its political and economic framework, and will hold its place among the free and liberal nations of the world.

Composed originally as a serial publication, *Facundo* lacks a unified plan. Sarmiento's enthusiasm and desire to make the work as comprehensive as possible may account for the discontinuity and diffuseness of some parts, especially when the author refers to involved historical events. However, what gives *Facundo* its warm appeal to a vast public is the spontaneity of narration, naturalness of expression, and sustained vigor of presentation. *Facundo* is real, palpable and moving, the fruit of a patriot's efforts to help the cause of political freedom.

Of paramount importance in *Facundo* is the association of Quiroga with the social and political atmosphere in which he lived. Sarmiento observes that he was a direct product of his environment, for his ideas and actions matched perfectly the rude mode of existence that surrounded him from infancy. The words *civilización y barbarie* are thus extremely significant and constitute a recurrent theme of the book. Quiroga fully represents *barbarie* in his rural crudeness and ignorance; Buenos Aires typifies *civilización* in its social advancement, cultivation of good taste, and correctness of manner. The clash of these two basic conceptions occasioned to a large measure the truculent civil war, and the temporary triumph of the Tyranny signified the victory of *barbarie* over *civilización*.

Facundo, as we have said, cannot be considered a novel, even in the broadest sense of the term. Its importance in our study, nevertheless, stems from several considerations. First, it is conceived almost in the fashion of a novel. "Confieso que nunca leí novela que me interesase como *Facundo*,"[44] states

---

[44] Rufino Blanco-Fombona, *Grandes escritores de América, siglo XIX*, Madrid, Renacimiento, 1917, p. 90.

Rufino Blanco-Fombona. Sarmiento moves the reader by a gripping narration of events centering around an interesting protagonist, as well as by an animated portrayal of secondary characters and occurrences which impinge upon the actions of the main figure. The conflict between *civilización* and *barbarie*, the bitter struggle for ascendancy among the *caudillos*, and the battle between Unitarians and Federalists, all contribute to form the colorful background against which is related the intense drama of internal strife. Secondly, *Facundo* was read and absorbed by later novelists, many of whose works revolve around ideas and incidents similar to those touched upon by Sarmiento. Thirdly, the work contains much descriptive material on the physical characteristics of Argentina, a feature that reveals the author's keen awareness of the significant relationship between setting and character. Lastly, the germ of the gaucho novel, in particular the dramatization of the clash between the nomadic dweller of the pampas and the uncompromising authorities, can be glimpsed from many passages depicting rural life and from accounts of Quiroga's activities.

. . .

Upon examining as a whole these early productions of fiction, we find that they fall into several classes. First, inasmuch as the precursory novelistic period was contemporary with the Tyranny, it is natural that some works reflected the conditions of the epoch and aimed to censure the Rosas government. The three works in this first group, *El matadero, Facundo,* and *Los misterios del Plata,* all written prior to the defeat of Rosas, were audacious attempts to aid with the pen the noble endeavors of valiant soldiers. A few years later, this series depicting the Tyranny reached its highest novelistic expression in *Amalia.*

Secondly, far from the irate cries of condemnation expressed in the preceding pieces, is a group of works exemplifying the romanticism of the era. *Soledad* and *El capitán de Patricios* represent the sentimental, lachrymose phase of the romantic trend; *La quena* illustrates the lugubrious and mysterious aspect; and *La familia del comendador* typifies the romantic taste for unusual, bizarre incidents. As narrations of pure caprice we may place in a third group *El hombre hormiga* and *Memorias de un botón de rosa*, written in lighter moments in the agitated lives of Gutiérrez and Mitre. Lastly, as isolated literary expressions of the versatile talents of Sastre and Alberdi stand *Cartas a Genuaria* and *Tobías o la cárcel a la vela*.

Two other observations relative to these precursory works may be mentioned. First, except for the Rosas theme, Argentina itself did not offer in this era sufficiently attractive material for writers of fiction, who consequently had to seek their inspiration elsewhere. Thus, it is significant that almost all of the more fully developed works of this period are of foreign setting—*La quena, Soledad,* and *La Familia del comendador*. Secondly, nearly all of the writers of these preliminary works were important national figures, either in the political or literary field. Echeverría, Sastre, Gutiérrez, Alberdi, Mitre, and Sarmiento figured among the leading personalities of their day and enjoyed considerable prestige before their fictional work appeared.

III

AMALIA AND THE ROSAS ERA
IN FICTION

The critics and public alike have long agreed that the first Argentine novel is *Amalia,* by José Mármol. The assertion is true if we qualify the term "Argentine novel," applying it only in a restricted sense, as solely referring to a work which is set in Argentina and has an Argentine theme. To explain this statement further it is necessary to consider again a few of the novels treated in the preceding chapter.

The first volume of *Amalia* was published in Montevideo in 1851,[1] one year before Rosas' defeat; the completed novel, consisting of two volumes, appeared in Buenos Aires in 1855.[2] If by the term "Argentine novel" we understand any novel written by an Argentine author, then *La quena,* published in 1845, *Los misterios del Plata,* composed in 1846, and *Soledad,* published in 1847, definitely precede *Amalia.*

In the case of *Los misterios del Plata,* certain bibliographical uncertainties prevent it from being regarded as the first Argentine novel. As we have seen, the work was written in 1846 and published, according to Juana Manso's own statement, before the fall of Rosas. This first edition has never been found, nor has any reference been made to it in newspapers or magazines. We are led to believe, therefore, that the work probably never reached the public, but was withdrawn from circulation for political reasons.

Concerning *La quena* and *Soledad,* several reasons may be offered to explain why neither of the two works is classified as the first Argentine novel. In the first place, both are completely

---

[1] José Mármol, *Amalia,* Vol. I, Montevideo, 1851.
[2] José Mármol, *Amalia,* Vols. I and II, B.A., Imprenta Americana, 1855.

devoid of Argentine elements, such as setting, characters and
ideas (*La quena* takes place in Peru, *Soledad* in Bolivia). Furthermore, the works were originally published in foreign
countries and did not reach the Argentine public until many
years later. *La quena* first appeared in a magazine in Lima in
1845, but it was not brought out in book form in Buenos Aires
until 1865; *Soledad* originally appeared in La Paz in 1847, but
not until 1907 was it published in the Argentine capital. If
either *La quena* or *Soledad* had met at the outset with re-
sounding success and had been recognized as a work of excellent merit, it would probably have been regarded as the first
Argentine novel, in spite of the fact that it contained no
Argentine elements. However, inasmuch as the works remained long forgotten by all and even after being revived were
judged as mediocre, rather elementary novels, with neither
outstanding literary qualities nor a significant social or political
background, they have been disregarded in considering the
exact chronology of the Argentine novel.[3]

The Argentines wished to present to the world as the first
rung in the ladder of novelistic productions a meritorious
work of undeniable Argentine savor, replete with elements
unmistakably Argentine—in short, a distinctly national novel.
Amalia fitted perfectly. Upon its appearance in Buenos Aires
in 1855, it was received with wide public acclaim, being heralded as a work that embodied the soul of a new Argentina. For
the first time Argentines read and discussed a novel which
centered around their country and which they could proudly
designate as their own. In view of the preceding considerations, we state that *Amalia* stands as the first full-fledged
novel of Argentine setting that reached the vast public.

José Mármol was born in Buenos Aires on December 2, 1817.
In 1839, while still a student in law school, he was imprisoned
as a result of his overt opposition to Rosas. Upon his release

---

[3] It should not be inferred from the reasoning set forth above that in the
category of an Argentine novel, a French novel, or a Spanish novel, we include
solely those works which deal specifically with the particular country concerned.
Salammbo is no less a French novel than *L'Assommoir*, merely because it treats
of the distant land of Carthage. Similarly, *La quena* and *Soledad* are no less
Argentine novels than *Amalia*.

he felt no inclination to continue his studies and in 1840 fled
to Montevideo, where he fraternized with noted political exiles
in whom he found a strong bond of interest. Through his
journalistic and literary work Mármol acquired a solid reputation as a staunch defender of justice and freedom. He founded
El Álbum, El Conservador and *La Semana,* and joined the
staff of the newspapers *El Comercio* and *El Nacional.* Mármol
was intensely active in Montevideo, to such an extent that almost all of his literary production—poetry, plays, criticism,
novel, and biography—was published in that city. With the
defeat of the Dictator in 1852, Mármol returned to Argentina
and began an active career in government, which culminated
in his election to the Senate. Moreover, his prestige as a distinguished man of letters gained for him the position of director of the Biblioteca Nacional of Buenos Aires. Mármol died
in the capital on August 9, 1871.

His life was dedicated to the struggle for political liberty.
His deeply inspired poems, such as *El peregrino,* placed him
among the most representative of the "poets of exile." The
publication of *Amalia* added another link to the impressive
chain of patriotic works which honored the name of José Mármol.

In a candid article appearing in *El Paraná* on October 25,
1852,[4] Mármol presents interesting bibliographical material
concerning *Amalia.* He declares that although arrangements
had been made for the appearance of the complete novel in
serial form in *El Paraná,* and notice to that effect had been
given to the public, a group of notable citizens thwarted the
plans on the grounds that the work might occasion too much
political disfavor and controversy. Mármol sums up the situation in these words:

> ....*Amalia* es un ataque demasiado violento al
> partido federal, hecho individual y descubierta-
> mente, para que deje de ser una grave inconve-
> niencia política su publicación en estos momentos;
> tanto más desde que esa publicación va a ser hecha

---

[4] *El Paraná,* B.A., October 25, 1852, p. 2. This publication, directed by
Mármol, was short-lived, appearing from October 25 to November 12, 1852.

> en un periódico, que todas las mañanas ha de dar
> ocasión a que alguien se disguste, cuando hoy no
> se debe disgustar a nadie.[5]

But Mármol was intent upon publishing the novel despite all opposition. He argued that the work, in addition to its political purpose, possessed literary merit which should also be taken into account. Apparently *Amalia* would have appeared in *El Paraná* if Mármol had toned down the more invective portions and had altered somewhat the shameful truth of history. Needless to say, the author preferred not to publish the novel in that newspaper than to accede to these demands. He thus had to wait three years, until 1855, before *Amalia* appeared in completed form in Buenos Aires.

Amalia is fundamentally a social and political document of a troubled era in Argentine history. As a novel it mirrors the events and personages which mark the period, recording its most salient and vivid characteristics through the unfolding of a fictional plot. Mármol was undoubtedly inspired by the works of Walter Scott, whose vogue in Hispanic America at this time was very great. Yet it is only by a broad extension of the term that we may place *Amalia* in the same category as those historical novels of which Scott is the accepted master. This distinguished English writer took history from the archives and clothed it in living form, glorified the events of the past, revived the important persons who shaped that past, and presented a colorful review of bygone manners and customs. In short, he recreated for his own and future generations what had occurred in previous eras. In contrast, Mármol conceived *Amalia* in a different mold, for his focal point was not the past, but the dynamic present. In *Amalia,* the era depicted was not unearthed from the pages of history, but was contemporaneous with the author's life: that is, Mármol actually lived through the incidents that he narrated, and the real people he portrayed affected directly his own existence. Rather than a reconstruction and interpretation of past events, *Amalia* stands as a tangible witness to history in the making. More logical it would be, therefore, to understand this work as a

[5] *Loc. cit.*

novel of contemporary affairs, rather than as a historical novel.

Amalia is the maximum effort on the part of a novelist to denounce the wickedness and inhumanity of the Federalist regime. Written during Mármol's exile in Montevideo, the novel seethes with the bitterness and intense hatred which come from personal suffering. As the center of interest Buenos Aires is admirably portrayed. On the one hand there is presented the struggle of the rebellious Unitarians, who are under the constant surveillance of the authorities, or are persecuted when they constitute a dangerous threat to the regime; on the other we see the efforts of the Federalists to remain in power and destroy all opposition. The tumultuous city is thus seen to be split by two hostile factions, but ruled by the iron hand of a dictator.

Although the activities of both Federalists and Unitarians are vividly revealed, the vantage point from which the moving drama of civil war is contemplated is life in Buenos Aires as lived by the resisting Unitarians. The novel is conceived largely in terms of the Unitarian minority in conflict with dominant Federalist forces. It was Mármol's contention, expressed clearly on many occasions and exemplified through the noble behavior of the protagonists, that the most effective means of combatting the Tyranny was to band together and fight, instead of running from danger and accepting the situation as beyond remedy. Inasmuch as Buenos Aires was the focal point of Rosas' power, emigration in large numbers from that city would have left it at the mercy of the Federalists, who then could have wielded their strength with little opposition. The dramatic story of the three principal characters is thus significant, in that it represents the heroic struggle of all the Unitarians who did remain behind in the capital to bear the brunt of Rosas' attack.

At homes, parties, and political meetings, in offices and secret reunions, at Rosas' headquarters, on the street, and wherever a slice of life may be captured and described—there Mármol penetrates to vivify his picture of the era. It is well to point out some of the scenes which reveal the conditions of the times. A gathering in Amalia's house gives occasion for the author to mention the contributions of notable Unitarians, such as Diego Alcorta, Félix Frías, Juan María Gutiérrez, and Juan Bautista Alberdi; while a conference in the Dictator's home concerning urgent problems of his administration introduces the reader to important Federalists, among them Corvalán, Cuitiño, and Victorica. The scenes are excellent which show the subservience and moral weakness of many of Rosas' officials, who have a deadly fear not only of their leader, but also of each other. At one point in the novel Mármol offers, in a purely expository form, an interesting synthesis of the Argentine political situation in 1840. In one chapter Rosas expresses concern over the struggle with the French, relations with the English, and increasing domestic hostility. At a meeting of the feared *Sociedad Popular Restauradora,* the members pledge total extermination of the *salvajes unitarios.* Lastly, we may mention Rosas' infamous black list of those opposed to the government, wherein are registered the occupations of the accused and the charges made against them.

Mármol succeeds in painting Rosas in the blackest colors, as one of the most ignominious and inhuman rulers that a nation ever had to endure. He affirms that the tyrant's cruelty can never be justified on the grounds that he governed in abnormal and difficult times, nor was his severity of command necessary to establish solidarity and a politically independent Argentina. So great is Mármol's hatred of the Dictator that he is not content with denouncing his political regime, but even criticizes his personal life. In a somewhat imaginative scene, the author enters Rosas' estate and describes him in the privacy of his family and close friends. To show his moral perversity Mármol dramatizes a painful episode where the Dictator, out of sheer baseness, forces a hideous idiot in his employ to kiss his modest daughter Manuela. Other passages reveal Rosas as a brute who takes a sadistic pleasure in the embarrassment, vexation, and physical suffering of others. Furthermore, the exaggerated picture of Rosas' uncouth manner of eating and speaking and of his crude behavior in general is an added indication of Mármol's utter contempt for the man as a ruler and as a private citizen.

Another member of the Rosas family is also portrayed in a most unfavorable light. María Josefa Ezcurra, the Dictator's diabolical sister-in-law, is pictured as a scheming political fanatic, who in her mad thirst for self-assertion becomes a formidable foe of the Unitarians. In María Josefa's service there are a few Negro spies who obtain needed information about enemy activities. On one occasion a Negress tells her that she saw Dr. Alcorta, a confirmed Unitarian, enter Amalia's house; also that she heard Amalia singing a Unitarian song and observed Eduardo limping as if he were wounded. This knowledge arouses María Josefa's suspicions that Amalia and her friends may really be Unitarians. Yet amid the bitter censure of Rosas and María Josefa appears the delightful praise of the tyrant's daughter,[6] for Mármol is not blind to the admirable qualities of Manuela, who stands apart from the baseness of the persons surrounding her.

From the initial scene of the novel, where several Unitarians are killed attempting to leave the capital, until the final massacre of the protagonists, there is terror at every turn, dramatic episodes of villainy and deception, and an over-all tenor of violence and confusion. Some of the most notable portions of the work are those scenes which depict the mistrust, deceit, fear, false homage, and forced loyalty among many of the characters. Amalia, Eduardo, Daniel, the French diplomat, Cuitiño, María Josefa, and the servants are all players in a vicious game of ingenuity and daring, where the penalty is death itself. This atmosphere of tenseness and restraint, where each person is suspicious of the other, where actions are often guided by false motives or are suppressed through fear of disapproval, is sensed at the outset of the work and is sustained until the close. There is a sly, almost painful humor each time that Rosas' officials, in pursuit of Eduardo, are duped by the Unitarians through a clever stratagem. Amalia and Daniel know that their best defense is the very insecurity and uneasi-

---

[6] In this respect it is significant to add that Mármol wrote a biography of this woman, entitled *Manuela Rosas—rasgos biográficos,* Montevideo, 1850.

ness of the Federalist agents, who, fearful of misinterpreting orders or committing other grave errors, are frequently turned from their sinister missions. Thus the Dictator's nefarious influence is constantly and frightfully perceived, since every citizen is ever on his guard and apprehensive for his life. Mármol further states:

> Una labor inaudita, empleada con perseverancia en el espacio de muchos años para relajar todos los vínculos sociales, poniendo en anarquía las clases, las familias y los individuos, estableciendo y premiado la delación como virtud cívica en la clase ignorante e inclinada al mal de sus semejantes; escudándose siempre con esa palabra federación, encubridora de todos los delitos, de todos los vicios, de todas las subversiones morales, es el sistema de Rosas; tales han sido los primeros medios empleados por él para debilitar la fuerza sintética del pueblo, cortando en él todos los lazos de comunidad, y dejando una sociedad de individuos aislados, para ejercer sobre ellos su bárbaro poder.[7]

In *Amalia* are combined both realistic and romantic elements. The most essential and enduring aspect of the work—the portrayal of a historic epoch—is conceived along definite realistic lines. In a faithful, lifelike manner Mármol dramatizes contemporary events and delineates key figures who shape these events. On the other hand, the plot of the novel—its fictional part—is conceived in a thoroughly romantic fashion. The love story of Eduardo and Amalia, devoid of motivation and analysis, is purely conventional and lacks interest, while the cat and mouse game between the Federalists and Eduardo at times assumes the proportions of high adventure and melodramatic action. Moreover, the three principal characters are typical romantic creations—Amalia, the noble and generous heroine, Eduardo, the unfortunate victim of persecution, and Daniel, the dashing and courageous hero. In addition, many individual scenes are exaggerated and even unlikely, such as those involving the timorous Cándido Rodríguez,

---

[7] *Amalia,* edition of Biblioteca de Clásicos Argentinos, B.A., 1944, Vol. I, pp. 403-404.

who at one time requests Daniel to have him jailed as a convenient solution to his distress; or those portraying the sly Nicolás Mariño, who uses his high political position to force his amorous attentions upon Amalia.

Mármol's interest in combatting the Tyranny is so absorbing that he frequently neglects the purely literary aspects of the novel. From an aesthetic standpoint *Amalia* lacks harmony of effect and beauty of composition. The work is long, too burdensome with an excessive number of episodes and protracted explanatory material. The many digressions in the form of historical analyses and lengthy declamations impede the progress of the story and delay the termination much beyond the reader's patience. Likewise, Daniel's extensive and weighty discourses, although significant in their expression of the ideals of a free Argentina, tend to be grandiloquent and overelaborated.

For the most part the style of the novel is ponderous and inflated. Mármol writes at times as if he were overwhelmed by the multitude of things he has to say and the urgency to say them. The solemnness of the detailed historical explanations and the uncontrollable vehemence of the attack against the Tyranny may account for the lack of ease and lightness of narration of many parts of the work. Yet on occasions Mármol breaks through his frequently heavy and cumbrous style and pens a pure and delicate literary description. Observe, for example, the author's picture of Amalia:

> Había algo de resplandor celestial en esa criatura de veintidós años, en cuya hermosura la Naturaleza había agotado sus tesoros de perfecciones, y en cuyo semblante perfilado y bello, bañado de una palidez ligerísima, matizado con un tenue rosado en el centro de sus mejillas, se dibujaba la expresión melancólica y dulce de una organización amorosamente sensible.
>
> En ese momento no era el sueño lo que cerraba los párpados de Amalia, entrelazando sus largas y pobladas pestañas; no era el sueño, era un éxtasis delicioso que embriagaba de amor aquella natu-

raleza armoniosa e impresionable, bajo la tibia
temperatura que la acariciaba, y en medio de los
perfumes, de la música y de los rayos blancos y
celestiales de luz que la inundaban blandamente.

Imágenes blancas y fugitivas, como esas mari-
posas del trópico que vuelan y sacuden el polvo
de oro de sus alas sobre las flores que acarician,
parecía que volaban jugueteando por el jardín de
su fantasía; pues dos veces su fisonomía se animó
y la sonrisa entreabrió sus labios, que se cerraron
luego como dos hojas de rosa a la que halaga y
conmueve el aliento fugaz que se escapa de los
labios de un amante que pone un beso sobre ella,
en recordación de la mano que se la envía.[8]

In the face of the dismal and horrifying days which he
brought alive in *Amalia*, Mármol was never pessimistic, but
expressed hope and faith that the dark clouds would pass over
and Argentina would emerge as a proud and prosperous nation. With prophetic longing he cried out:

Cada pueblo tiene su siglo, su destino y su imperio sobre la tierra. Y los pueblos del Plata ten-
drán al fin su siglo, su destino y su imperio, cuando las promesas de Dios, fijas y escritas en la naturaleza que nos rodea, brillen sobre la frente de
esas generaciones futuras que verterán una lágri-
ma de compasión por los errores y por las des-
gracias de la mía. Sí, tengo fe en el porvenir de
mi patria. Pero se necesita que la mano del tiempo haya nivelado con el polvo de donde hemos
salido la frente de los que hoy viven.[9]

. . .

With *Amalia* as the initiator and model, several other novels dealing with the epoch of Rosas appeared in Argentina in
the years closely following the Dictator's defeat in 1852. These
works reveal a poignant denunciation of the Tyranny, which
the writers recall with anger and horror. The plots are primarily designed to punctuate the cruelties of Rosas and his hench-

[8] *Ibid.*, Vol. I, pp. 210-211.
[9] *Ibid.*, Vol. I, pp. 389-390.

men, as well as the heroic action and sacrifices of the Unitarians. Although these works are grouped apart in this chapter, they contain many of the same elements found in the romantic novels of exaggerated and exalted sentiment, to be treated in subsequent portions of this study.

In 1856 appeared *La huérfana de Pago Largo*,[10] by Francisco López Torres (1839-1871), popular journalist and minor poet. The highly involved plot concerns a diabolical plan of revenge of which the heroine, her family, and sweetheart are the unfortunate victims. Innocent Unitarian partisans thus fall prey to the malevolently warped mind of a cruel and lustful Federalist army officer, who uses his favored position in the Rosas ranks for personal ends. The story is in part quite improbable, yet it does illustrate a romantic pattern that many Argentine novels of the period follow; namely, after the malefactor executes a series of horrendous crimes, he repents and relates the circumstances which impelled him to commit such acts. Thus, in *La huérfana de Pago Largo* the villain seeks to justify his evil deeds of vengeance on the grounds that he now retaliates against society for the horrible privations and mistreatment he suffered during imprisonment for a crime he did not commit.

In 1857 there appeared *El prisionero de Santos Lugares*,[11] by Federico Barbará (1828-1893). The author, a professional soldier almost all his life, took part in the battle of Caseros (1852) and in the campaigns of Cépeda (1859) and Pavón (1861), and also lent valuable service to the government in the frontier wars with the Indians. His close contact with the aborigines of Calfucurá led to the writing of two important works: *Usos y costumbres de los indios pampas* (1856) and *Manual y vocabulario de la lengua pampa* (1879). Barbará died in the province of Buenos Aires on March 25, 1893. The plot of *El prisionero de Santos Lugares* purports to show how the Federalists were able to use their political power to satisfy personal desires. The author selected the site of Santos Lugares, with all the cruelty of its detention camps, as the embodiment of

[10] Francisco López Torres, *La huérfana de Pago Largo*, B.A., Imprenta del Plata, 1856.
[11] Federico Barbará, *El prisionero de Santos Lugares*, B.A., Imprenta de Las Artes, 1857.

Rosas' inhumanity. There are scenes which portray the mental and physical suffering of the prisoners, the torture chambers, and the callous, brutal behavior of the camp attendants. Among the shocking episodes is one which describes preparations for the execution of a number of clergymen.

In the novel entitled *Aurora y Enrique, o sea la Guerra Civil* (1858),[12] by Toribio Arauz, it is a woman who releases the invective against the Dictator. When this heroine learns that savage members of the *Mazorca* have murdered her father, she seeks revenge and contemplates slaying Rosas. Yet the thought of killing another human being, even a tyrant, terrifies her; she atones for her evil notion and hopes merely for his defeat. The work, in addition to lashing a bitter diatribe against Rosas, directs sharp criticism against the Paraguayan dictator, Carlos Antonio López.

Lastly, it is important to note that the Rosas theme aroused interest even in foreign writers: *Misterios de Buenos Aires* (1856)[13] and *Camila O'Gorman* (1856),[14] both novels written originally in French by Felisberto Pelissot, were immediately translated into Spanish and published in Buenos Aires; and *Los mártires de Buenos Aires, o el verdugo de su república*,[15] by a Spanish author named Manuel María Nieves, was first published in Madrid in 1857 and subsequently reprinted in Buenos Aires in 1861.[16]

---

[12] Toribio Arauz, *Aurora y Enrique, o sea la Guerra Civil*, B.A., Imprenta de Mayo, 1858.

[13] Felisberto Pelissot, *Misterios de Buenos Aires*, traducida al castellano para La Tribuna por uno de sus colaboradores, B.A., Imprenta de La Tribuna, 1856.

[14] Felisberto Pelissot, *Camila O'Gorman*, trans. Heraclio C. Fajardo, B.A., Imprenta Americana, 1856.

[15] Manuel María Nieves, *Los mártires de Buenos Aires, o el verdugo de su república*, Madrid, Librería Española, Barcelona, El Plus Ultra, 1857.

[16] M.M.N., *Los mártires de Buenos Aires, o el tirano Juan Manuel Rosas*, B.A., 1861. Notice that in this edition the author's initials appear, not his full name; also that the second half of the title is altered.

IV

THE HISTORICAL NOVELS OF
VICENTE FIDEL LOPEZ

The novel in Argentina reaches deep into the roots of Hispanic-American civilization with *La novia del hereje, o la Inquisición de Lima,* by the illustrious historian Vicente Fidel López. In this work the author is not concerned with an account of contemporary history, as is Mármol in *Amalia,* but rather with a recording of life in a bygone age. The vigor and intensity of narration of *La novia del hereje* attest to López' fervent dedication to the history and traditions of America.

Vicente Fidel López, son of the famous Vicente López y Planes,[1] was born in Buenos Aires on April 24, 1815. After preparatory classical studies he enrolled in law school, receiving his degree in 1839. A year later, oppressed by the Tyranny, he voluntarily left the capital and took up residence in Montevideo. From there he traveled to Chile, where he initiated his literary career as a journalist for several newspapers —*El Heraldo* and *El Progreso* of Santiago, and *El Comercio* of Valparaiso. After his return to Buenos Aires in 1852, López emerged as an imposing figure in the public and cultural life of Argentina. In 1853 he was appointed minister of education; and in later years he became president of the Banco de la Provincia and rector of the University of Buenos Aires. He founded in 1871 the important literary and historical magazine, *La Revista del Río de la Plata,* and together with Juan María Gutiérrez and Andrés Lamas he directed its publication. Much of the talent and greatness of Vicente López lies in his accomplishments as a historian. Most significant are the many

---

[1] Statesman and poet, López y Planes is perhaps best remembered as the author of the Argentine national hymn.

volumes on Argentine history,[2] which still stand as authoritative reference works.

The first edition of *La novia del hereje* appeared in Buenos Aires in 1854.[3] In September of that same year and continuing until July, 1855, the novel was presented in serial form in *El Plata Científico y Literario*. In 1870 the famous publicist, Carlos Casavalle, came out with the second edition of the work, in two volumes.[4]

In the prologue to the 1854 edition[5] López offers enlightening information concerning the writing of *La novia del hereje* and other historical novels which he planned. He states that fiction can assume a vital function in awakening an interest in the national traditions of a country; and that precisely in England and the United States, where the past is revealed through the novels of Scott and Cooper, the people hold a deep respect for their customs and traditions. In consideration of this, López nourished in his youth the idea of creating for Argentina a national historical novel, which might thus earn for him in his own country such literary esteem and significance as Scott and Cooper hold in theirs. As he confesses, however, he soon abandoned these illusions, judging that his natural bent lay more with a pure expression and interpretation of history than with a novelized account of it. Accordingly, when he did write *La novia del hereje*, he pessimistically called it the "fruto de una ilusión renunciada."[6]

It may seem strange, in view of his desire to form a national historical novel, that López should select Lima as the setting for his work. The author explains that the cultural heritage of Argentina is essentially a product of colonial Spain, and

---

[2] We may mention by way of example: *La revolución argentina*, 1881; *Historia de la República Argentina*, 1883-1893; and *Compendio de la historia argentina*, 1889-1890.

[3] Vicente Fidel López, *La novia del hereje, o la Inquisición de Lima*, B.A., Imprenta de Mayo, 1854.

[4] Vicente Fidel López, *La novia del hereje, o la Inquisición de Lima*, ed. Carlos Casavalle, B.A., Imprenta de Mayo, 1870, 2 vols. Subsequent editions include that of La Cultura Argentina, B.A., 1917, and that of the Biblioteca La Tradición Argentina, B.A., 1933, Vols. 23 and 24.

[5] This prologue is in the form of a letter, dated Montevideo, September 7, 1854, which López directed to his friend Miguel Navarro Viola, residing in Buenos Aires.

[6] *La novia del hereje*, 1854 edition, *op. cit.*, prologue, p. 4.

that by presenting the customs, traditions, and ways of life of that vital city in the flourishing Spanish Empire, that heritage can be readily envisaged. He states:

> Yo pretendía entonces consignar en *La novia del hereje* la lucha que la raza española sostenía en el tiempo de la conquista, contra las novedades que agitaban al mundo cristiano, y preparaban los nuevos rasgos de la civilización actual.[7]

Concerning the series of national novels which he planned in his youth but never terminated, López offers a brief account. First, he refers to a work (no title is mentioned) which was to deal with Pedro de Zeballos and his successful efforts in opening up the Plata River to European commerce by wresting La colonia del Sacramento (Uruguay) from the Portuguese. López explains:

> Esta revolución, consumada por un hombre como Zeballos......, habría sido de cierto un vastísimo campo para la novela histórica. En ella habría podido hacerse servicios eminentes a la nacionalidad argentina, reponiendo el espíritu de los pueblos, aturdidos por los escesos y las calamidades de las guerras incesantes, a la vía sana de su nacionalidad, y de su único desarrollo posible.[8]

López further mentions in the prologue that he outlined and began writing a romance entitled *El conde de Buenos Aires,* which was to treat of the events leading to the memorable Independence Day of May 25, 1810. Lastly, the author refers to a group of three novels which remained in outline form— *Martín I, Capitán Vargas,* and *Guelfos y Gibelinos.* The first was to deal with the conspiracy perpetrated by Alzaga in 1822;[9] the second was to glorify the victories of Chacabuco and Maipú; and the third was to depict the Uruguayan insurrection of the rural class against the central government of Artigas and Ramírez.

[7] *Ibid.,* p. 5.
[8] *Ibid.,* p. 8.
[9] In 1807, Martín Alzaga brilliantly organized the defense of Buenos Aires against the English invaders. Some years later, in June, 1812, he led a conspiracy to overthrow the triumvirate (at that time the main executive body in Argentina) and establish a monarchy ruled by Carlota of Portugal. However, the plot failed and the conspirators were executed.

Thus, of the many works of fiction which the author set out to write in his youth, only *La novia del hereje* was completed; and this work stands as one of the outstanding historical novels of Argentina. The principal conflict of the novel revolves around the consequences of the ill-fated relationship between a proud Spanish girl (María) and a valiant English naval officer (Lord Henderson). Unrelenting foe of these lovers is Padre Andrés, cruel, ignoble chief Inquisitor of Lima, who shrewdly uses to advantage María's transgression as he contrives to gain possession of her father's vast fortune.

In *La novia del hereje* López masterfully places in action diverse elements of American colonial society. On the one hand, Spanish authority is represented in the viceroy, in the Inquisition, and in the many public offices which maintained the colonial organization strong and efficient; on the other hand are presented forces hostile to the motherland—operating externally in the person of Sir Francis Drake, the famed English navigator and pirate who undermined Spain's supreme power, acting internally through the people's dissatisfaction with Spain's colonial policy. In addition, the various social groups of Lima are brought into play, from the aristocracy, high office holders and religious leaders, down through the middle-class merchants and druggists, and finally to the common masses and even outcasts of the community. There appear functionaries, administrators, actuaries, lawyers, clerks, and other officials who render important service to the crown. Among the notable characterizations is that of the irresolute prosecutor of the Inquisition, Marcelín Esteca, who has a mania for interjecting an excess of Latin words and phrases during legal argumentation. Also, at Bautista's pharmacy there congregate *tertulianos, cholos,* and other common folk of Lima, to discuss, among other affairs, the Inquisition and María's imprisonment. Furthermore, political reunions, business transactions, royal councils, social and religious customs, and the everyday life of the masses, with their markets, eating places, dress, and festivals—are all graphically presented in the novel. As an example of the colorful descriptions of colonial

Lima, we offer the following paragraph which paints the public square of the city:

> Desde aquel tiempo hasta ahora muy pocos años, la plaza de Lima se cubría por las mañanas de toda clase de gentes. Los vendedores de los comestibles necesarios al alimento o al lujo de las familias venían a pasar allí sus surtidos en paños o canastos estendidos por el suelo a la orilla de las cuatro veredas que la cuadraban. Como en aquel tiempo toda la semana era de días de misa y allí estaba la Catedral, todo el concurso de la iglesia se desparramaba de paseo por la plaza, que servía así de mercado. Era allí el lugar del primer desayuno de las familias, el del primer saludo o la primera sonrisa de los amantes. Junto con la carne de puerco y las verduras, se vendían los picantes adovados y otras mil manufacturas saturadas con el agí, que es el néctar todavía de los hijos de la vieja Lima. En las mismas mesas en que todo esto estaba a la vista del comprador, se hacía y se despachaba el mate y el mentado chocolate de abolobamba que bebían con deleite en gícaras espumosas los alegres y matinales círculos de damas y caballeros que rodeaban las mesas, o puestos más acreditados, de aquella especie de café público tenido bajo el esmaltado pavimento del cielo luminoso del Perú.[10]

Alongside important historical events, political dissension, and religious controversy there are depicted such routine concerns of life as activity in a public square (described above), local chatter, and the particular manner of dress. When a council convenes to review María's imprisonment, López picturesquely relates how the populace responds to the event. A portion of that description follows, where mention is made of women's attire:

> Las señoras acudían al espectáculo con todos los atavíos del lujo. Adornadas de anchas y tiezas golillas, que rodeaban sus cabezas como una redoma

---

[10] *La novia del hereje*, 1854 edition, *op. cit.*, p. 198.

de pliegues, arrastraban enormes vestidos de cola,
que tres o cuatro lacayos renegridos como el éba-
no iban suspendiendo por detrás para que no to-
casen con la finura de sus telas el pavimento de
las veredas: y como acudían por familias iban pre-
cedidas de dos o más lacayos, que llevaban bien
desplegadas por delante riquísimas alfombras de
tripe.[11]

In a quite obvious manner López reveals himself as fundamentally opposed to the tremendous power of the Inquisition
and in general to the entire Spanish colonial regime. The denunciation of the evils of Spanish policy permeates the work
in the form of a steady and potent undercurrent, yet the author
is careful not to convert his novel into a mere diatribe. He
frequently explains causes and effects of political and social
events in order to make the era depicted more comprehensible.
The opening chapter of *La novia del hereje,* for example, contains a revealing picture of the Spanish Empire and a description of Lima in 1578. Through these historical and social exposi-
tions, set forth more for the purpose of clarification than for open
censure, the characters and situations of the novel are developed in a clearly defined milieu. To substantiate his account of
a historical incident which is incorporated into the plot, or to
confirm the exactness of a particular point of information,
López on a few occasions cites other references which treat
of the same material. Thus, lest he be accused of exaggeration
or untruth in his description of the terror in the streets of Lima
upon Drake's arrival there, the author quotes that part of a
poem by Barco Centenera which deals with the same occur-
rence and corroborates his narration.[12]

It is well to consider now the characterizations of the principal persons of the novel. The heroine, María, symbolizes the
unfortunate victim of the Inquisition. Although her romance
with Lord Henderson provides the work with a most important conflict, the love affair itself—the development, expres-

---

[11] *Ibid.,* p. 215.
[12] *Ibid.,* p. 33. The full title of this poem, published in 1602, is *La Argentina y conquista del Río de la Plata, con otros acaecimientos de los Reynos del
Perú, Tucumán, y estado del Brasil.* The stanzas quoted by López are taken
from Canto XXII.

sion, and analysis of it—is treated in a hasty and superficial fashion. María's active role in the story is very slight; her reactions to her imprisonment and to the various problems arising from it are seldom made a part of the narration. Padre Andrés, as the ruthless and scheming chief Inquisitor, is symbolic of the evils of unlimited and misused power in the colonies. He is the most fully developed character of the novel; his unyielding persecution of María, which envelops him in numerous complicated situations with many secondary figures, amply reveals his cruelty and cunning.

As a constant, impending menace to peace and order in Lima appears the dreaded figure of Sir Francis Drake, whose daring activities may be said to mirror the opposition to the closed and restrained colonial spirit, and to act as a counterpoise to the unchallenged will of Spain. Although Drake's active and physical presence is seldom overtly felt, the very atmosphere of Lima is saturated with his awesome name and the terrible reality of his exploits. The author considers Drake a noble, just, and praiseworthy individual, despite his tarnished reputation as a pirate. López states:

> Verdad es, que aunque pirata, su renombre no ha quedado manchado ante la justicia de la humanidad, con los actos atroces de barbarie, a que, por lo común, deben su negra celebridad los hombres de su oficio. Él, muy al contrario, se distinguió no menos que por los grandes resultados, por la esquisita benevolencia y urbanidad con que suavizó la desgracia, harto terrible, de los que cayeron bajo la rapacidad de sus banderas. ¡Y cosa rara! A su vida y a sus actos de pirata, este hombre unía la más estraña pretensión de ser tenido por un perfecto cristiano; y siendo uno de los guerreros cuya fortuna y cuyo arrojo causaba más pavor en su tiempo, oraba con la devoción y la humildad de un niño.[13]

One of the few characters in the novel who dares to oppose openly Padre Andrés' will is the colorful Mercedes, at one time a devoted lover of the chief Inquisitor. This perilous de-

---

[13] *La novia del hereje,* 1854 edition, *op. cit.,* p. 222.

fiance is the more striking and dramatic because it places in
juxtaposition the pomp and importance of a high church official and the plainness and humility of a downtrodden woman.
Mercedes' dauntless resistance to forces far superior to her own
and her rigorous determination to save María despite overwhelming odds, form some of the most impressive and moving
scenes of the novel.

In his earnest desire to render a full account of colonial
Lima at the close of the sixteenth century, López includes too
much material. The work suffers from a superfluity of incidents and detailed descriptions. Too many things happen; too
many episodes are presented, some of which, although enhancing the comprehensiveness of the scene, tend to be tedious
and inconsequential. Especially, the innumerable accounts of
conspiracy and inveiglement centering around Drake's activities, Padre Andrés' schemes, and María's imprisonment become at times too minute and involved.

Despite this overabundance of material, *La novia del hereje*
is well developed and adeptly carried to its conclusion. The
narration proceeds rather slowly through the mass of intrigue
and hidden motives. The language, correct, straightforward
and non-pretentious, possesses vigor and, above all, descriptive
expressiveness. *La novia del hereje* stands as a skillful literary
interpretation of colonial America, a work which combines
significant historical matter with rich imaginative elements.

· · ·

The second historical novel of Vicente López, *La loca de la
guardia,* appeared in Buenos Aires in 1896,[14] more than forty
years subsequent to the first edition of *La novia del hereje.*
The work, which treats of a demented woman's efforts to aid
the patriots during the struggle for independence, is set in
the Andean region, where heroic Argentine forces, under the
command of Colonel Juan de Gregorio Las Heras, are engaged in fierce battles. Around the military events is built the
strange and pathetic story of the protagonist Teresa, who de-
termines at all cost to exact personal vengeance on the cruel

[14] Vicente Fidel López, *La loca de la guardia,* ed. Carlos Casavalle, B. A.,
Imprenta de Mayo, 1896.

and lecherous Spanish army officer, San Bruno. Evidently
López had a real person in mind in characterizing the heroine
and added fictional elements of his own imagination. A certain Father Félix Pico, in a letter to the author,[15] states that
a Colonel Ramón Dehesa related to him that such a woman
as "la loca de la guardia" did exist, and that she became deranged as a result of mistreatment at the hands of the Spaniards, but always received the respect and protection of the
patriots.

In this novel López turns from the comprehensive examination of a historic era, which characterizes *La novia del hereje,*
and deals primarily with the military aspects of the period
treated. Figuring importantly in *La loca de la guardia* are
lengthy explanations of strategic plans and preparations for
battle, as well as detailed accounts of the action itself. In these
narrations López proves himself well versed in military science
and reveals a deep understanding of the independence movement. Many imposing patriots of the period, such as San
Martín, O'Higgins, and Las Heras, appear in the work, not
only by way of mere mention, but by actual participation in
the story. In addition, López evokes celebrated events in
Hispanic-American history: the victory of Chacabuco on February 12, 1817, whereby Santiago and the northern half of
Chile regained their independence; the decisive battle of Maipú on October 5, 1818, by which all of Chile was made free
except for a few scattered regions in the south. The author
also follows the reactions and activities of the townsfolk as
military operations are in progress. Illustrating this feature of
the novel is a paragraph depicting the populace's state of confusion during the struggle for possession of Valparaíso:

> Cuando el pueblo se apercibió de todo esto se-
> rían como las nueve de la noche. Alborotada la
> plebe, se lanzó a las calles armada de hachas, ba-
> rretas y picos, vociferando en un desorden atroz,
> y atacando a mano armada las casas que tenían
> por más opulentas y ricas, sin distinción de parti-
> do. A esta horrible confusión se agregó que las

[15] *Ibid.,* prologue, pp. 3-5. The letter is dated November 21, 1887.

bandas de realistas derrotados, creyéndose ataca-
dos ya por el ejército vencedor, corrían por las calles, disparando sus fusiles y atacando también
todo lo que encontraban al paso, en su deseo de
ganar pronto los caminos por donde pensaban es-
capar. Andaban revueltas con los unos y con los
otros familias enteras, mujeres y niños, que trata-
ban de seguir a sus deudos; y mujeres y pilluelos
de la clase baja que robaban y mataban sin piedad.[16]

The deranged Teresa, although a vague and unprecise character, casts a protective and guiding light over the efforts of
the noble insurgents. Her role in the novel is symbolic of
anti-Spanish sentiment and of the intense passion of the patriots; that is, her vengeance on San Bruno is indicative not
so much of a personal triumph, as a realization that the Spanish regime, incarnate in San Bruno, will be entirely over-
thrown. Teresa's incoherent and raving talk reveals her constant fanatic preoccupation with the progress of battle and
the welfare of the soldiers, which she understands as the only
reality and significant affair of her life.

[16] *Ibid.*, p. 197.

V

THE DEVELOPMENT OF THE
ROMANTIC NOVEL AFTER *AMALIA*

(*Part one*)

1. BACKGROUND: THE ROMANTIC NOVEL THROUGHOUT HISPANIC AMERICA

All the literatures of Hispanic America fell under the influence of European models, in particular the French. Most continental literary currents were late in reaching the New World, but their influence as a directive force was not on that account diminished. Romanticism arrived at America's shores in 1820 with the poetry of the Cuban José María Heredia,[1] and following him with eager strides appeared other notable writers who adapted to their particular land the principles and techniques of romantic literature. Esteban Echeverría, for example, introduced romanticism in his native Argentina with three volumes of poetry,[2] in which he revealed himself an inspired disciple of the English and French romantic artists, whom he had read avidly during his five-year stay in France from 1826 to 1830.

Hispanic America in the post-independence era was an ideally suitable land for the development of romanticism. Unshackled from the rigid and disciplined colonial regime, the recently formed nations were able to enjoy the freedom, liberty, and individuality that characterized so intimately the essence of the romantic spirit. In addition, this new status of independence brought forth vehement struggles for power and

---

[1] His work *En el Teocalli de Cholula*, 1820, is generally accepted as the first romantic poem composed in the Spanish language.

[2] We refer to the volumes *Elvira*, 1832, *Consuelos*, 1834, and *Rimas*, 1837, the last of which contains the celebrated piece *La cautiva*.

bitter political dissension, a situation that gave ample motive for the romantic expression of dynamic self-assertion so well exemplified in the ambitious rule of the *caudillos*. It was thus amid the turbulent efforts of Hispanic-American countries to offset the effects of previous colonial restraint and come into their own as sovereign nations, that the birth and flourishing of romanticism in America took place.

The romantic novel—our special concern—had its vogue in Hispanic America from about 1840 to 1870, although in isolated instances it continued to subsist side by side with realistic and naturalistic works. The general development of the novel in America gives evidence of the superposition of types—romantic, realistic, naturalistic, modernistic—rather than of a succession in strict chronological order. Furthermore, in a given novel the presence of one type does not necessarily exclude that of another; fusion of romantic and realistic elements, for example, may be seen in such works as *Cecilia Valdés, Amalia,* and *Astucia*. It appears that the American novel never completely disregards old or outworn forms, but preserves them and grafts them to newer, less developed ones.

The romantic novel in America assumed various distinct forms in the course of its development, several of which might be clearly traced to the works of the European masters. The effusively sentimental and highly idyllic novel had its prototype in Bernardin de Saint-Pierre's classic piece, *Paul et Virginie;* the novel of the land, with its awareness and glorification of the American scene, had as antecedent Chateaubriand's influential *Atala;* the writers of the romantic historical novel could look with emulation at the stirring works of Walter Scott, who enjoyed wide public acclaim in America from 1820 to 1860. Lastly, feuilletonistic novels of adventure, rapid and exciting in their endless stream of romanesque episodes, had their continental forerunners in the popular works of Dumas, Sue, and Ponson du Terrail.[3]

To many European romantic artists, especially the German,

---

[3] Furthermore, it is important to note that the adventure novels of frontier life of the North American James Fenimore Cooper were also absorbed by many Hispanic-American writers.

the Middle Ages were a compelling source of inspiration. Hispanic America lacked this theme, but in its place turned an impassioned view toward the exaltation of the Indian. *Atala,* splendid in its warm tribute to the Indian, may be seen as a harbinger of subsequent American novels of similar subject matter. The history, legends, traditions, and customs of the various indigenous groups formed a picturesque background for the imaginative mind of the American writer in search of native material. To romantic fiction was thus added the *indianista* novel, completely idealistic and sentimental in conception, wherein appeared poetic and heroic Indians in an artificial and strained environment. *Cumandá* (1871), by the Ecuatorian Juan León Mera stands as the masterpiece of this romantic *indianista* novel.[4] Written in a beautiful prose, the work is saturated with admirable descriptions of the American scene, although the portrayal of the Indian appears affectedly majestic and falsely chivalrous. The Indian theme also runs through several romantic novels of historical background, as in *Los mártires de Anáhuac* (1870), by the Mexican Eligio Ancona, and in *El Enriquillo* (1882), by the Dominican Manuel de Jesús Galván.

Another important manifestation of the romantic novel—the novel of customs—appeared principally as an outgrowth of the varied forms of writing in the New World that sought to portray the ways and manners of a developing society. These essays, satires, journalistic articles, and short stories that dotted the literary field in the first half of the nineteenth century, were developed more fully in a novelistic framework and ultimately evolved into the novel of customs. Although richly steeped in regional color, with a careful portrayal of local types, national traditions, and everyday modes of living, this form of novel was clearly romantic in conception, execution, and treatment of story and characters. The works generally contained a rather mediocre, insipid, and painfully trite plot, un-

---

[4] This same *indianista* novel in the twentieth century became harshly realistic and evinced a marked social tendency. With such works as *Raza de bronce,* 1919, *Huasipungo,* 1934, and *El mundo es ancho y ajeno,* 1941, it has come to constitute one of the most significant and meritorious types of American fiction.

developed and unmotivated, serving fundamentally to reveal the customs of the epoch.

In widely separated portions of Hispanic America, from the sturdy land of Mexico to the Andean nation of Chile, the novelistic manifestation of romanticism made its way. In most cases this fiction brought into view the first attempts at novel writing; it appeared not within the sphere of a clearly outlined literary movement, but as an undirected and irregular form of imaginative composition. Cuba, although not gaining independence until the very end of the century, gave early evidence of the development of the novel. Outstanding among the early novelists of that country are Cirilo Villaverde, author of *Cecilia Valdés* (1839),[5] and Gertrudis Gómez de Avellaneda, who wrote such romantic works as *El mulato Sab* (1841) and *Guatimozín* (1845). Mexico, credited with having introduced the first three novels in Hispanic America with the works of Fernández de Lizardi,[6] also cultivated the romantic novel quite extensively. As the foremost figures of this type of fiction may be cited Manuel Payno, Fernando Orozco y Berra, Juan Díaz Covarrubias, and Luis G. Inclán;[7] while the renowned Ignacio Manuel Altamirano represents the transition from romanticism to realism, as may be noted in his famous *Clemencia* (1869).

In Chile, early cultivators of the romantic novel were Wenceslao Vial and Manuel Bilbao, whose works[8] remain obscure even in their native land. As Chile's first real novelist, history records the name of Alberto Blest Gana. Although his importance stems from his realistic novels, Blest Gana's early works of fiction, such as *El primer amor* (1858) and *La aritmética en el amor* (1860), reveal a purely romantic tone. The mountainous country of Colombia, where interior communication was exceedingly difficult, developed a host of romantic

---

[5] In 1839 appeared the first part of *Cecilia Valdés*. Not completed until 1879, it was published in final form in 1882.

[6] See Chap. II, note 3.

[7] Payno, *El fistol del diablo*, 1845; Orozco y Berra, *La guerra de treinta años*, 1850; Díaz Covarrubias, *Gil Gómez el Insurgente*, 1859; Luis G. Inclán, *Astucia*, 1865.

[8] Vial, *La vida de un amigo, o un primer amor*, 1845; Bilbao, *El Inquisidor Mayor*, 1852.

costumbrista writers, whose interest lay principally in portraying selected regions of their nation. The novel was cultivated only secondarily; and those minor romantic works which preceded *María* are now virtually forgotten.[9] In other Hispanic-American countries—Venezuela, Peru, Bolivia—the beginnings of fiction may similarly be traced to a few isolated and obscure novels of romantic nature.[10] Owing to their lack of genuine artistry in conception, structure, development, and over-all literary technique, most of these initial romantic works remain as mediocre, second-rate efforts, having far more chronological significance than intrinsic merit.

The romantic novel reached its highest point in the year 1867 with the publication of *María,* by the Colombian Jorge Isaacs. Although the work appeared belatedly when considered within the chronology of romantic literature, it represents the purest and most artistic expression of romanticism in the American novel. The author's conception and presentation of the idyllic love story reveal his intimate affiliation with the French romantic masters; and the poetic and almost ethereal relationship between the young lovers sentimentally calls to mind the romances in *Atala* and *Paul et Virginie.* Yet despite the clearly discernible European influence in María, it is a thoroughly American novel—in its love of the land and people of America, and in particular in its colorful portraiture of the Cauca valley.

This, then, is the substance of the romantic novel. It represents the callow child in the growth of American fiction: prior to its appearance the novel was practically nonexistent; after its vogue ended and this period of fictional preparation and exploration was over, the stage was set for the advent of a more artistic and more fully developed novel in the realistic and naturalistic currents. Viewed in its entirety, the romantic

[9] Among such minor works we may cite *María Dolores,* 1841, by José Joaquín Ortiz, and *El oidor,* 1848, by José A. Plaza.

[10] In Venezuela: Fermín Toro, *La sibila de los Andes,* 1849; Rafael María Baralt, *El hábito hace al monje,* 1849. In Peru: Narciso Aréstegui, *El Padre Horán,* 1848; Luis B. Cisneros, *Julia, o escenas de la vida de Lima,* 1861. In Bolivia: Sebastián Dalence, *Los misterios de Sucre,* 1861; Manuel María Caballero, *La isla,* 1864. The first novel of note in Bolivia was the romantic historical work of the independence period entitled *Juan de la Rosa,* 1885, by Nataniel Aguirre.

novel can not claim outstanding merit; only a few superior pieces tower above the general level of satisfactory but not distinguished fiction. Not before the twentieth century could America turn with pride to a truly excellent array of novel writing.

The romantic novelist, in a virgin field of art, depended to a large degree upon European direction. Much of the artificiality and mediocrity of many romantic works stemmed from the attempt to apply European literary formulas to an American background. A true artistic expression of America's spirit could not come from a servile imitation of continental masters, or from an adaptation of European psychology to the native mind; it had to spring spontaneously from a genuine appreciation and understanding of its traditions and customs. Romantic fiction writers, although keeping one eye reverently on European models, proudly viewed with the other their own magnificent America. These artists strove to capture the native scene in all its beauty, to understand the past by evoking the Indian and colonial heritages, and to penetrate into the customs and manners of society. All this, undertaken within the framework of the romantic novel, constituted the initial and at times awkward strides toward the uncovering of America's identity.

The romantic novel in Argentina, as in other Hispanic-American nations, was born under the influence of European precepts. Yet within that very broad band of similarity, it revealed distinctive elements that gave it a character quite its own. These particularly Argentine manifestations of romantic fiction will be brought out as we discuss individual authors and their works.

Those elementary and rather undivulged novels that preceded *Amalia,* such as *La quena, Soledad,* and *La familia del comendador,* evinced a purely mellifluous and sentimental type of romanticism. Yet the first notable work in Argentine fiction, and in truth the first romantic novel of significance and acclaim—*Amalia*—derived from more substantial and vigorous stock, from the very lifeblood of a nation in political chaos.

Hispanic America honored Mármol's work, and recognized that the best in Argentine romantic fiction had its roots not in honeyed sentimentality and artificial idealization, but rather in the vigor and vitality of national problems. *Amalia* sounded the keynote for subsequent novels denouncing the Tyranny, wherein the hatred of oppression and the love of individual freedom stood as fiery expressions of romanticism.

Yet the robust romanticism of *Amalia* and its followers, although representing one of the most significant phases in Argentine romantic fiction, was certainly not the only one. The romantic novel in Argentina displayed many facets and included works of exalted passion and exaggerated sentiment, stories of foreign setting, and narrations of the mysterious, supernatural, and legendary. Hitherto, this romantic novel has been lightly passed over; in most commentaries on Argentine fiction there is only scant or incidental mention of such authors as Miguel Cané (father), Juana Manuela Gorriti, Eduarda Mansilla de García, and Pedro Echagüe, while other writers of less importance are hardly ever even named. In the remainder of this chapter and the following one, the totality of Argentine romantic fiction will be treated.

2. THE NOVELS OF MIGUEL CANÉ

An early cultivator of Argentine fiction, Miguel Cané (father) enriched the scope of the romantic novel with the publication of four short works in the 1850's. Born in Buenos Aires on April 26, 1812, he emigrated to Montevideo as a young man to escape persecution. There he practiced law and collaborated on several anti-Rosas newspapers, as well as associating himself with important figures of the era, notably Mitre, Lamas, Mármol, and Rivera Indarte. In 1843 and 1844, during the siege of Montevideo, Cané served as a captain in the Argentine forces fighting against Oribe, who a few years previously had imprisoned him. In 1847 Cané parted for Europe, where he traveled extensively through France, Belgium, Italy, and Switzerland, in part to soothe his nerves, tense and worn owing to personal grief and distress over his nation's plight. After Rosas' defeat he returned to Argentina and began to assume an active part in public affairs. Death came on July 5, 1863. His reputation is to a large extent obscured by that of his son, of the same name, whose work *Juvenilia* (1882) ranks as one of the most popular pieces of Argentine literature. In fact, not infrequently are the works of the father grouped with those of his more famous son, as if to deny the literary existence of the former and to understand that there is only one Miguel Cané.

By far the most important of Cané's novels is *Esther,* a short work laid amid the aesthetic delights of Italy, where the author lived for a short time and which he grew to admire greatly. Concluded in May, 1851, in the city of Florence, *Esther* was first published fully in 1858, in Volume IV of the Biblioteca Americana.[11] It was not published again until 1929, when it appeared as one of the selections of the Instituto de Literatura Argentina.[12] The thin plot, autobiographical in part, centers around an idealistic Argentine youth[13] and an emotionally unsatisfied English woman. The two meet in far-off Italy. Esther, painfully enduring an unhappy marriage, quickly finds in the highly cultured and inspiring Argentine the

[11] Miguel Cané, *Esther,* in Biblioteca Americana, ed. Magariños Cervantes, B.A., Imprenta de Mayo, 1858, IV, 25-105. This volume bears no date, but a notice in *La Tribuna,* November 29, 1858, p. 3, states that Volume IV was published on November 28, 1858. Previously, a section of the novel, Chapter V, appeared in *La Tribuna* on February 1, 1856, with the title *Fragmento de un viaje—Esther.* This fragmentary part differs slightly, in regard to wording and sentence structure, from the corresponding Chapter V in the final text of the Biblioteca Americana. In addition, the completed novel is written in the third person, while the fragmentary portion is in the first person.

[12] Miguel Cané, *Esther,* in Instituto de Literatura Argentina, *op. cit.,* 1929, serie 4, tomo I, No. 7.

[13] In *Esther,* the youth's name is Eugenio Segry. However, Manuel Mujica Láinez, in a work entitled *Miguel Cané (padre), un romántico porteño,* B.A. Ediciones C.E.P.A., 1942, p. 121, note 4, states that in the original manuscript the protagonist is not called Eugenio Segry, but Tomás Gallardo; and that Cané, associated in Montevideo with Dr. Manuel Bonifacio Gallardo, changed the name perhaps to avoid difficulties.

Furthermore, it is of interest to note that an obscure story by Cané bears the title *Eugenio Segry, o el Traviato.* This work was completed in Montevideo in June, 1857, and published in serial form in *La Tribuna* of Buenos Aires from March 21 to April 13, 1858. The story relates Eugenio's amorous affair in Paris with a charming Austrian woman who is resignedly married to an alcoholic.

companionship and spiritual affinity she craves so much. The two lovers, with a perfect union of interests, live blissfully in a world of aesthetic sensations—journeying through Italy, visiting the renowned museums, libraries and churches, admiring famous works of art, and exchanging opinions on Italian literary masters.

The plot of *Esther* is extremely meager and external action is decidedly limited. It is clear that the author composed the novel not so much for the story as for the aesthetic effect it was to produce. *Esther* is indicative of Cané's literary creed of art for art's sake, and is in many respects an early manifestation of the modernistic novel cultivated at the turn of the century in America by such authors as Manuel Díaz Rodríguez and Pedro César Dominici. In Argentina this type of intellectual, artistic, and highly refined novel, of limited plot and movement, was to be skillfully developed by Ángel de Estrada and Enrique Larreta.

Cané's admiration of Italian civilization is manifested in *Esther* through exquisite paragraphs on painting, sculpture, and the fine arts in general, which reveal him as an author of delicate artistic sensibility. The political turbulences which compelled Cané to take temporary refuge in Europe could not dull his keen awareness and appreciation of the beauty around him; and despite his deeply felt apprehension for the future of Argentina, he composed *Esther,* wherein the cult of beauty and harmony seems to rise above the cruelty and intrigue of the Tyranny.

In his next work Cané turned his attention to the Argentine independence movement and wove a tragic drama ending in violence and bloodshed. Written in September, 1854, during the author's stay in Montevideo, *Una noche de boda* first appeared as the daily serial of *La Tribuna* from April 14 to 18, 1858, and in August of the same year it was published in Volume III of the Biblioteca Americana.[14]

The plot revolves around a bitter rivalry of love between an

---

[14] Miguel Cané, *Una noche de boda,* in Biblioteca Americana, ed. Magariños Cervantes, B.A., Imprenta de Mayo, 1858, III, 215-256. This short novel has never been republished and to the general public remains practically unknown.

impetuous captain of a rebel grenadier regiment and a wealthy but ignoble Spaniard. The story is slight and offers no particular originality. The melodramatic conclusion comes swiftly, yet is consistent with the rashness of the protagonists. Correct and elegant is the language; artificial and flowery is the dialogue. The two opponents in love are seen contending not only for a woman's affection, but for an ideology that each one believes basic in his existence. The insurgent captain, risking his life for freedom, embraces the revolutionary ideas proposed on the memorable date of May 25, 1810; while the influential Spaniard, fighting to preserve an Empire and the benefits and privileges it grants him, scorns the new generation of patriots who clamor for liberty. Thus he cries out:

> ¡Oh! es infame esta generación mestiza — la
> sangre salvaje de las pampas corre furiosa en esos
> corazones también salvajes.[15]

Completely different in subject matter from the two preceding works, *La familia de Sconner* treats of the usurpation of an inheritance by an unscrupulous relative and the legal action taken to restore the property to the rightful owners. The work was published, together with *Esther,* in Volume IV of the Biblioteca Americana.[16] A few days after the author finished the novel, *La Tribuna,* receptive to all literary work from the pen of Miguel Cané, inserted the following commentary:

> Ha concluído la novela jurídica del D. Cané, y
> con ella la solución histórica de un pleito en que
> la esplotación, el robo y la mentira coaligados con-
> tra la inocencia de los niños, han sido vencidos.[17]

Among the novels of Cané, *La familia de Sconner* shows the highest development of plot. In *Esther,* not only does the main interest lie outside the story, but that story itself is very limited and unsubstantial; while in *Una noche de boda* the plot is ingenuous and conventional. On the other hand, the subject matter of *La familia de Sconner*—a legal struggle—

---

[15] *Ibid.,* p. 241.
[16] Miguel Cané, *La familia de Sconner,* in Biblioteca Americana, *op. cit.,* 1858, IV, 106-219. It was not until 1930 that the work was re-edited by the Instituto de Literatura Argentina, *op. cit.,* 1930, serie 4, tomo I, No. 10.
[17] *La Tribuna,* B.A., September 4, 1858, p. 2.

quite easily lends itself to interesting and diversified elements of plot, which add a fresh note to the many hackneyed stories of the early romantic period. Furthermore, for the first time in the Argentine novel the plot centers around the vital force of money in human affairs. Hitherto, the motivating and impelling drives were patriotism, lust for power, revenge, and love; the desire for money received little consideration, or, as in *La novia del hereje,* it was not made prominent because of the more significant issues involved in the novel.

The sheepraising industry, in which Pedro Sconner amassed his fortune, is seen as constituting an important factor in the economic development of the nation. In this respect, Cané explains:

> Ese hombre se proponía introducir en la ganadería de Buenos Aires, ramo principal de su riqueza propia, una mejora radical......
>
> Pocos o ninguno antes que él habían pensado en que la mejora de la hacienda lanar podría aumentar la riqueza del país y llegar a ser uno de los artículos de esportación de primera importancia, y conocedor, como lo era por estudios prácticos, por sus viajes en los países productores y consumidores, de que ese ramo era una mina no esplotada todavía, fué a Inglaterra, se procuró corresponsales inteligentes, capitales bastantes, e importó a Buenos Aires las primeras ovejas Sajonas que se han conocido.[18]

Pedro Sconner's fine estate serves as a haven for the less fortunate people of the surrounding region and also as a gathering place for groups of gauchos. This rustic atmosphere, only very scantily touched upon in this novel, will play an important role in later works of the nineteenth and twentieth centuries. In Cané's estimation, the gaucho is a child of nature —heroic, spontaneous, enigmatic, embracing at once the noblest virtues and the most shameful vices. In addition, it is interesting to note that the author regarded the gaucho of his time as a cultural group that was gradually dying out, victim of an advancing civilization.

---

[18] *La familia de Sconner,* 1858 edition, *op. cit.,* p. 113.

3. The Novel of Exaggerated and Exalted Sentiment

A host of minor writers[19] tried their hand at the romantic novel during the years immediately following the publication of *Amalia* in 1855. Their names are now forgotten and their works remain stacked on the shelves of the Biblioteca Nacional or other libraries, where occasionally some curious reader or literary investigator will consult them. Yet these works are significant, for they indicate one of the early trends in the Argentine novel.

After the fall of Rosas a new and vital interest in the cultural life of the nation began to be kindled. The public was ready to assimilate novels by even the most obscure Argentine author; the important thing was that the work should be the product of an Argentine, and not of a foreign writer. In view of the growing demand for national novels, newspaper editors saw fit to advertise the appearance of new works. The public was not only informed as soon as a novel was available at the bookstores, but it even received advance notices, at times concerning a work in the process of preparation, at times in regard to an unforeseen delay in publication.

True critical reviews were seldom offered. Most often criticism was limited to a few short, vague, and ingenuous statements about the author and work; in other cases no qualifying remarks at all accompanied the announcement of publication. After this brief newspaper publicity, the majority of these novels were hardly ever referred to again and remained forgotten by all.

. . .

As one of the characteristics of romanticism we have the exaltation of the individual personality—the concentration on the ego, the releasing of the wide gamut of emotional states through which the mind passes. Around this expression of

[19] The only available biographical material concerning many of these authors is that found in the newspapers and magazines where some of their literary production appears. Yet even from that source information is extremely scanty in most cases. Moreover, for dates of birth and death, we had to resort frequently to the obituary columns of newspapers, the registers of parishes, and the indices of cemeteries.

romanticism center many Argentine novels of the early period. As a group these works reveal several definite features, which we may point out to advantage. Foremost, the majority of the novels invest human sentiment and action with a highly exaggerated and overplayed quality. In life, emotional disposition of one human being toward another is generally modulated, controlled, or even restrained; and except under very trying conditions violent outbursts and impetuous displays of feeling remain at a minimum. Yet in these romantic works there occurs either one of two things: general and undue intensification of sentiments regardless of motivating force; or a deliberate presentation of the most unusual experiences or circumstances, whereby behavior, of necessity, is guided by impulsive and irrational thinking. Not even in the latter case, nevertheless, are ordinary modes of behavior in life so excessively vehement and precipitous.

Such qualities as love, friendship, honor, and sacrifice are idealized to the extreme and are presented in an exceedingly artificial and disproportionate manner. In a similar vein, weaknesses and vices of mankind are shown in colors completely black. By either the most horrible vices or the most exalted virtues are the majority of protagonists thoroughly and inexorably controlled. No middle of the road hues, no intermediary shades of gray. Angelic, poetic creatures, consummating noble and sublime acts, or wicked and treacherous men, planning and executing the most barbarous deeds—such individuals are typical in these novels. Common themes revolve around frenetic love, hate, jealousy, vengeance, and lewdness; and neither reason nor fear of punishment can restrain the impulsive protagonists from the fulfillment of these passions.

Among the first works in this group is *Camila, o la virtud triunfante* (1856), written by Estanislao del Campo (1834-1880),[20] the famous author of *Fausto*. Many of the elements which we have just cited as characteristic of this type of ro-

[20] E. del C., *Camila, o la virtud triunfante,* B.A., Imprenta de La Revista, 1856. There is no indication in the work for whom the initials "E. del C." stand, but we know that the author is Estanislao del Campo from the following

mantic novel are clearly discernible in *Camila*. Exaggerated
emotions, exalted passion, unusual incidents, and aberrant personalities all combine to produce the fanciful plot. We see a
wicked and revengeful libertine finally murdered in a manner
as diabolical as his own machinations for personal satisfaction.
No less evil is this villain's partner, who possesses a mind just
as devilishly warped. The scene in the cellar, where the re-
probate is helplessly awaiting death, is sickening, offensive to
fine sensibility, and calculated to stimulate interest by means
of spectacular and brutal action. Set in opposition to these
fiendish characters we find Camila and her female companion,
who represent the idealized and sentimental aspect of the work.

　　Laurindo Lapuente. Although better known and far more
successful as a poet, Laurindo Lapuente (1835-1870)[21] also es-
sayed the field of prose fiction. In 1856, Lapuente published
La aerostática en Buenos Aires,[22] a curious novelistic account
of a Frenchman's attempt to ascend in a balloon. The book
opens with a description, penned in a cynical and mocking
fashion, of a multitude gathered together to witness the aerial
stunt. The crowd is disappointed as the balloonist fails in his
first try; and when subsequent attempts likewise prove unsuc-
cessful, the once enthusiastic throng solemnly withdraws, voicing displeasure at the entire affair. Intercalated in this narration is a simple love story of young sweethearts who become

information. In *La Voz de Pueblo*, May 17, 1860, p. 3, there was published a
poem entitled *Mi sobrina*, below which appeared the letters "E. del C." The
editor of the newspaper prefaced the poem as follows: "Nuestro amigo, Estanislao del Campo, nos ha autorizado para publicar los que a continuación in-
sertamos." Furthermore, in a work by Alfredo Lovell y Sainz de Aja, entitled
*Seudónimos, anagramas, criptónimos, alónimos, títulos nobilarios, etc., usados
por escritores,* Rosario, 1950, p. 250, our statement is corroborated.
　[21] Born in Montevideo in 1835, at an early age Lapuente was left an orphan
and had to struggle alone through his formative years. He came to Argentina
in 1853 and served as a lieutenant in the naval forces of the then independent
province of Buenos Aires. Subsequently, he earned his livelihood at teaching,
but at the same time published volumes of poetry, political treatises, and newspaper articles. An indefatigable worker despite chronic ill health, he enjoyed
a solid reputation both as a man of letters and as a staunch defender of civil
liberties. Death came in Buenos Aires on November 16, 1870.
　Laurindas, 1865, is Lapuente's most important volume of poetry. In addition, he published the following: *Ensayos poéticos,* 1856; *Poesías,* 1865; *Re-
publicanas,* 1865; *La virtud,* 1867. In prose he wrote: *La gran política del
Presidente Mitre,* 1867; *Frutos de una gran política,* 1868; *Las profecías de
Mitre,* 1868; *El gobierno de Sarmiento,* 1869.
　[22] Laurindo Lapuente, *La aerostática en Buenos Aires—capricho histórico y
novelesco,* B.A., Imprenta de El Eco, 1856.

reconciled at this event. The original feature of *La aerostática en Buenos Aires* lies in its satirical portraiture of selected social types, such as the dandy and the newsmonger, as well as in the bitter criticism of other more objectionable groups of individuals. Note in the following paragraph Lapuente's censorious tone:

> ¡Y los varones! Si tienen, creen que todos los demás hombres son sus esclavos y que están obligados a rendirles homenaje, aunque sean pícaros o asnos. Si valen les parece que su posición social les autoriza para abusar de ella; se vuelven despreciativos y orgullosos, fruncen el ceño; en fin, llegan a ser odiados de todo el mundo. Si es algún gefe de importancia, derecho como una estaca, seco como un escupido, arrogante como un necio, en todas partes le parece que está mandando su ejército o batallón; pues para él todos son sus soldados.[23]

Lapuente's love for the land of his birth is clearly manifested in the novel *El Herminio de la Nueva Troya*,[24] which treats of the important role that Uruguay played in the struggle against Rosas. In 1834, Manuel Oribe became president of Uruguay and then proceeded to form an alliance with Rosas. When his term of office ended in 1838, he became a high-ranking officer in the Federalist army, and in that capacity committed many civil and military crimes. In 1843, Argentine forces under Oribe's command invaded Uruguay, and in the battle of Arroyo Grande decisively defeated the defending troops. Against this tense background *El Herminio de la Nueva Troya* relates a tender story, in which the protagonists are a self-exiled Argentine girl residing in Montevideo to avoid

---

[23] *Ibid.,* pp. 39-40.

[24] Laurindo Lapuente, *El Herminio de la Nueva Troya*, B.A., Imprenta de La Reforma Pacífica, 1857. This novel received considerable publicity in the newspapers of Buenos Aires. *El Nacional* and *La Prensa* gave notices when each of the three parts of the work appeared. On September 25, 1857, the first part went on sale; on October 10, the second; and on November 13, the last part. On August 13, 1857, the following advance notice was made in *La Prensa*, p. 3: "*Herminio*, novela histórica contemporánea, original de Laurindo Lapuente, dedicada a los valientes defensores de la Plaza de Montevideo, sitiada por el ejército de Oribe. Esta publicación, que contendrá varios episodios del sitio de Montevideo, se hará por entregas."

political persecution, and a noble Uruguayan soldier who defends his country against Rosas' hordes. The most interesting feature of the work is the narration of the military campaign in Montevideo. The formation and position of the armies, the types of munitions, the tactics employed, the untold suffering of the troops—these things are all described in faithful detail. Lastly, Oribe and Rosas are portrayed vividly, in all their ignominy.

In Lapuente's second novel, entitled *Virtud y amor hasta la tumba*,[25] the romantic story of love, hate, and vengeance is carried to fanciful excess, and involves a strange entanglement in which the villain is none other than the virtuous maiden's licentious uncle. In this work Lapuente's romanticism is revealed in the exaggerated story of overwrought emotions; while in *El Herminio de la Nueva Troya* it is seen in his ardent love of liberty and justice.

Ángel Julio Blanco. From the pen of Ángel Julio Blanco (1831-1898)[26] came three of Argentina's most bizarre and inordinately imaginative novels.[27] In 1856, Blanco published *Una venganza funesta*,[28] and the following year its sequel, *Emeterio de Leao*.[29] The closely interrelated plots of both works are extremely lengthy and complicated, involving a multitude of incidents and characters that become fancifully entwined. Throughout the pages appear mysterious people and persons of double identity. Blanco's romanticism is further indicated in these two novels by his vigorous shout of

[25] Laurindo Lapuente, *Virtud y amor hasta la tumba*, B.A., Imprenta de La Reforma, 1858.

[26] These dates of birth and death were taken from the records of the Recoleta Cemetery in Buenos Aires, year 1898, folio 174, line 13.

[27] Besides these novels, he published many articles, poems, and stories in newspapers and magazines. As a journalist he discussed political and social questions of the day, revealing himself as an enthusiastic supporter of liberal and democratic government. In addition, he held several political positions, which he fulfilled with dignity and devotion. In 1880, Blanco retired from public life, yet worked for some time afterward as an actuary. Death came on April 6, 1898. This biographical information was obtained from an article by Álbano Honores, which appeared in *El Tiempo*, p. 3, on April 9, 1898, a few days after Blanco's death.

[28] Ángel Julio Blanco, *Una venganza funesta*, B.A., Imprenta Americana, 1856.

[29] Ángel Julio Blanco, *Emeterio de Leao*—continuación de *Una venganza funesta*, B.A., Imprenta Americana, 1857. At the close of *Emeterio*, the editor states that a third and final part is to appear shortly, containing many characters previously met in the first two sections. This work has not been found, having never been published or having been lost completely.

protest against existing social conditions. Within the highly extravagant plot, two basic points of focus may be noticed: the ultimate moral regeneration of the once lawless protagonist, and the bitter upbraiding of the negligent society that brought about his criminal behavior as a youth. The author further lashes out at the wealthy class, censuring its disdain of the common man and the hypocritical way in which it so neatly conceals vice, corruption, and ignorance under a coat of riches and false manners.

> En todas partes lo que llamamos "pueblo, clase baja, chusma," es esa gran parte de la sociedad universal, condenada a sufrir pasivamente los privilegios y desmanes de esa otra más pequeña que se llama "clase alta, aristocracia, gente de tono."[30]

Blanco's third novel, *Luis y Estevan,* appeared in the magazine *Museo Literario* on January 20, 1859, and treats in a most lurid fashion of the immorality and viciousness of two youths. The author's introduction to this work is significant, for it reveals a budding interest in portraying the national scene. Blanco states that although he sought in this novel and the preceding ones to describe customs distinguishably Argentine, he was always faced with a lack of suitable material. He affirms "que no tenemos nada nuestro: que somos como los monos, imitadores..., o nos estacionamos, o copiamos; ésa es nuestra vida."[31] Therefore, blocked in his desire to reproduce typical Argentine customs, he turned to depicting passions— love, lust, vengeance, and greed—and pointing out the foibles of society. In *Luis y Estevan,* nevertheless, Blanco does succeed in presenting a very elementary characterization of Buenos Aires. Centers of reunion, such as hotels and restaurants, are briefly mentioned, and an occasional reference is made to social types, streets, and churches. Yet the author's fleeting picture of the capital is not a very complimentary one, as he considers it only a third-rate city in commerce and among the most unattractive in architectural design.

· · ·

[30] *Una venganza funesta, op. cit.,* Vol. I, pp. 102-103, note.
[31] Ángel Julio Blanco, *Luis y Estevan,* in *Museo Literario,* B.A., January 20, 1859, p. 9.

Numerous other novels of exaggerated and exalted sentiment were written during the 1850's and 1860's. In many of these second-rate works[32] the story is unfolded in a virtual environmental vacuum; that is, either the locale remains indefinite and completely undescribed, or the depiction of setting is so slight and insignificant as to render negligible its effect in enhancing the meaning of the novel. In short, conspicuously absent is the portraiture of the Argentine scene, with its varied landscape, its social types, and its vital traditions and

[32] We mention the following works in chronological order:

a. Margarita Rufina Ochagavia, *Un ángel y un demonio, o el valor de un juramento*, B.A., Imprenta de Mayo, 1857. The author, born in 1840, wrote this insignificant novel of love at the age of seventeen.

b. José V. Rocha, *Un drama de la vida*, B.A., 1857. The author (1830-1898) weaves a complex but frivolous plot around a youth's heroic struggle to save his sister's honor. Records of the Recoleta Cemetery, year 1898, folio 187, line 21, reveal that Rocha died on October 22, 1898.

c. Carlos L. Paz, *Santa y mártir de veinte años*, B.A., Imprenta de La Reforma, 1857. The author (1837-1874) was a poet, journalist, lawyer, and soldier. His novel relates the sad experiences of a young woman whom misfortune seems to have sought out, until a magnanimous army officer, touched with deep compassion, offers to marry her and accept her newborn child as his own.

d. Tomás Gutiérrez, *Carlota, o la hija del pescador*, in serial form in *La Tribuna*, April 20 to 28, 1858. In this work, two sisters are rivals for the love of a young man. Gutiérrez (1838-1881), poet, dramatist, and fecund contributor to many newspapers and magazines, also wrote *El destino, o la venganza de una mujer*, a novel which was announced to the public in *La Prensa* on December 11, 1857, but has not been found.

e. Francisco López Torres, *La virgen de Lima*, B.A., 1858. The author (1839-1871) spins a fanciful story of a young man's double life as priest and bandit.

f. Eusebio F. Gómez, *Angélica o una víctima de sus amores*, Paraná, Imprenta de El Nacional Argentina, 1859. A spurned lover acts as executioner of his former sweetheart, who once committed murder to avenge her brother's death.

g. Ernesto O. Loiseau, *Hojas de mirto*, B.A., Imprenta de La Reforma, 1860. The author (1816-1863) concludes a tender love story by having a girl murdered by her own father because she did not consent to his prearranged marriage. Records of the Recoleta Cemetery, year 1863, folio 180, line 5, indicate that Loiseau died on October 23, 1863.

h. Tomás N. Giráldez, *Vengador y suicida*, B.A., Imprenta de P. Gautier, 1860. The author (?-1871) narrates the loves of a fickle man about town. A notice in *El Nacional* on March 8, 1871, p. 3, states that Giráldez died on February 12, 1871.

i. M. Sasor, *María de Montiel*, B.A., Imprenta de La Revista, 1861. M. Sasor is the anagram of Mercedes Rosas de Rivera, the Dictator's sister. The long and tiresome novel unfolds a trite love story, in which interminable declarations of affection and devotion are made through an exchange of letters.

j. R. El Mugiense, *Emilia, o los efectos del coquetismo*, B.A., Imprenta de La Bolsa, 1862. The author, whose real name was Ramón Machali, narrates the affairs of a frivolous and mercenary woman.

Also in the year 1862 there appeared a notice in *La Nación Argentina*, September 21, p. 3, of the coming publication of a novel by Luis Veras, entitled *Una víctima del poder de la plata, o el capricho de un millonario*. "La primera edición de esta novela histórica de la época verá la luz pública tan luego como se haya conseguido otros pormenores que falta por la segunda." However, we have not been able to locate the work, nor do we know whether it was ever actually published.

customs. Yet a few works contain selected features which indicate the author's interest in original Argentine subject matter. These novels we shall briefly consider in the paragraphs that follow.

Manuel Romano (1825-1878)[33] glorifies a rude but noble gaucho in his novel *El isleño* (1857).[34] At first scorned by his sweetheart's haughty father, he finally gains acceptance upon proving himself a hero during a battle for Argentine independence. The author's defense of the gaucho is revealed in those scenes in which the protagonist's unrefined manner comes in conflict with the pompous and overbearing demeanor of his fiancée's father. The single military episode around which the novel centers is well written and carefully developed. The vivid and detailed descriptions of preparations for battle, as well as of the actual fighting, are excellent. The stalwart patriotism and cooperation of the citizens of San Lorenzo are clearly and forcibly demonstrated. No less ably portrayed is the figure of San Martín, whose personal report of the battle adds a graphic note to the narration.

From the inspiration of Argentina's history and traditions came the novel *El pirata, o la familia de los Condes de Osorno* (1863),[35] by Coriolano Márquez, an Argentine military officer involved in political disorder in his own country as well as in Uruguay and Paraguay. The author wrote the work while imprisoned in Buenos Aires for having ordered unauthoritatively the arrest and execution of several officials. In October, 1864, he escaped from jail and fled to Montevideo, where he took part in the revolution to depose Atanasio Aguirre. Later, charged with conspiracy against the Paraguayan dictator Francisco Solano López, he was condemned to death and executed in 1867. The novel treats of the sad fate of several members of the wealthy Osorno family, kidnapped by an infamous pi-

[33] Records of the Recoleta Cemetery, year 1878, folio 224, line 15, reveal that Romano died on July 3, 1878.
[34] Manuel Romano, *El isleño—episodio de la guerra de la independencia,* B.A., Imprenta Americana, 1857.
[35] Coriolano Márquez, *El pirata, o la familia de los Condes de Osorno,* novela histórica, escrita en la cárcel pública de Buenos Aires, en el calabozo No. 5, en octubre de 1862, B.A., Imprenta de La Bolsa, 1863.

rate as they proceeded to a region of Chile formerly settled by their ancestors. The many episodes in the work lack unity, and frequently motives of action remain unclear. Inserted in the novel is a facsimile of a historical document which reveals that Spanish explorers encountered the lost city of Los Césares, founded by the Osorno settlers and later destroyed by Araucanian Indians. The manuscript discloses that this city is located in Argentina, and not in Chile as previously supposed. In the last thirty pages of *El pirata,* the author refutes the charges made against him as an officer. Through the presentation of indisputable evidence and logical deductions, Márquez hopes to convince all Argentines of his innocence.

Concern over the possible pernicious effects of Argentina's expanding economy is seen in Enrique López' *El indicador positivista* (1869),[36] a work which appears as an elementary forerunner of the subsequent novels of the financial crisis of 1890. Intercalated in the plot (which concerns the tragic fate of each one of the heroine's three eager suitors) are numerous digressions that serve to praise virtue and condemn vice. López sharply criticizes those who sacrifice the finer values in life for material possessions; and in this respect he mentions the California gold rush as indicative of the extremes to which men may go to satisfy their passion for money. The author's antipathy to a purely materialistic philosophy may be summed up in the following observation made by the most noble of the heroine's admirers:

> Una educación que no reconoce otro punto de partida que el de un positivismo repugnante, el cual no tarda en descender hasta el más grosero materialismo, que petrifica el alma y corrompe el corazón acaso.[37]

Lastly, it is important to mention Bernabé Demaría's[38]

[36] Enrique López, *El indicador positivista, o la novela enciclopédica,* B.A., Imprenta Española, 1869.

[37] *Ibid.,* pp. 18-19.

[38] Demaría, born on January 17, 1824, belonged to a well-established family of the capital. Persecuted by the Tyranny, he emigrated to Montevideo in 1844, and there continued his academic studies and cultivated his talent for painting. In 1847 he traveled to Madrid, where in many artistic circles his paintings won high acclaim. After returning to Argentina in 1852, Demaría became active for a brief period in journalism and politics, but then soon retired to private life. He died in Buenos Aires on May 25, 1910.

sprawling and undisciplined novel entitled *Revelaciones de un manuscrito* (1869),[39] which centers around the unbridled amorous adventures and dissipative life of leisure of an Argentine youth who takes up residence for many years in fashionable Europe. The author's desire to portray Argentine civilization in fiction is quite evident; yet with his limited novelistic skill he could do no more than reveal this culture in a purely expository fashion, wholly detached from the narration of events and without any identification with the action of the novel or the behavior of the characters. Demaría dedicates one entire section of the work to the geographical, historical, and sociological background of Argentina. He carefully treats of its physical features, social classes, customs, traditions, and peculiarities of language. He bestows lavish praise on the gaucho's crude but sincere mode of life, writing of his daily activities, home atmosphere, characteristic dress, and forms of diversion. Lastly, nature's splendid scene is exposed through beautiful descriptions of the immense pampas and the Paraná and Tigre Rivers, as well as through brief sketches of many indigenous birds, fish, and trees.

[39] The work appeared for the first time as the serial of *El Nacional,* from July 5 to December 7, 1869. The same year it came out in book form, B.A., Imprenta Argentina de El Nacional, 1869, and all copies were sold within three months. In 1906, the novel was published in an anthology of the author's works, in *Obras literarias de Bernabé Demaría,* B.A., Imprenta Europa de M. A. Rosas, 1906, pp. 163-383.

In the preface to *Revelaciones de un manuscrito,* the author explains the title. He possesses the diary of a close friend who recently passed away, in which the writer refers particularly to his meditations, problems, and disillusions. This manuscript constitutes the basis of the work, but Demaría alters many elements to suit his novelistic purpose and to hide the identity of the real people in the story.

VI

THE DEVELOPMENT OF THE
ROMANTIC NOVEL AFTER *AMALIA*

(Part two)

1. THE ROMANTICISM OF JUANA MANUELA GORRITI

Owing to its chronological significance we formerly set apart
one novel—*La quena* (1845)—of Juana Manuela Gorriti. We
shall now consider her works in general and the character of
her romanticism. Gorriti is the most distinguished woman
writer of her generation and one of the most noteworthy and
original cultivators of the Argentine romantic novel. Born on
June 15, 1818, in the province of Salta, she was the daughter
of José Ignacio Gorriti, an important general of the independence movement. In 1831 the Gorriti family emigrated to
Bolivia to escape political persecution. There, two years later,
Manuela married Manuel Isidro Belzu, who in 1848 became
president of Bolivia. However, despite a happy beginning the
matrimony ended in failure. Gorriti then took up residence
in Lima, where she dedicated herself assiduously to literature
and teaching. To her *salones* came the renowned and obscure
of Peruvian letters, and within a short time she earned a widespread reputation as a prominent writer and cultivator of the
fine arts. In point of fact, the many years she spent in Peru
constitute the period of her greatest literary productivity. To
gauge the great esteem in which Gorriti was held in Lima, we
may note that during the years 1876 and 1877 no less an outstanding figure than Ricardo Palma presided over many of
these popular literary gatherings, where assuredly the counsel
and example of both these artists gave fresh stimulus to the
cultivation and appreciation of literature in Peru. In 1879,

when hostilities broke out between Peru and Chile, Gorriti left Lima and returned to Argentina, where she lived until her death on November 6, 1892.

Gorriti's principal works of fiction are included in *Sueños y realidades* (1865)[1] and *Panoramas de la vida* (1876).[2] These two productions consist of novels, short stories, fantasies, anecdotes, legends, historical episodes, and picturesque descriptions of American life, wherein Gorriti reveals the wild, unbridled romanticism that was quick to arrest the attention of the critics and public throughout America.

How do we define Gorriti's romanticism? In the first place, like other Argentine novelists of the period, Juana Manuela displayed the common inclination toward exaggerated and exalted sentiment, and themes of vengeance and atrocious crimes of passion. To this aspect of romanticism Gorriti added others, hitherto undeveloped in the Argentine novel. Juana Manuela, who, it is related, "danzaba misteriosos ritos a la luz de la luna en su jardín limeño,"[3] possessed an unrestrained imagination and a brilliant fantasy, of which she availed herself freely in her literary works. Her novels and stories indicate a predilection for the mysterious, the unknown, the eerie, and the suggestive. Gloom, darkness, shadows, premonitions, fatidic words, and weird sounds frequently fill the scene of action. As revealed in her fiction, strange, inexplicable, and dreadful forces often influence man's passions and lead him to execute his deeds. Gorriti's world is not a peaceful, pleasant, or lucid one; it is chaotic, appalling, and unfathomable. As an illustration of the lugubrious and mystifying atmosphere that she excellently creates, we may cite the closing paragraphs of *La quena,* which describe the hero's eternal bereavement.

[1] Juana Manuela Gorriti, *Sueños y realidades,* ed. Vicente G. Quesada, B.A., Imprenta de Mayo, 1865, 2 vols. In 1907, this work was republished by La Biblioteca de la Nación, Vols. 280 and 281.

[2] Juana Manuela Gorriti, *Panoramas de la vida,* ed. Carlos Casavalle, B.A., Imprenta de Mayo, 1876, Vols. I and II.

In 1888, Gorriti issued separately a short novel entitled *Oasis en la vida,* ed. F. Lajouane, B.A., 1888, in which she put aside her rich fantasy, and around the life of a struggling young journalist wove a story wherein were included such mundane concerns as an inheritance, a bankruptcy, and a life insurance policy. Written in an epoch of national prosperity, the work extols industriousness and frugality, virtues which are exemplified in the life of the protagonist.

[3] Ricardo Rojas, *Historia de la literatura argentina,* B.A., Editorial Losada, 1948, VIII, 492.

Mas la tempestad había pasado. Una noche lóbrega cubría las montañas, el pueblo y la llanura; y la doble oscuridad que nivelaba todos los objetos sólo era interrumpida a largos intervalos por la luz amarillenta y fugaz de los lejanos relámpagos. La naturaleza entera parecía dormitar después de la terrible crisis que la había agitado; y todo lo que tenía vida sufría la reacción del miedo; reposaba.

Ningún ruido esterior revelaba la vida en aquel negro hacinamiento de edificios, y sin embargo en lo alto de uno de ellos se veía la luz brillando como un faro en aquel océano de tinieblas.

De repente una melodía estraña, dulce, desgarrante y aterradora a la vez, se elevó de aquel sitio, atravesó los aires, llenó los ámbitos del valle, y fué a despertar los ecos de las montañas.

Era una música sublime, cuyos mágicos acentos, ora tiernos y apasionados como el adiós de un amante que se aleja, ora melancólicos y dolientes como los suspiros de la ausencia, ora sombríos y lúgubres como la voz del "De profundis," remedaban, uno a uno, todos los gemidos que el amor o el dolor pueden arrancar al corazón humano. ¿Era una voz? ¿Era un instrumento? Ángel o demonio; ¿quién era el autor de esa melodía?

Era un hombre que sentado a los pies de una mujer en un gabinete enlutado y alumbrado por una gran lámpara de plata, tañía un instrumento de forma estraña.

Aquel hombre vestido de negro, como todos los objetos que lo rodeaban, era de estatura alta y llena de distinción, de facciones bellas, aunque cubiertas de una palidez sepulcral.....

La mujer a cuyos pies se hallaba, envuelta en una túnica blanca, y recostada en un ancho diván, tenía medio cubierto el rostro con las ondas de su cabellera negra, que descendiendo a lo largo de los pliegues de su ropa llegaba hasta el suelo. Una de sus manos descansaba en su rodilla, y la otra sostenía su cabeza reclinada sobre los cogines del diván.

Nada más plácidamente bello que el grupo que formaban, la mujer vestida de blanco como la virgen que sube al lecho nupcial y el hombre que puesto a sus pies y alzando hacia ella sus tan hermosos y apasionados ojos, parecía dirigirla todas las notas de aquella celeste armonía. Pero si algún ser viviente hubiera podido penetrar en ese sitio y mirar de cerca aquel grupo, habría sentido erizarse los cabellos sobre su cabeza y hubiera huido espantado: porque la larga cabellera de aquella mujer tenía una aridez metálica; sus manos de forma tan bella, estaban secas; aquella alba túnica era un sudario; el rostro que el jóven contemplaba había recibido hacía largo tiempo el horrible sello de la muerte, y el instrumento mismo cuya voz tenía una tan divina melodía, era un despojo de la tumba, era el fémur de aquel esqueleto.[4]

For more individual consideration we may select two of Gorriti's works, *El guante negro*[5] and *El tesoro de los incas*,[6] both of which originally appeared in the volume *Sueños y realidades*. In *El guante negro* Gorriti presents a moving story of a youth's intense struggle between solemn duty and love of a woman. Once again the Rosas era forms the background. The heroine is a fervent Unitarian supporter, while her sweetheart is a staunch Federalist, whose father wields a powerful hand as an influential officer of the Dictator's army. The conflict reaches an acute stage when the jealous girl demands from her lover an act of sacrifice to prove his real devotion and allay her misgivings—namely, that he should be a traitor to the Federalist forces and join the Unitarians. An object, the black glove, adds a symbolic and bewitching note to the work. The hero receives this glove from a charming woman as an eternal remembrance, with the understanding that he keep it always near his heart. Months later, when his fiancée discovers his body on the battlefield (he did not betray Rosas), she notices on the mortal chest wound the same fatal black glove.

[4] *La quena*, in *Sueños y realidades*, 1865 edition, *op. cit.*, I, 63-65.
[5] Juana Manuela Gorriti, *El guante negro, Ibid.*, I, 69-106.
[6] Juana Manuela Gorriti, *El tesoro de los incas, Ibid.*, II, 87-133.

El guante negro is one of Gorriti's best developed works.
Each scene, brief and compact, is carefully executed and forcibly presented. Among the many moving episodes we may
signal out that in which the jealous heroine urges her lover
to forsake his political allegiance; the scene in which maternal
love triumphs over marital love, as the hero's mother slays her
husband to save her son; and the one in which the heroine
lovingly clings to the corpse of her faithless sweetheart. The
works moves swiftly and acquires much dramatic impact as
dominating passions are placed in conflict with one another.

Gorriti's interest in American folklore and legend is well
revealed in *El tesoro de los incas,* which narrates how loyal
members of an Indian family of Cuzco stubbornly refuse to
disclose the location of an ancient hidden treasure. When
greedy Spanish officials inflict untold torture on his daughter
to force her to break her vow, the august chief painfully cries
out, "Calla y muere." The girl dies happily in writhing agony
within full sight of her father, who then throws himself into the
fire that his torturers prepared for him, thus perishing with
the secret of the treasure forever sealed on his lips. Gorriti
appropriately sets the scene for the somber drama, describing
Cuzco as a city of fantastic legends, marvelous traditions, and
closely guarded secrets, of unmeasured beauty and grandeur,
of extraordinary wealth and brazen ostentation. The mystery
of the *tesoro de los incas* is just one of the many obscurities of
the magnificent city that was Cuzco; while the venerable chief
represents the proud defender of the Indian tradition.

Gorriti selected material for her novels and stories from a
wide variety of sources: traditions, legends, and customs of the
American autochthonous population, as in *La quena* and *El
tesoro de los incas;* the history of Argentina, with particular
reference to the independence period and the Tyranny, as in
El lucero de Manantial[7] and *El guante negro;* social types,
folklore, and characteristic scenes of Argentina, as in *Gubi-
Amaya;*[8] recollections of her own past life in Argentina, Peru,

[7] Juana Manuela Gorriti, *El lucero de Manantial—episodio de la dictadura
de don Juan Manuel Rosas, Ibid.,* I, 277-303.
[8] Juana Manuela Gorriti, *Gubi-Amaya, Ibid.,* I, 107-200.

and Bolivia, with vivid impressions of relatives, friends, local folks, landscape, and memorable events, as in *Peregrinaciones de una alma triste;*[9] and lastly, the intemperate passions of men, presented in an exaggerated and overplayed manner, as in *Juez y verdugo,*[10] *El pozo del Yocci,*[11] and *El ángel caído.*[12] We recognize Juana Manuela Gorriti as a writer of powerful creative instincts and an intensely vivid imagination, who interpreted in her fiction the glorious America she loved so well. She proudly availed herself of the American scene in general for the picturesque background of her works; yet in the portrayal of selected sections of America she never forgot her native Argentina, which despite prolonged absence she always regarded with deep admiration and sincere sentiment.

2. OTHER WOMEN NOVELISTS: EDUARDA MANSILLA DE GARCÍA
AND ROSA GUERRA

A frequently discussed romantic novel was *El médico de San Luis,*[13] published in 1860 under the pseudonym of "Daniel," in reality Eduarda Mansilla de García.[14] The work was enthusiastically applauded by the public in general, and notable critics, among them Juan María Gutiérrez[15] and Ventura de la Vega,[16] offered their favorable comments. *El médico de San Luis* purports to show that true happiness and contentment are achieved only through the family unit, trustworthy

[9] Juana Manuela Gorriti, *Peregrinaciones de una alma triste,* in *Panoramas de la vida, op. cit.,* I, 17-238.
[10] Juana Manuela Gorriti, *Juez y verdugo, Ibid.,* I, 239-347.
[11] Juana Manuela Gorriti, *El pozo del Yocci, Ibid.,* I, 349-450.
[12] Juana Manuela Gorriti, *El ángel caído,* in *Sueños y realidades, op. cit.,* II, 3-86.
[13] Daniel, *El médico de San Luis,* B.A., Imprenta de La Paz, 1860. In 1879 the novel was republished with the author's real name: Eduarda Mansilla de García, *El médico de San Luis,* precedida de apuntes por M.N.V., y de un estudio sobre la autora por Rafael Pombo, B.A., 1879.
[14] Eduarda Mansilla (1835-1892) was the daughter of General Lucio Mansilla, active in the independence movement, and Agustina Rosas, the Dictator's sister. Her brother was the famous Lucio V. Mansilla, author of *Una excursión a los indios ranqueles.* An esteemed figure in literary circles, she contributed many articles and stories to newspapers and magazines.
[15] Juan María Gutiérrez, "El médico de San Luis," *Revista de Ciencias y Letras del Círculo Literario de Buenos Aires,* B.A., 1864, I, No. I, 69-79.
[16] Ventura de la Vega, "El médico de San Luis," *Ibid.,* pp. 79-87.

friends, and diligent work. The novel presents episodes in the life of a kindly and unpretentious country doctor, dear to the hearts of all, who by virtue of his confidence in the love he inspires nobly surmounts many difficulties. Mansilla de García was undoubtedly stimulated by Oliver Goldsmith's *The Vicar of Wakefield*. At the beginning of her novel she cites this English writer, the quotation stating that his book reveals the soul of a humble and sincere provincial dweller living simply and guilelessly in an era of luxury and wealth. The protagonist of Mansilla's novel may be characterized in a similar fashion.

In the intimate portrayal of this devoted father and dutiful husband lies the principal interest and merit of *El médico de San Luis*. The over-all peaceful and harmonious tone of the novel represented a welcomed change for the Argentine public, which by 1860 had read its share of fiction containing villainous characters, crimes of vengeance, and scenes of violence. The protagonist himself narrates the story solemnly and unassumingly, as a person deeply moved by the action he relates. Sincerity of emotion, exemplary conduct as the head of a closely knit family, hospitality, helpfulness, and self-sacrifice are among the fine qualities of this hero. Ventura de la Vega makes the following comment concerning the novel: "¡Qué ternura! ¡Qué delicadeza de sentimientos! ¡Qué filosofía tan práctica! ¡Qué moral tan pura!"[17]

El médico de San Luis contains many interesting considerations on the progress of Argentina, a subject with which Mansilla de García was ever concerned. The author felt that the nation was advancing too rapidly along materialistic lines, to the detriment of moral and social values. Furthermore, Mansilla attacked what she considered the superficiality and falseness of high society, while she showered words of praise on poor and humble folk. She cried out against venal and corrupt magistrates who use their influence to make a mockery of justice, while she lauded upright and ethical conduct in all of life's activities. Lastly, apprehensive that the far-flung rural

[17] *Ibid.*, p. 80.

regions might be neglected in favor of the advancing urban civilization, Mansilla stated that the savage gaucho, if given proper education, could greatly contribute to the future importance of Argentina.

Under the pseudonym of "Daniel," Mansilla de García also wrote *Lucía — novela sacada de la historia argentina,* which appeared as the serial of *La Tribuna* from May 10 to July 4, 1860. In 1882, the work was published again, with the title *Lucía Miranda*[18] and under the author's real name. The novel reaches far back to the days of the first Spanish settlement in the Paraná region—the fort of Espíritu Santo—and interprets the celebrated story of the noble and beautiful Lucía Miranda, who, alone among members of an Indian tribe, is finally executed at the hands of the malicious chief, Siripo. The novel as a whole lacks artistry in composition and development. The interest of the main story lags because of long and detailed descriptions, tedious digressions, and a multitude of minor episodes and anecdotes.

The theme of Lucía Miranda was also treated by Rosa Guerra (? -1894), whose novel (1860)[19] is a much more artistic and masterly creation than the one published by Mansilla de García the same year.[20] The author, who divided her activities

---

[18] Eduarda Mansilla de García, *Lucía Miranda,* B.A., Imprenta de Juan A. Alsina, 1882. The novel was subsequently published in Biblioteca La Tradición Argentina, 1933, Vol. XXXV.
    Under the name "Eduarda," Mansilla de García published a novel entitled *Un amor,* B.A., Imprenta de El Diario, 1885. Although the author's name is indicated only as "Eduarda," it unquestionably refers to Eduarda Mansilla de García, for on the inside cover there are mentioned other works of the same novelist—*El médico de San Luis* and *Lucía Miranda. Un amor* narrates the story of a wealthy girl who falls in love with twin brothers.
[19] Rosa Guerra, *Lucía Miranda,* B.A., Imprenta Americana, 1860.
[20] Within the brief period of one month both Mansilla de García's *Lucía Miranda* and Rosa Guerra's novel of the same name were made available to the public. The former appeared as the serial of *La Tribuna* from May 10 to July 4, 1860, while the latter was placed on sale on June 9, 1860. On May 12, 1860, *La Tribuna,* p. 3, inserted the following comment about Guerra's work: "Hay otra novela basada sobre el mismo argumento y que lleva el mismo título de *Lucía Miranda.* Su autor es la señorita Rosa Guerra. ¿No publicará esta señorita su obra, para que la juzgue el público?"
    In 1879 there appeared a third novel treating this same theme: Malaquías Méndez, *Lucía,* Santa Fe, Imprenta de El Santafesino, 1879. In this work, the interpretation of the story differs from that given in the other two novels. The villain Siripo plays no part but Mangora himself kills Lucía and Sebastián. Moreover, there figures an important additional person named Lola, who, married to a Spanish officer, suffers the same fate as Lucía.

between literature and teaching, composed *Lucía Miranda* in 1858 for a contest sponsored by *El Ateneo del Plata*. To obtain the opinion of a reputable man of letters, she sent the completed manuscript to Miguel Cané (father), who then stated in a letter to the author that the work was "una de las producciones de nuestra literatura que más gusto me haya causado."[21] Unfortunately, the contest never materialized and the novel remained unpublished until 1860.

Rosa Guerra's *Lucía Miranda* is a well-written and carefully executed novel which recreates the impressive story of love and abnegation taken from the pages of Argentina's early tradition. The work, narrated with beauty, simplicity, and lucidness, is almost entirely devoid of involved historical explanations which may tend to divert the reader's attention. Lucía is colorfully portrayed through a series of skillfully developed and united scenes. In her relationship with the persistent Indian leader Mangora, whom she sees as an ingenuous, confiding, almost childlike individual, there is at once stateliness, pathos, and understanding; with the brutal and licentious Siripo, however, Lucía's manner is appropriately indignant and defiant; and for her loyal husband there is no greater evidence of eternal love than the sublime sacrifice of her own life to join him in death.

3. THE REGION OF SAN JUAN IN THE NOVELS OF PEDRO ECHAGÜE

The first author to introduce regional novels into Argentine literature was Pedro Echagüe (1821-1889). Hitherto, the scene of action was generally focused in or around Buenos Aires, or occasionally in a distant site in America or Europe. Untreated in the novel except for incidental references were vast and picturesque sections of Argentina. Yet by 1865, thanks to the pen of Echagüe, one such area received attention in fiction. San Juan, in northwestern Argentina, was the particular concern of this author, who sought to capture the traditions and customs of this colorful and historic region.

---

[21] This letter is reproduced on page iv of Rosa Guerra's novel.

Echagüe was born in Buenos Aires on October 8, 1821. Persecuted by the Tyranny, he fled to Montevideo in 1839 and enlisted in the military forces of General Lavalle. For a period of ten years, beginning in October, 1841, Echagüe lived in exile in Chile, Bolivia, and Peru. After Rosas' defeat in 1852, he returned to Buenos Aires, where he became editor of *El Nacional*. Largely through the persuasion of his intimate friend Sarmiento, he left the capital in 1862 and took up permanent residence in San Juan.[22] There he edited *El Zonda* (founded by Sarmiento himself in 1839), collaborated on many other newspapers, and also served as inspector of schools, a post which Sarmiento created especially for him. Besides his novelistic work, Echagüe wrote many plays which are of historical significance and serve to mark him as a precursor of the national theater. The author died in San Juan on July 5, 1889.

La Rinconada, Echagüe's initial novel, was first published in San Juan in 1865, under the title *Elvira, o el temple de alma de una sanjuanina.*[23] La Rinconada is an expanse of barren land, situated directly to the south of the city of San Juan and within the limits of the department of Pocito. Several times this section was the scene of bitter battles fought in defense of liberty and justice, both during the post-independence era and the years of national reorganization subsequent to the Tyranny. The background of the historical events which Echagüe portrays in *La Rinconada* is the following: President Derqui refused to recognize Antonio Aberastain as governor of the province of San Juan, and accordingly sent Colonel Saa to occupy that region. Aberastain, a sincere and capable statesman, had no intention of relinquishing his authority, even in the face of overwhelming pressure. He rallied together unprepared local troops and then set out to meet the approaching Federal forces. On January 11, 1861, the combatants clashed at

[22] It will be recalled that Sarmiento was born in San Juan, which he always held in fond memory, and in whose cultural and political life he ever maintained an avid interest.

[23] The second edition, San Juan, Imprenta de La Unión, 1880, also carried the title *Elvira, o el temple de alma de una sanjuanina.* Under the title *La Rinconada,* the novel was published three times: B.A., Coni, 1924; Instituto de Literatura Argentina, *op. cit.,* 1931, serie 4, tomo I, No. 12; and Grandes Escritores Argentinos, B.A., 1931, XXXIX, 29-90.

La Rinconada; the makeshift soldiers of San Juan defended their land with the fury of fanatics, but they were no match for the well-trained national army and were mercilessly slaughtered. Aberastain was taken prisoner and promptly executed, while Saa entered San Juan in triumph aad savagely sacked the city.

Around these events Echagüe wove a story of vengeance and murder. The novel, written in a simple, unadorned, and straightforward prose, is related with much interest. Of pure fantasy, but illustrative of the romantic taste for exaggerated sentiment and unusual occurrences, is the fictional element of *La Rinconada,* which reaches its most extravagant point when the heroine, dressed in ethereal white against the blackness of the night, plunges a dagger into the villain's back—the same weapon with which he killed her sweetheart.

In *La Rinconada* Echagüe succeeds in portraying vividly the anguish and resentment of the *sanjuaninos.* The city of San Juan is pictured in all its heroism and humility, with its valiant and determined inhabitants struggling to preserve their liberty. Echagüe narrates with sympathy and understanding the unfortunate plight of the self-sacrificing improvised local forces, and in particular the noble action of Aberastain. With the city vanquished and its leader slain, a black cloud of sadness and mourning hung over the ill-fated people, who in future years would recall with horror the truculent massacre at La Rinconada.

After a lapse of almost twenty years, Echagüe issued his second novel in 1884, also in the city of San Juan. The work, entitled *La Chapanay,*[24] relates the adventurous life of a virile and dynamic woman, Martina Chapanay, whose name to this day remains imbued in the traditions and legends of the province of San Juan. Concerning the protagonist one Argentine critic states:

> Vida larga y azarosa la de esta mujer hombruna, que vestida de gaucho, jinete insuperable, recorría en eterno vagabundear la región, primero

[24] Pedro Echagüe, *La Chapanay,* San Juan, Sanda y Yofré, 1884. The novel also appears in Grandes Escritores Argentinos, 1931, XXXIX, 95-215.

como bandido y luego como hada buena de las
travesías cuyanas. El pueblo rodeó de un halo terrible y misterioso sus proezas y la convirtió, en
otras ocasiones, en un personaje grotesco.[25]

Most of the action of *La Chapanay* takes place in the mountainous rural section of San Juan, which Echagüe describes
with much color and vividness. Regional types, customs, traditions, and the everyday life of the inhabitants are all effectively portrayed in the novel. In the rustic and rude atmosphere of this area Martina Chapanay lived from infancy, and
her forceful, resolute, and independent personality was molded
in a large measure by the severity and rigor of the region.
Furthermore, around the principal action of the novel are narrated many interesting incidents that serve to define clearly
the milieu in which the characters move. For its strong love
and deep concern for the region of San Juan, *La Chapanay*
quickly calls to mind *Recuerdos de provincia* (1850), the famous work of Echagüe's close friend Sarmiento, from whom
he undoubtedly received noble inspiration and guiding example.

La Chapanay is richly steeped in the legends and traditions
of San Juan. On one occasion the author states that the fecund
imagination of the common folk created peculiar and even
fantastic versions of how Martina's mother had been assaulted
by a group of vicious highwaymen. In another section there is
narrated the legend of Pata de palo, a mysterious giant whom
the indigenous population recognized as a master and to
whom they paid tribute. Even after the giant died, his wor-
shipers persisted in believing that his artificial leg wandered
about through the hills.

La Chapanay encompasses the entire life of Martina and
presents as well an introductory account of the adventurous
lives of her mother and father, and the circumstances that
brought them together. Martina is well drawn and excellently
envisaged in relation to her physical surroundings. We see her
first as a rebellious and stubborn young girl with a resolute
and manly temperament, committing all sorts of roguish and

[25] Margarita Mugnos de Escudero, prologue to *La Rinconada* and *La Chapanay* in Grandes Escritores Argentinos, *op. cit.*, XXXIX, 17.

malicious acts which frequently scandalize the inhabitants of San Juan. Subsequently, we follow her as a member of a ruthless band of highwaymen, whose audacious and vile leader plunges her to the very depths of degradation. Finally, after she awakens to a realization of her miserable and sinful existence, we notice her as a contrite woman aiding the forces of justice. Yet at the close of the novel we seem to have forgotten the protagonist's evil past, and we understand her only as a noble, praiseworthy, and very extraordinary person.

The significant and original feature of both *La Rinconada* and *La Chapanay* is the portrayal of one particular region of Argentina—San Juan. It is interesting to note that Echagüe neither was born in that section nor did he spend there his early, formative years, but arrived at San Juan at a mature age. Yet within a short time he closely identified himself with the cultural and political life of the people, established a laudable reputation as a writer, and gleaned from its history, traditions, and customs much inspiring material for his novelistic work.[26] In *La Rinconada* Echagüe evoked a memorable historical event, while in *La Chapanay* he narrated a colorful story of an unusual inhabitant of this rural region.

4. LATER ROMANTIC NOVELISTS

The romantic novel in Argentina did not come to an abrupt end with the advent of realism and naturalism in the 1880's and 1890's; rather, novels of romantic tone continued to be composed simultaneously with those offering a realistic depiction of life. The authors of these late romantic works did not respond to the new and predominant current in Argentine fiction that centered around the faithful portrayal of the developing nation. Not at all, or on occasions only superficially, did they touch upon the grim affairs of national life; instead

---

[26] Besides *La Rinconada* and *La Chapanay*, Echagüe also wrote the novel *Cuatro noches en el mar, o sea Amalia y Amelia*, San Juan, Tipografía de La Unión, 1886. In this work the author narrates the tragedy that befalls identical twin sisters who are in love with the same man.

they retained most of the extravagant romantic trappings of the previous period, but in some cases demonstrated a more detailed development of story and characters.

Among these later romantic writers we may designate Manuel Bahamonde (1842-1916), José Victoriano Cabral (1822-1915), and Lola Larrosa de Ansaldo (1859-1895), all of whom turned a deaf ear to the clamor of Argentine reality. Bahamonde[27] preferred novels containing melodramatic and unusual action, as is seen in *Mareos* (1892); Cabral's most ambitious work is entitled *Amelia de Floriani, o el castillo del diablo* (1887), a rambling, tedious, and complex novel set in Milan, Italy, towards the close of the eighteenth century;[28] and Larrosa de Ansaldo, in such novels as *Hija mía* (1888) and *El lujo* (1889), sought to express her high moral principles and teach the precepts of good living.[29]

· · ·

In this chapter and preceding ones, the development of the Argentine romantic novel has occupied our attention. Beginning with *La quena, Soledad,* and *La familia del comendador* of the introductory period, to *Amalia* and subsequent fiction

---

[27] Bahamonde was born in Uruguay, but resided in Argentina for many years. His novels are the following: *Buenos Aires novelesco*, B.A., 1889; *El último Dobaiba*, B.A., Imprenta de M. Biedma, 1890; *Abismos*, B.A., Imprenta de M. Biedma, 1890; and *Mareos*, B.A., 1892.

[28] Cabral, one of the most respected notaries in Buenos Aires, started fiction writing at a relatively advanced age. His three novels are *Lina Montalván, o el terremoto que destruyó el Callao y la ciudad de Lima en 1746*, B.A., Imprenta del Porvenir, 1880; *Amelia de Floriani, o el castillo del diablo*, B.A., Imprenta de M. Biedma, 1887; and *La campana de San Telmo y la conspiración de 1839 contra el dictador Rosas*, B.A., Imprenta de M. Biedma e hijo, 1897.

[29] Larrosa de Ansaldo wrote four novels: *Las obras de misericordia*, B.A., Imprenta Ostwald, 1882; *Hija mía*, B.A., Imprenta de Juan A. Alsina, 1888; *El lujo*, B.A., Imprenta de Juan A. Alsina, 1889; and *Los esposos*, B.A., Compañía Sud-Americana de Billetes de Banco, 1895.

Other minor romantic works published in the 1880's and 1890's are the following:

a. Ricardo Gutiérrez, *Cristián*, B.A., Imprenta de La Patria Argentina, 1880. This author (1836-1896), doctor, poet, and journalist, was the brother of the more famous Eduardo, whom we shall study in a later chapter.

b. Miguel Browne, *La primera conquista de Esther*, B.A., 1888. According to the records of the Recoleta Cemetery, year 1898, folio 186, line 44, Miguel Browne (1844-1898) was a teacher by profession.

c. Teodoro Y. Marques, *Tragedia de la vida*, La Plata, Imprenta Americana de M. Cerdeña del Río, 1890. Marques died on May 24, 1891, at the age of twenty-one, according to information taken from *La Nación*, May 25, 1891, p. 5.

d. Amaranto T. Rivero, *Guantes blancos y conciencias negras*, ed. Ángel S. Maranta, B.A., 1899.

depicting the Rosas era, down through the myriad other works of the 1850's and 1860's, the novel was basically romantic. Many authors tried their hand at purely sentimental novels or those of exaggerated passion; some writers sought romantic stories in Argentina's past, in far-off Italy, and in simple home life; while one artist, Juana Manuela Gorriti, combined a rich imagination, vigorous prose, and excellent narrative skill to present scenes from the history, traditions, and legends of Argentina and America in general.

VII

THE DECADE OF THE 'SEVENTIES

1. THE NATION'S CHANGING TEMPO

The decade of the 1870's opened up new vistas in fiction. The romantic novel, although still to appear in this and subsequent periods, had run its major course during the 1850's and 1860's. As we have seen, Argentina was just emerging in the 1870's as a progressive, rapidly expanding nation, but as yet the changing picture of the country—in particular, Buenos Aires —did not come into sharp enough focus to provide material for novelistic purposes. Not until the 1880's did the novel begin to reflect the great strides attained in Argentine civilization. Meanwhile, the novelists of the 1870's, writing in a period that witnessed the beginning of what may be called modern Argentina, sought to weave their plots around subject matter lines which were different from those of the 1850's and 1860's. The new themes which thus made their way into the novel of the 1870's dealt with scientific and pseudo-scientific phenomena, with crime and its social implications, and with the nation's small indigenous element.

Before considering the general development of the novel in the 'seventies, it is well to note the social, political, economic, and cultural growth of the nation during this period. We shall start by going back a few years to 1862, when Argentina finally achieved political unity with the inauguration of Bartolomé Mitre as president of the nation. During the six years of his office, Mitre succeeded in initiating Argentina on the path of economic prosperity. Relative political stability was secured and a respect for law and order was obtained; commerce with Europe was strengthened considerably by virtue of amendments in customs regulations; transportation, recognized as an essential factor in the development of the nation, became of vital concern to the government, and in 1863 construction was started on the Argentine Central Railroad; telegraph and cable service was introduced; the task of establishing an adequate school system began to take form; and immigration, considered indispensable to further progress, was zealously promoted.

Yet simultaneously with this economic progress there raged the bitter war against Paraguay.[1] Hostilities started in March, 1865, when Mitre refused to permit Paraguayan troops, then engaged in a war with Brazil, to cross the province of Corrientes. Uruguay hastened to join Argentina and Brazil against the Paraguayan dictator Francisco Solano López. Mitre assumed supreme command of the allied armies, entrusting the internal affairs of the Republic to Vice-President Marcos Paz. Despite the apparent inequality of the opposing forces, the struggle was prolonged for five years, and when Paraguay finally capitulated in 1870, it found itself in a state of almost complete ruin.

In 1868, Sarmiento succeeded Mitre as president. One of the outstanding contributions of his six-year administration was the promotion of education, a task which earned for him the nickname of the "schoolmaster president." Throughout the nation Sarmiento constructed many public schools, and following the example of the great American educator Horace Mann, he instituted a training program for teachers. In addition to the development of education, railroads were further extended, foreign capital was welcomed into the country, and immigration was encouraged as in the previous administration. Also, Argentina's great epic poem, *Martín Fierro,* appeared in 1872, at a time when the crude and unrestrained way of life of the gaucho contended in bitter struggle with the modern, progressive forces in the nation. Lastly, as unfortunate occurrences of this period we cite the epidemics of cholera (1868)

---

[1] Manuel Gálvez, distinguished Argentine novelist of the twentieth century, treats the theme of the Paraguayan War in a series of novels which bears the general title of *Escenas de la Guerra del Paraguay.* The trilogy is composed of *Los caminos de la muerte,* 1928, *Humaitá,* 1928, and *Jornadas de agonía,* 1929.

and yellow fever (1871), and the murder of Urquiza in Entre Ríos (1870).

In 1874, Nicolás Avellaneda assumed the office óf president, although the validity of the election was at first questioned by his opponent, Mitre. In general, Avellaneda's administration was an era of relative tranquillity and progress. The financial situation of the country was strengthened; the value of exports exceeded that of imports; large numbers of immigrants entered the nation; and government grants for railway construction were liberally extended. Moreover, one of the most significant events of his presidency, as far as the future development of Argentina was concerned, proved to be the extension of the habitable southern frontier by virtue of successful campaigns against bands of menacing Indians. Rosas himself on several occasions had attempted to push back hostile indigenous tribes, and although he had met with some victories, damaging incursions still remained to beset the neighboring provinces. In 1879, General Julio Roca, minister of war under Avellaneda, commanded a triumphant military expedition against groups of belligerent natives in the southern part of the Republic. The Indians, driven back to the Negro River, were so reduced in number that the danger of future raids on a major scale was averted. As a result of this achievement, the region of Patagonia was made available for settlement and cultivation by both nationals and foreigners. Toward the close of Avellaneda's term of office, on September 20, 1880, the city of Buenos Aires became a federal district, separate from the province of the same name. At the same time the province selected the near-by city of La Plata as the new site for its capital. This federalization of Buenos Aires ushered in a glorious era of material progress which characterized the 1880's and 1890's.

Along with the forementioned economic and social advancement, this period of national reorganization and political consolidation from 1852 until 1880 witnessed a vital growth in cultural and artistic pursuits. The intellectual life of the nation, stifled by so many years of tyrannical government, responded avidly to the pulse of freedom and progress and hummed busily with the talent of gifted men. After the fall of Rosas Argentina proudly and thankfully welcomed to its shores that illustrious group of *proscritos,* who by virtue of their genius and application served as a directive and inspirational force in the development of the nation's cultural life. Such men as Mitre, Alberdi, Mármol, Gutiérrez, and Vicente F. López achieved great personal success with their varied intellectual endeavors, and by these same efforts stimulated many a youthful or repressed talent in the direction of cultural attainment. Fruits of their conscientious labor were such meritorious works of thought and analysis as *Historia de Belgrano y de la independencia argentina* (1858), *Bases* (1852), *Noticias históricas sobre el origen y desarrollo de la enseñanza pública superior en Buenos Aires* (1868), and *Introducción a la historia de la República Argentina* (1881), all of which contributed in part toward the aggrandizement and flourishing of culture in the young Republic.

Significant also during this period of cultural and academic enrichment was the splendid array of statesmen, orators, historians, publicists, and scholars, who in congressional assemblies, lecture halls and public meetings, in pamphlets, treatises and published material of all sorts, displayed brilliant eloquence, vast erudition, and superior intellect. By virtue of their writings and speeches, the names of Félix Frías (1816-1881), Pedro Goyena (1843-1892), Fray Mamerto Esquiú (1826-1882), José Manuel Estrada (1842-1894), Dalmacio Vélez Sarsfield (1801-1875), to mention but a scant few, made a deep impress in the mold of the evolving Argentine culture.

It was during this period also that popular gaucho poetry reached a high degree of merit with Del Campo's *Fausto* (1866), Ascasubi's *Santos Vega* (1870), and especially with Hernández' *Martín Fierro* (1872). The poetry of other notable artists revealed a variety of tendencies and themes: the sensitive romantic soul of Ricardo Gutiérrez (1836-1896) spoke out nobly in such poems of intimate emotion as *La fibra salvaje* and *Lázaro;* of robust and impetuous inspiration, grandiloquent in style and sonorous of word, Olegario Víctor Andrade (1838-1882) sang the glories of his country and the future of America in his fiery poems *San Martín, Nido de cóndores,* and *Atlántida;* while the classic cut of the poetry of Carlos Guido Spano (1827-1918) evinced a studied harmony of form, a purity and beauty of expression, a majestic serenity of tone, and general elegance of style.

Lastly, the energy of this intellectual surge was also strongly manifested in the establishment of many literary and cultural institutions, as well as in the founding of important newspapers and periodicals.[2] Among those publications that quickened the pace of cultural advancement, and on which many of the most alert and distinguished minds of the day collaborated, may be cited *La Prensa* (1857), *La Nación* (1862), *La Revista de Buenos Aires* (1863), *El Correo del Domingo* (1864), and *La Revista del Río de la Plata* (1871.)[3]

2. *Peregrinación de Luz del Día*

One of the most unusual novels of this decade, if not of the entire nineteenth century, is *Peregrinación de Luz del Día, o viaje y aventuras de la Verdad en el Nuevo Mundo* (1871),[4] by the eminent political theorist and legislator, Juan Bautista

[2] Careful investigation of the periodicals and newspapers established in this era reveals the following data: during the years 1852 to 1859 approximately forty-five publications were founded, ten of which were in the year of Rosas' defeat, 1852; the decade 1860-1870 witnessed the appearance of only twenty-five new publications, the decline resulting perhaps from the enervating and demoralizing Paraguayan War (1865-1870); while the period from 1870 to 1880, years of considerable economic progress, was quite prolific in new publications, the total being approximately seventy-five.

[3] Other periodicals include the following: *La Ilustración Argentina,* 1853; *La Espada de Lavalle,* 1857; *La Revista de Ciencias y Letras,* 1864; *La Revista Argentina,* 1868; *La Ondina del Plata,* 1875; *La Alborada del Plata,* 1877.

[4] A, *Peregrinación de Luz del Día, o viage y aventuras de la Verdad en el Nuevo Mundo,* B.A., 1871. Notice that the author is indicated by the initial "A" alone. At the close of the work Alberdi reveals that he finished the novel in February, 1871, in London. Other editions of this work are the following: *Obras Completas de Juan Bautista Alberdi,* B.A., Imprenta de La Tribuna Nacional, 1887, VII, 176-393; ed. Carlos Casavalle, B.A., Imprenta de Mayo, 1906; *Obras Selectas de J.B.A.,* ed. Joaquín V. González, B.A., Librería La Facultad de J. Roldán, 1920, Tomo II, Vol. II, pp. 1-304; Biblioteca Argentina, preliminary note by Ricardo Rojas, B.A., 1916; Editorial Choele-Choel, prologue by José María Rosa, son, B.A., 1947.

Alberdi (1810-1884). The work is an ingenious and acrimonious satire on political and social conditions in South America. It will be recalled that in 1852 Alberdi idealistically offered to the Argentine people his monumental *Bases,*[5] which laid the groundwork for the formulation of the Constitution of 1853. Yet the resolute optimism that Alberdi displayed during the years immediately following the Tyranny—expressed in *Las Bases* and other treatises—was soon to turn to bitter disappointment as he sadly observed the pungent, contentious situation existing in Argentina in the 1860's, precisely at a time when the need for national unity and political solidarity was most urgent. This disillusionment at the failure of his political ideals to be implanted in Argentina motivated the writing of *Peregrinación de Luz del Día,* in which Alberdi waged a rancorous attack against what he considered the deceitful, unsubstantial, inept, and bungling American society.

The protagonist of the work is the allegorical figure of Truth, who travels to America when he can no longer endure the hypocrisy and sham of European nations. In the New World, Truth, disguised as a woman under the name of Luz del Día, encounters many of the same objectionable conditions from which he has just fled. He soon comes upon Tartufe, Basilio, and Gil Blas, and in the course of intriguing conversations he learns that they hold offices as astute and ruthless politicians who have acquired power, fortune, and fame by maliciously duping the people and using them to their own advantage.

In the second part of the novel Luz del Día is apprised that the celebrated Spanish heroes El Cid, Pelayo, Don Juan Tenorio, and Don Quixote, all now residing in South America, have morally degenerated as a consequence of the unpropitious political and social atmosphere. To such a point has the insanity of Don Quixote reached that he has organized in Patagonia a Republic of sheep, called *Quijotanía, o la colonización socialista en Sud-America.* The *carnero,* Alberdi paradoxically

<hr>

[5] The complete title of this work is *Bases y puntos de partida para la organización constitucional de la República Argentina,* Valparaíso, Imprenta del Mercurio, 1852.

points out, represents liberty and progress, by virtue of the fact that this animal's gentle and defenseless state obviates the need to restrict his movements or place him in chains, as is done to the rebellious and fierce lion. Alberdi further adds that the meekness and docility of the sheep can accomplish more for liberty than the impetuousness and violence of the tiger (the military man). When the progressive *República de Quijotanía* fails, Luz del Día delivers a public lecture on concepts of liberty and government and the conditions that a nation must fulfill to be free and strong. Finally, disappointed at not finding such liberty and ideal government in America, in the land which promised so much, he sadly resolves to return to Europe.

Through a caricatural depiction of such characters as Tartufe and Basilio, analysis of government proceedings in the fictitious *República de Quijotanía,* and inquiry into the nature of liberty, Alberdi lays bare the gross defects and flagrant misconceptions of the South American Republics. For Alberdi the gravest error in which Americans can incur is to believe that the sword, so effective in bringing about independence from Spain, can likewise be suitably employed in guaranteeing domestic liberty and peace. Consequently, the military man, the soldier-statesman and the *caudillo,* standing as principal obstacles to the tranquil settlement of internal differences and the establishment of an equitable and competent government, must be removed as the leaders of nations before true liberty can be achieved.

3. THE INDIGENOUS ELEMENT IN THE ARGENTINE NOVEL

The Indian in Argentina has never constituted a numerically important group, much less a culturally significant one in the nation's development. The wild bands of Indians that inhabited the marginal areas of Argentina were considered not only as an element apart from the country as a whole, but as a hindrance to economic growth and social progress. Yet these native groups occupied the attention of several novelists, who sought in the main not to censure their primitive mode of life, but to understand it and divulge it to the public. The year 1870 saw the initial publication of one of the most widely read books in Argentine literature—*Una excursión a los indios ranqueles*,[6] by Lucio V. Mansilla. Although not a work of fiction in the true sense of the term, but rather a detailed account in novelized form of the author's experiences among those Indians, it does stand as the forerunner of a later group of novels which treats the colorful Argentine indigenous element.

Mansilla, a distinguished professional soldier, spent long and arduous years among autochthonous groups, and through intimate association with their everyday life he acquired detailed knowledge and profound understanding of this native population. The conflict between hostile Indian bands and the national government was a constant and unrelenting one. A particularly stubborn group was the Ranqueles, a tribe of Araucanian Indians who emigrated from the western part of the Andes Mountains to the eastern and finally settled in the territory between the Negro and Colorado Rivers. With the utmost skill and tact Colonel Mansilla succeeded in drawing up a peace treaty with the Ranqueles, but several difficulties still had to be resolved before it might be executed effectively. In the interim, Mansilla audaciously penetrated the domain of the Ranqueles, with the intention of examining their customs, traditions, dress, food, native language, ideas, and religion. Fruit of this extensive study is the appealing *Una excursión a los indios ranqueles,* written in an informal, spontaneous fashion. The narration of events to a large measure assumes the form of sprightly and natural conversations between the author and the various persons he encounters during the course of his adventures, to which are added succinct but telling descriptions of the physical surroundings, social types, and particular modes of living of the Ranqueles.

    [6] Lucio V. Mansilla, *Una escursión a los indios ranqueles,* B.A., Imprenta y litografía y fundición de tipos—Belgrano 126, 1870, 2 vols. Other editions of the work are the following: Brockhaus, Leipsig, 1877; B.A., 1890; B.A., Biblioteca de la Nación, 1905, Vols. 197 and 198; Biblioteca del Sub-oficial, 1927, Vols. 33 and 34; La Cultura Popular, 1928; Biblioteca Mundial Sopena, 1939; Atlántida, 1940; Grandes Escritores Argentinos, 1944, Vols. II and IV; Tor, 1948.

The idealized and falsely heroic treatment of the indigenous theme may also be seen in the short story *La chiriguana*.[7] Published in 1877 by Josefina Pelliza de Sagasta (1848-1888), the work narrates a cloyingly sentimental and tragic story of love, hate, and vengeance among members of the Chiriguano Indians. From early womanhood Pelliza de Sagasta was a reputable figure in the literary circles of Buenos Aires. She was noted particularly for her lyric poetry, but in addition she wrote stories and novels,[8] narrative prose, and numerous newspaper and magazine articles. The scene of *La chiriguana* is set near the banks of the Bermejo River, in the Gran Chaco region of northern Argentina. The romantic tale is narrated simply, almost ingenuously. There is no attempt either to describe the civilization of the Chiriguano Indians or to penetrate even superficially into the character of the protagonists. The hero and heroine are two delicate, ethereal creatures who might easily fit into the pages of *Atala* or *Paul et Virginie*. Nature is majestic, grandiose, truly inspiring for these two lovers who live in close communion with it. Not without reason, then, does the Bermejo River, splendidly painted at the beginning of the work, proudly serve as the hero's tomb.

Life among the indigenous population was not further used as a theme in fiction until the 1880's, but to preserve the unity of subject matter it is well to treat of this later development at this point. Estanislao S. Zeballos (1854-1923),[9] in part availing himself of historical figures and events and in part using imaginative material, produced two novels which reflect the social state of groups of Araucanian Indians. In *Painé y la dinastía de los zorros* (1886)[10] and its continuation *Relmu, rei-*

---

[7] Josefina Pelliza de Sagasta, *La chiriguana*, in Novelas Americanas, B.A., Imprenta y administración, Santiago del Estero 176, 1877, pp. 3-32.

[8] Her novels include the long and complicated *Margarita*, B.A., Establecimiento tipográfico de El Orden de W. Muntaner y Cía., 1875; and an unfinished work of the Rosas theme, *La favorita de Palermo, o el prisionero de Santos Lugares*, eight chapters of which appeared in the literary magazine *La Alborada del Plata*, from February 10 to May 1, 1878.

[9] A distinguished Argentine statesman and prolific writer on national affairs, Zeballos fulfilled with dignity and success many high official positions, notably minister of government, plenipotentiary, treaty representative, and congressman. In addition, he served as dean of the Law School of the University of Buenos Aires.

[10] *Painé* first appeared serially in *La Prensa* from June 15 to July 10, 1886, but remained unfinished. That same year the complete work was published in

na de los Pinares (1887),[11] the author colorfully pictures the determined struggle of the federal government in the 1840's to bring under submission the numerous bands of primitive Indians in the southern regions of Argentina. In the little known novel *Salvaje* (1891),[12] survivors of a shipwreck take up refuge in an isolated section of southern Argentina, inhabited by a wild Indian tribe. The author's purpose was to refute the widespread belief of the viciousness and inhumanity of the Argentine indigenous population, and to show that savage races, through proper education, could readily be civilized and might progress rapidly.

An important cultivator of the indigenous theme was Filiberto de Oliveira Cézar (1856-1910), who in addition to holding several important public offices served with distinction on an exploratory mission to the Chaco region. In *Amores de una india* (1892),[13] the author recounts the experiences of two adventurers who penetrate into the territory of the Tobas Indians, situated near the banks of the Paraná River. The slight plot, which revolves around the unrequited love of the heroine for one of the explorers, asumes much less interest and significance than the detailed descriptions of the region and the picturesque sketches of native customs. In *El cacique blanco* (1893),[14] Oliveira Cézar relates the adventures of two Englishmen in the land of the Pampa Indians. Evident in the work is the author's deep respect for this native group, whose traditions, language, and ways of life he carefully studied. In the preface of the novel Oliveira Cézar mentions some fifteen books which he profitably consulted to obtain pertinent data.[15]

---

book form, B.A., Imprenta de J. Peuser, 1886. J. Peuser also put out the second and third editions in 1889. It is interesting to note that *Painé* was soon translated into French under the title *Paîne, et la dynastie des Renards,* trans. Mme. Menjou, Paris, Maison Quantin, Compagnie générale d'impression et l'edition, 1890.

[11] Estanislao S. Zeballos, *Relmu, reina de los Pinares,* B.A., La Plata, Imprenta de J. Peuser, 1887. J. Peuser republished the work in 1893.

[12] C. M. Blanco, *Salvaje,* B.A., Barcelona, Casa editora Franco-Española, 1891.

[13] Filiberto de Oliveira Cézar, *Los amores de una india—viaje al país de los Tobas,* B.A., La Plata, Imprenta de J. Peuser, 1892.

[14] Filiberto de Oliveira Cézar, *El cacique blanco—costumbres de los araucanos en la pampa,* B.A., Casa editora de J. Peuser, 1893.

[15] Among these books may be mentioned the following: *Una excursión a los indios ranqueles,* by Mansilla; *Historia de Chile,* by Barros Arana; *Cuadros de la naturaleza,* by Humboldt; *La lengua pampa,* by Federico Barbará; *Origen del hombre en la Plata,* by Ameghino; and *La Araucana,* by Ercilla.

Furthermore, inserted at the close of *El cacique blanco* are two appendices, one containing a grammar of the Araucanian language and the other a Spanish-Araucanian vocabulary.

4. Eduardo L. Holmberg — Science and the Supernatural in the Novel

An interest in science began to manifest itself in the novel of the 1870's. This theme took on several forms: scientific and pseudo-scientific explanations of phenomena, imaginary journeys into the unexplored universe, predictions of things to come, and an inquiry into supernatural forces. During the 1870's the scientific novels of Jules Verne and the adventure stories of Mayne Reid started to make their appearance as the daily serials of newspapers. For the Argentine reader, accustomed to the extremely romantic and sentimental novels of native writers and such foreign authors as Pérez Escrich, Fernández y González, Tárrago y Mateos, and Ponson du Terrail, the works of Verne and Reid served as a welcomed innovation; and the steady succession in which they were offered to the public during the years 1872-1875 attests to their popularity. Among the novels of Jules Verne that appeared in serial form may be mentioned *Les Anglais au pole Nord — Voyages et aventures du Capitaine Hatteras*,[16] *Une ville flottante*,[17] *Le tour du monde en quatre-vingts jours*,[18] and *Le pays des fourrures*.[19] Of Mayne Reid there appeared *The Finger of Fate*,[20] *Osceola the Seminole, or The Red Fawn of the Flower Land*,[21] and *The White Gauntlet*.[22] Lastly, we note that during this period

[16] Trans. D.A. Ribot y Fontsère, as *Los ingleses en el Polo Norte—Aventuras del Capitán Atteras*, in *El Nacional*, afternoon edition, June 1 to August 31, 1872.

[17] Trans. D.G.R. y M. (*sic*), as *Una ciudad flotante*, *Ibid.*, November 2, 1872 to January 11, 1873.

[18] Trans. Vicente Guimera, as *La vuelta al mundo en 80 días*, *Ibid.*, October 7 to December 12, 1873.

[19] Trans. Vicente Guimera, as *El país de los pieles*, *Ibid.*, April 14 to June 29, 1874.

[20] Trans. F.N., as *El dedo del destino*, *Ibid.*, February 3 to March 30, 1874.

[21] Trans. Ribot y Fontsère, as *Aventuras de mar y tierra—Oceola, el gran jefe de los Seminoles*, *Ibid.*, August 20 to October 9, 1874.

[22] Trans. D.J. Sala, as *Aventuras de mar y tierra—El guante blanco*, *Ibid.*, December 28, 1874, to February 17, 1875. Also, *El capitán Scarthe*—segunda parte de *El guante blanco*, appeared from February 24 to April 21, 1875.

there appeared in serial form *La novela del Egipto—viaje imaginario a la apertura del canal de Suez*,[23] by the Spanish author José de Castro y Serrano—a novel of adventure and inquiry, of the type that readers avidly devoured to stimulate their curiosity about the world they inhabit.

The first and most important Argentine figure who carried this interest in science to the novel was Eduardo Ladislao Holmberg (1852-1937). In 1880 he received the degree of Doctor of Medicine, but he never practiced his profession. Instead, he obtained a position as instructor of natural history, physics, and chemistry in a normal school in Buenos Aires. In 1882 he became a member of the Academy of Sciences of Córdoba; in 1885 and 1886 he headed a scientific expedition to the Chaco region and the province of Misiones; from 1888 to 1896 he fulfilled with distinction the office of director of the zoological garden in Buenos Aires. In 1890 Holmberg was named professor of botany at the University of Buenos Aires. In later years he held the position of inspector of secondary and normal schools in the capital. An industrious and talented research scholar, Holmberg published many articles and books on such subjects as evolution, zoology, botany, and chemistry.

The rich, inquiring, and exploring spirit of Jules Verne, and the interest in the supernatural of the German novelist Hoffmann,[24] undoubtedly left a lasting impression on Holmberg and contributed to the particular line of development that his fiction was to follow. Although Holmberg's novelistic production extends beyond the 1870's, reaching until the end of the century, it is more convenient and advantageous to treat all of his works in this one section.

Holmberg's first novel, *Viaje maravilloso del Sr. Nic-Nac al planeta Marte* (1875),[25] is indicative of the author's concern with problems of the physical universe and his attempt to fathom the unknown. The work aims to divulge the hypothesis that Mars is not only inhabitable, but also inhabited. The pro-

[23] *Ibid.*, September 2 to October 22, 1872.
[24] It is significant that Holmberg's ancestry was German.
[25] After its publication in book form in 1875, the work appeared serially in *El Nacional,* from November 29, 1875, to February 25, 1876.

tagonist, an inmate of a mental institution, and his companion, an eccentric spiritualist, land on the planet to carry out a scientific expedition. The two travelers observe the *martografía* of this heavenly body—its surface, mountains, and other physical features—as well as the social organization of the planet. At length, after a fire destroys a vast section of the principal city, the voyagers return home to Earth.

In its conception and execution, *Viaje maravilloso del Sr. Nic-Nac* stands as an original piece of fiction, cleverly presented within its framework of scientific fantasy. Holmberg does not endeavor to explain his thesis that Mars is inhabited, but merely sets forth his unsubstantiated belief as the starting point for the weird tale of Sr. Nic-Nac. It would seem that the author seeks to whet the reader's natural scientific curiosity, to provide the stimulus for his imagination to wander, and to make him ponder over the complexities of the universe.

Holmberg's next work, *La pipa de Hoffmann* (1876),[26] is significant as the forerunner of his novels of the supernatural and visionary that were to appear in the 1890's. In this short story, one of the author's friends, Isaac, owns a strange pipe that formerly belonged to the German writer Hoffmann. Upon Isaac's death, the pipe is bequeathed to Holmberg. The first time he smokes it he witnesses a fantastic illusion: Isaac arises from the grave and informs Holmberg that he possesses one of Hoffmann's inedited manuscripts. The vision then disappears as rapidly as it came and Holmberg miraculously finds the manuscript in his room. In *Horacio Kalibang, o los autómatas* (1879),[27] Holmberg fancies to what length scientific progress may reach. In this story, a German manufacturer is engaged in the production of various types of automatons which can sing, dance, paint, fight, and perform other acts with amazing ability and precision. One robot, Horacio Kalibang, is particularly astounding because it is able to defy the natural laws of gravity. The work ends as one of the charac-

[26] *La pipa de Hoffmann* appeared in serial form in *El Plata Literario*, a monthly periodical of Buenos Aires, from June 15 to September 15, 1876.
[27] Eduardo L. Holmberg, *Horacio Kalibang, o los autómatas*, B.A., Imprenta de El Álbum del Hogar, 1879.

ters expresses the mad hope that some day he will rule the world by controlling the actions of a multitude of these automatons.

The year 1896 witnessed the publication of three novels of Holmberg, all of which involve the mysterious and the eerie. In *La casa endiablada*,[28] a house supposedly bewitched keeps the community in a state of nervous fright and uncertainty. At length the authorities are summoned to investigate, and they encounter in the house the corpse of a man who disappeared five years previously. It is significant to point out that on one occasion Holmberg refers with respect and admiration to the great master of the mystery story, Edgar Allan Poe, whom he undoubtedly read with avid interest. Holmberg's knowledge of the field of medicine is turned to use in the novel entitled *La bolsa de huesos*,[29] in which an examination of two skeletons reveals the brutal murder of two medical students. The interest of this work lies in the detection and solving of a criminal case through scientific proceedings.

Holmberg's most accomplished work of fiction is *Nelly*, first published in 1896 as a serial of *La Prensa*[30] and that same year offered to the public in book form.[31] Joaquín V. González first focused attention on the novel in an article in *La Prensa* on January 26, 1896, in which he stated that Holmberg was one of Argentina's most original writers and merited high praise for his rich imagination, his agreeable and charming style, and his power to interest the reader. The scene of *Nelly* is an old secluded house in an unidentified part of Argentina, where a group of young men are spending a few days of leisure. Yet the proposed peaceful and enjoyable stay is short of realization, as there takes place in the house a series of mysterious and even fantastic happenings. In turn, these strange events provide motive for the narration of the equally bizarre story of a dead woman's revenge on her unfaithful husband.

[28] Eduardo L. Holmberg, *La casa endiablada*, B.A., Compañía Sud-Americana de Billetes de Banco, 1896.
[29] Eduardo L. Holmberg, *La bolsa de huesos*, B.A., Compañía Sud-Americana de Billetes de Banco, 1896.
[30] *Nelly* appeared in *La Prensa* from January 27 to February 6, 1896.
[31] Eduardo L. Holmberg, *Nelly*, B.A., Compañía Sud-Americana de Billetes de Banco, 1896.

Particularly noteworthy in *Nelly* is the skillful development of the unnatural and weird atmosphere surrounding the characters. Among those things which help to produce this air of mystery may be mentioned the following: the very physical appearance of the old house; the delirium of one youth, appropriately named Edwin Phantendom, who is frequently so transported by his inner thoughts that at night he carries on a strange dialogue with his deceased wife Nelly; an old man's apparition that requests his grandson to examine carefully some worn maps and manuscripts; a woman's frightful and anguished groans echoing through the walls; several unusual anecdotes, one of which concerns the fatidic reappearance of the number "22" in the life of one of the protagonists; Edwin's trip to India, where he was exposed to the teachings of the fakirs; the divulgation of the secret of Edwin's birth by his grandfather's spirit; and finally Nelly's revelation to her husband as he sleeps beside her dead body.

The elements of the supernatural and subconscious seldom appear in a haphazard or isolated fashion, but represent in part the hidden and incomprehensible motives, fears, and desires of the characters. Holmberg clearly recognizes the complexities involved in human emotion, as is noted in the following paragraph, which may be taken as indicative of his view concerning the role of the supernatural in the lives of men:

> Hay miles, centenares de miles de personas muy razonables en todos los actos de su vida, para quienes la materialización de Nelly, la aparición del General, los gemidos y otros fenómenos más espeluznantes aún, son la realización innegable de un mundo que no conocemos, por haber seguido, en la evolución de nuestro progreso, rumbos que nos han acercado al ideal de lo que llamamos civilización de Occidente; mientras que los indios del Indostán y del Tibet, sin tantos canones, ni logaritmos, ni telescopios, ni telégrafos, han seguido otro rumbo que los aproxima a la vida espiritual y que realizan en los misterios de sus pagodas y en sus cavernas mil veces seculares.[32]

[32] *Ibid.*, p. 101.

Two other writers also channeled an inquiring mind into the realm of fiction. Luis V. Varela (1845-1911),[33] in a novel entitled *El doctor Whüntz* (1880),[34] enters into the field of scientific theory and practical experimentation. The work treats in part of the phenomenon of the nerve centers and its relation to human actions. The doctor's project entails not only a study of anatomy and psychology, but also experimentation with frogs as an aid to explaining nervous spasms after death. Áquiles Sioen (1834-1904),[35] a French journalist residing in Argentina, published in Spanish a whimsical novel that bears the title *Buenos Aires en el año 2080* (1879).[36] This author, seeing in the Argentina of 1879 auspicious signs of a future great nation, ventured to foretell conditions in the Republic in the year 2080. Sioen's interesting prognostications center around scientific progress, economic development, agricultural growth, and increased immigration.

5. LUIS V. VARELA—THE NOVEL OF CRIMINAL INVESTIGATION

Another of the themes initiated in the decade of the 1870's was that of crime detection and solving. Luis V. Varela, writing under the anagram of Raúl Waleis, deals in two novels with several murders and the operation of the police department in apprehending the criminals. *La huella del crimen* (1877)[37] and *Clemencia* (1877),[38] containing such items of a

[33] We shall treat of this author more fully in the next section of this chapter.

[34] Raúl Waleis, *El doctor Whüntz*, ed. Carlos Casavalle, B.A., 1880. Notice that Raúl Waleis is an anagram of Luis Varela.

[35] Sioen arrived in Argentina in 1878 or 1879, according to information given in the prologue to his novel, p. 7. He was employed as an instructor of French in the Colegio Nacional de Buenos Aires, as we learned from a booklet entitled *Memoria de la secretaría y tesorería del Colegio Nacional de la Capital, año 1884*, B.A., Taller Tipográfico de la Penitenciaria, 1885, p. 38. Sioen died in Buenos Aires in March, 1904, according to information from the Recoleta Cemetery, year 1904, folio 64, line 43.

[36] Áquiles Sioen, *Buenos Aires en el año 2080*, ed. Igon Hermanos, B.A., Librería del Colejio, 1879.

[37] Raúl Waleis, *La huella del crimen*, novela jurídica original, in Biblioteca Económica de Autores Nacionales, B.A., Imprenta de Mayo, 1877. That same year, 1877, the novel appeared serially in *La Tribuna*, from July 23 to August 30.

[38] Raúl Waleis, *Clemencia*—continuación de *La huella del crimen*, novela jurídica original, in Biblioteca Económica de Autores Nacionales, B.A., Im-

police case as suspects, clues, and evidence, stand as the first works in Argentine fiction which fall into the category of the detective novel. Luis Vicente was the son of Florencio Varela, the eminent patriot whom Manso de Noronha glorified in *Los misterios del Plata*. At an early age he began his journalistic career by publishing miscellaneous articles in *La Tribuna,* the newspaper which his brothers Héctor and Mariano then directed. In later years Varela distinguished himself as a brilliant jurisconsult, fulfilling many important official positions, as well as producing numerous volumes on law and government.

It is significant to observe that both *La huella del crimen* and the continuation *Clemencia* bear the words *"novela jurídica"* after the title. Varela states that just as Jules Verne made the public aware of scientific possibilities, he himself aims in these novels to popularize the laws which govern society.[39] He further adds: "El derecho es la fuente en que beberé mis argumentos. Las leyes malas deben conocerse por los efectos que su aplicación produzca. Yo formo el drama en que aplico la ley vigente. Sus fatales consecuencias probarán la necesidad de reformarla."[40] The popular French writer of detective stories, Émile Gaboriau (1835-1873), served as his model, and that author's characterization of the detectives Monsieur Lecoq and Père Tabaret was used as the prototype for Varela's creation of L'Archiduc, the protagonist of *La huella del crimen*.

In *La huella del crimen* the body of a young woman, cleverly disguised in masculine garb, is found by two French villagers in a wooded area near Boulogne. Largely through the efforts of the astute and efficient police commissioner, Andres L'Archiduc, the investigation is brought to a successful conclusion with the conviction of the killer, who turns out to be the victim's jealous husband.

---

prenta de Mayo, 1877. On the closing page of *Clemencia* the editor states that Varela wrote a third novel in this series: "La continuación de esta novela es la del mismo autor, titulada *Herencia fatal.*" There is no indication that the novel was ever published; certainly it has never been found. Juan Carlos Gómez, in a letter to the author which is included in *La huella del crimen,* praises his two novels, and then adds that he has not read *La herencia fatal,* "por no haberse publicado."

[89] Information taken from *La huella del crimen,* 1877 edition in book form, *op. cit.,* p. 5, in the form of a letter to the editor by the author of the novel.

[40] *Loc. cit.*

The characterization of L'Archiduc as a clever, sharp-tongued, fearless, and persistent detective is lively and well defined. We follow him step by step in his relentless endeavor to solve the mystery surrounding the victim's death: the meticulous examination of the body for important clues; the interrogation of the two youths who discovered her corpse; L'Archiduc's meeting with the villain at the morgue and the refutation of his story by carefully retracing his actions prior to the murder; his inquiries at hotels and private homes to check essential facts; and finally the fruit of this diligent investigation—the murderer's confession. L'Archiduc attacks the problem of crime in a systematic and scientific fashion, painstakingly gathering pertinent material for the case and intelligently weighing every shred of evidence. The author's awareness of the importance of detail in detective work is seen in the following paragraph, which describes the various objects collected at the scene of the crime:

> ......el pedazo de lienzo a que se había referido L'Archiduc, una herradura de caballo, un cordón de lana encarnada como de tres pulgadas de largo, la punta de un cigarro habano ya fumado, una pequeña lima para limpiar las uñas, y un vidrio de ventana, cuadrilongo, de poco más de veinte centímetros de largo por diez de ancho, el que, para evitar que pudiera ser roto por la herradura, había sido envuelto en un diario.[41]

Although *Clemencia* was published as the continuation of *La huella del crimen,* the work is practically an independent novel. Two characters reappear, however, in the story—Clemencia, who in the preceding work is briefly mentioned as the villain's paramour, and the commissioner, whose role in this novel is much less significant and engaging. The main portion of *Clemencia* treats in retrospect of the murder of a young woman, the subsequent police investigation, an account of the private lives of individuals connected with the crime, and the confession of the victim's husband, who slew his wife when he could no longer endure her brazen adultery. It is to

[41] *Ibid.,* pp. 76-77.

be noted in *Clemencia* that the author advocates the recognition of divorce for the general welfare of society. The crime
committed by the deceived husband, Varela believes, may in
part be attributed to the harmful social legislation which pro-
hibits divorce. When the murderer is finally apprehended, he
cries out in his own defense: "¿Por qué, si la sociedad no me
daba los medios de vengarme de la muger infiel, no me daba,
al menos, el medio de separarme para siempre de ella?"[42]

F. MINOR NOVELS OF THE 'SEVENTIES

The remaining novels published in the decade of the 1870's
reveal a wide range of subject matter, but rather limited artistic
merit.[43] Among these we may signal out *Elisa Lynch*,[44] published in 1871 by Héctor F. Varela (1833-1896), under the
pseudonym of "Orión." The protagonist of this novel was the
charming mistress of the Paraguayan dictator Francisco Solano
López. The author, a popular journalist and brilliant orator
who fervently sang the praises of democratic and liberal government, viewed with wrathful indignation the tyrannical rule
to which López subjected his people. Varela acrimoniously

[42] *Clemencia, op. cit.*, p. 325.

[43] We may list these minor novels in chronological order:

a. Fortunato A. Sánchez, *El ciego Rafael*, B.A., Imprenta E. Coni, 1870. In
this short novel a blind beggar relates the sad story of his life to a peaceful
family who welcomes him as a temporary guest. According to the records
of the Recoleta Cemetery, year 1884, folio 215, line 27, Sánchez died on
September 18, 1884, at thirty-nine years of age.

b. Nicanor Larrain, *El alma de Jesús Pérez, o la justicia del terror*, San Juan,
Imprenta de D. A. Luna, 1871. Larrain (1840-1902), reputable historian,
statesman, and educator, narrates the story of a seamstress who is executed
for implication in a series of robberies. The author uses this case to express
poignantly his condemnation of capital punishment, and to plead for a more
effective penitentiary system.

c. Luis J. Albert, *Lía*, B.A., Tipografía Borghese, 1879. The work narrates
how Rosas' henchmen force a young girl to wed the son of a prominent
newspaper editor. Albert (? -1926), a successful journalist, was also the
author of two unfinished novels that appeared in serial form in magazines
of Buenos Aires: *Rojelia* was published in *El Correo de las Porteñas* from
October 15 to December 3, 1876; and *Berta, la querida del jugador*, came
out in *La Aurora* from August 17 to November 15, 1879.

[44] Orión, *Elisa Lynch*—precedida de una semblanza del autor por Emilio
Castelar, B.A., Imprenta de La Tribuna, 1870. This biographical sketch by the
celebrated Spanish writer was originally published in *La Igualdad*, a newspaper
of Madrid, on July 25, 1870. Castelar recognizes Varela (who was the brother
of Luis Vicente) as a noble crusader for liberty and justice in the South American Republics.

impugns this inexorable despot, who partly because of egotisti-
cal motives waged to the point of futility the disastrous Paraguayan War. In novelized form Varela narrates episodes in
the life of the intriguing Elisa Lynch, and to this the author
adds much imaginative writing. Furthermore, he expounds
lengthily on the contemporary political situation in Argentina
and Paraguay, discusses important public figures, and rambles
diffusely about such themes as the Tyranny, democracy, and
Mitre's administration. It is clear that this digressive material,
presented with a firm conviction and an unswerving devotion
to the tenets of free and just government, occupied the author's
attention more fully than the development of a unified and
artistic account of Elisa Lynch's adventures.

. . .

It is apparent from the preceding paragraphs that Argentine
fiction of the 1870's unfolded in the absence of any clearly defined novelistic current. Already spent was the impelling force
of romanticism, and not yet mature was the bud of realism.
Most of the novels of this decade appeared as undisciplined,
unguided pieces of literature, without a definite trend in subject matter or a distinctive literary technique; and in many
cases the development of the work and the prose employed in
it were by the same token disorderly and careless. Yet despite
the very irregular nature of the novel during this decade, many
original elements in fiction writing were introduced. The
scope of the novel was extended greatly to include such diverse
material as scientific experimentation, supernatural phenomena, medical knowledge, criminal investigation, penitentiary
systems, divorce laws, and political satire. The treatment of
this material brought about an enrichment of words and
phrases, of incidents of plot, of ideas and motives, and of types
of characters. This revelation of new horizons in fiction stands
as one of the most salient features of the 1870's.

VIII

THE GAUCHO NOVEL

The gaucho, if not always regarded with favor, certainly occupied the attention of the nation at all times and was closely identified with its culture and progress. Disdained by some for his so-called barbarism and viciousness, admired by others for the humbleness and sincerity of his mode of living, he was a source of constant controversy even as far back as the colonial period. We have already noted the far-reaching influence of *Facundo* (1845), in which Sarmiento placed the gaucho's nomadic and crude existence in unfavorable contrast with the more disciplined and advanced civilization of the cities. Yet other important literary works of the nineteenth century considered the gaucho in a more sympathetic light, to the extent that his virtues were greatly exalted and his defects interpreted as the result of his inferior social position. Such classic pieces as *Diálogos patrióticos* (1822) by Bartolomé Hidalgo, *Fausto* (1866) by Estanislao del Campo, *Santos Vega* (1870) by Hilario Ascasubi, and the culminating work *Martín Fierro* (1872) by José Hernández, portrayed the gaucho in idealized tones, as endowed with a nobleness of spirit and genuineness of manner that made him worthy of an esteemed place in the hearts of all.

The appearance of the gaucho in the Argentine novel dates from an early period. In a few of the romantic novels of the 1850's and 1860's the gaucho is mentioned in a purely incidental manner, or he plays a small and insignificant active role. *Amalia* contains brief passages expressing Mármol's love and understanding of the gaucho; *Los misterios del Plata* presents an interesting gaucho type in the person of Miguel; *La familia de Sconner* makes casual reference to a friendly meeting of gauchos; *Revelaciones de un manuscrito* enters into the gaucho's

social and cultural characteristics; and *El médico de San Luis*
and *Emilia, o los efectos del coquetismo* offer laudatory remarks concerning his honest and wholesome vision of life. *El
isleño* proceeds one step further and deals in part with the conflict between an unrefined but noble gaucho and a dignified
city-bred gentleman; yet even in this work the author's principal focus is not upon a portraiture of the gaucho. With the
appearance of *El hogar en la pampa* (1866) and *Aventuras de
un centauro de la América meridional* (1868), the gaucho's
particular mode of life assumes a primary part in the story and
becomes the direct concern of the novelist. These two works,
which may be called the forerunners of the actual gaucho
novel, will occupy our attention in the next few pages.

1. *El Hogar en la Pampa*

El hogar en la pampa, published in 1866,[1] was written by Santiago Estrada (1841-1891), brother of the well-known congressman and author, José Manuel Estrada. Santiago fulfilled a
notable career as critic, journalist, and editor of several publications of his day. His complete writings were gathered together in seven volumes in 1889, but Estrada omitted his youthful novel *El hogar en la pampa,* without doubt not considering it of sufficient importance. Discourses, biographical studies,
dramatic criticism, and voyage narrations form the contents
of the books of this versatile and elegant writer.

The action of *El hogar en la pampa* takes place in an unidentified rural region of Argentina, in the year 1856. In this
quiet and modest atmosphere the author develops a love story,
in which a warmhearted *mayordomo* of a small ranch finally
wins the daughter of a humble sheepherder. The structure of
the novel is flimsy and the characters are only slightly developed; yet its powerful redeeming feature—the interesting
picture of rural life—gives this work an important place in

---

[1] Santiago Estrada, *El hogar en la pampa,* B.A., Imprenta del Siglo, 1866.
The novel was republished in 1931 by the Instituto de Literatura Argentina,
op. cit., 1931, serie 4, tomo II, No. 1.

the growth of the gaucho novel. As one contemporary writer succinctly explained: "...es que el marco es demasiado rico para el cuadro."[2]

The author's intention, as he states in the preface of his novel, is to glorify the beauty, wholesomeness, and sincerity of rural life, to laud the simplicity and honesty of the gaucho, and to demonstrate that true happiness and satisfaction may just as readily be found in the humble homes of farmers, herdsmen, and ranchers, as in the false and ostentatious medium of a large city. Furthermore, Estrada recognizes that these rural sections, frequently held in disparagement by pretentious and hypocritical urban dwellers, are to a large measure the source of Argentina's wealth, the very backbone of the nation.

It would be well to point out those elements in *El hogar en la pampa* which form the picturesque representation of Argentine gaucho life. The first chapter describes the *Fiesta de la Milagrosa Virgen de Luján,* a commemoration in which are revived some of the old gaucho customs that by the middle of the 1850's were beginning to disappear under the weight of the advancing civilization. Estrada laments that the onrush of material progress has altered many of the gaucho's habits of living.

> La bota de potro huye avergonzada a la sola presencia del poblado, para ser sustituída en los días de fiesta por la de becerro, y en los de trabajo por la alpargata; el chiripá se cae de las piernas del gaucho, ya acostumbrado a la comodidad del pantalón de piel del diablo; el cielo se hace perdiz en los bailes, porque los guitarreros entienden más de polkas y mazurkas, y el coñaque y el vermouth han fundido a los importadores de caña y jiniebra.[3]

There follows an interesting and lively account of the activities that are carried on during this celebration in the small town of Luján. The gauchos put together the traditional *barracas,* a sort of "rancho sin pared al frente, o mejor dicho, un

[2] L. D. Desteffanis, "El hogar en la pampa," *El Correo del Domingo,* August 19, 1866, p. 85.

[3] *El hogar en la pampa,* edition of the Instituto de Literatura Argentina, *op. cit.,* p. 9.

galpón de tablas con techo de lo mismo o de ramas secas."[4]
In the rear of the *barraca,* the *pulpero* constructs a crude coun-
ter and shelf, on which he places the food and drink to be
consumed by the revelers. Within the *barraca,* tables and
equipment are set up for the *juego del monte* and the *juego
de bolos.* By the light of the *vela de baño,* members of the
merry group amuse themselves by singing folk songs, playing
the guitar, dancing the *gato* and the *cielo,* or just being passive
spectators. Lastly, the more talented individuals of the company engage in a popular pastime called *una payada por cifra,*
in which each participant, in turn, improvises and sings short
verses of three or four lines.

Throughout the novel there appear comments on the customs, dress, food, and daily activities of the gaucho, as well as
brief references to popular Argentine rural types—the *peón,
payador, pastor-soldado,* and *esquilador.* Furthermore, in several sections the expressive gaucho vernacular is vividly employed. Particularly interesting is the conversation carried on
by a group of gauchos upon learning of the sadness and despair of the protagonist, who has just been rejected by his
sweetheart's mother:

> Desde la pulpería se veía el campo de Luis, al
> cual pertenecía alguno de los interlocutores, pues
> dijo:
> —¡Pobre mozo! ya le ha entrau la manía de
> dirse......
> —Eso es viejo, contestó otro, desde la muerte de
> la dijunta, él no anda bueno.
> —Ni la casa tampoco...... De valde hemos
> puesto la cruz a la entrada de la Estancia......
> Las ánimas no se van......
> —¡Qué ánimas, amigo! Los que se mueren no
> vuelven pó acá....
> —Pues yo digo que sí. A las noches cuando
> silba el viento y pasan las lechuzas del Cemente-
> rio, se ven luces en la casa de D. Luis......
> —Ya se ve, ¡cómo la deja sola y se va quien sabe
> aonde!

[4] *Loc. cit.*

—Ustedes se engañan, señores.

—¡Diaonde! ¿Ud. no ha visto las luces?

—Yo no he visto más luces que las que salen de
los caballos muertos......

—¿Y esas luces que andan?

—Es amigo porque las corren los caballos.

El pulpero abrió los ojos y dijo:

—Yo también he visto luces en la casa de don
Luis.

El que sostenía la oposición a la mayoría, repli-
có diciendo:

—Yo también las vide la otra noche y juí a la
casa con mi compadre Juan.

—¿De veras? preguntó con tono de increduli-
dad uno de los oyentes.

—¡Pues no, amigo! ¿Que cree que a mí me
asustan las ánimas?

—Siga el cuento, don Pedro.

—Pues, señor, juimos. Encendimos un jósforo
en el cuarto de la dijunta y al dentrar el viento
nos lo apagó...... Oímos un ruido y nos echa-
mos atrás...... les aseguro que con miedo......

—¡Ahí está......!

—¡Qué ahí está ni que vaca gorda! Salimos
y trujimos una vela, la encendimos, y nos encon-
tramos con un gato encerrau en el cuarto......
La luz que ustedes ven, a la cuenta son los ojos
del gato......[5]

2. Aventuras de un centauro de la América meridional

In 1868, from the pen of José Joaquín de Vedia,[6] came the
novel *Aventuras de un centauro de la América meridional.*[7]

[5] *Ibid.*, pp. 48-49.

[6] This author was the brother of Delfina de Vedia de Mitre, wife of Bartolomé Mitre.

[7] José Joaquín de Vedia, *Aventuras de un centauro de la América meridional,* ed. Santiago R. Pilotto, B.A., Imprenta del Orden, 1868. According to information supplied incidentally in the text, p. 184, the novel was written in
1864. To be sure, on May 27, 1864, there appeared in *El Nacional,* p. 4, a
notice of the coming publication of the work. However, it was not until four
years later, in 1868, that it actually was published.

Fundamentally, the work treats of the conflict between a gaucho and the national government during the revolutionary furor of the 1820's. Attempts to subject the gaucho to the regulations and form of life demanded by the new society met with his dogged and resentful resistance, for he clung tenaciously to his traditionally unhampered existence. Concerning the gaucho, Joaquín de Vedia states in his novel:

> Término medio entre la índole agreste del hombre de la naturaleza y los primeros refinamientos del fluido civilizador, el capricho de su voluntad era su ley y la norma de sus procederes.[8]

One such gaucho is the protagonist of the novel, a youth of many virtues, strong and noble of heart, who values beyond measure the free and nomadic life on the pampa. A fugitive from military service because of its discriminatory and harsh practices, the hero lives a precarious life, sweetened only by his wife's devoted love. The opening pages of the novel, with the account of the protagonist's flight from justice and his refuge at the homes of friendly gauchos, promise a more engaging and meaningful plot than that which is finally evolved. The work lacks concrete and purposeful action, as well as a unified plan of execution. True, the conflict is nicely set forth and the character of the hero is adequately revealed, but the movement of the novel is sluggish and at times aimless. What abounds in the work is lengthy passages which moralize and philosophize on all sorts of themes, from social progress, Americanism, and politics, to justice, customs and traditions, and love.

El centauro is significant in the development of the gaucho novel in that it stands as the first work which presents the gaucho as a fugitive, persecuted and hunted by the authorities. In more famous novels, notably *Juan Moreira* and *Santos Vega,* this conflict is to recur with frequency, forming the major interest of the plot. As portrayed in *El centauro,* the gaucho of the 1820's, rebellious and menacing, represented a group hostile to organized society, and by his nonconformity acted even

---

[8] *Aventuras de un centauro . . . . , op. cit.* p. 4.

as a deterrent to the economic and social progress of the country. Yet the author sustains that the gaucho's way of thinking and behaving must be comprehended in the light of his upbringing and environment, rather than peremptorily condemned. Educate the gaucho, give him an adequate understanding of his rights and duties as an Argentine, cries out the author, and then he will respect and revere his country's laws and institutions and will acquire a sense of responsibility in the community.

3. The Novels of Eduardo Gutiérrez

This incipient portraiture of gaucho life presented in the forementioned books evolved fully into the gaucho novel with the works of Eduardo Gutiérrez. His was neither a haphazard nor scant endeavor, but rather a conscientious and full-scale task of offering to the Argentine public a series of novels which would colorfully picture an important and deeply rooted national group. In these novels the gaucho approached full stature, came into his own as an absorbing protagonist, and with all his virtues and vices, angel or devil, bared his head unashamed before the world.

Eduardo Gutiérrez (1851-1889) started his literary career in his youthful years by composing varied articles for *La Nación Argentina,* which his brothers tirelessly and efficiently published.[9] His essays, narrations, critical reviews on the fine arts, and sketches of native customs, appearing in that newspaper and also in *La Tribuna, La Época, El Nacional,* and *Sud-América,* served to establish Gutiérrez as a keen and observing interpreter of contemporary Argentine life. In addition to journalistic pursuits, Gutiérrez' early manhood included active military service, which he later used to advantage in many novels. In 1874, as a member of the garrison at Fort General Paz, located to the west of Buenos Aires, he experienced the rigors of army life and became acquainted with military pro-

---

[9] These brothers were José María, Carlos, and Ricardo.

cedures; and from 1876 to 1879 he fought valiantly at Blanca Grande, Guaminí, and Monte Laguna to subdue savage Indian bands.

The reception accorded Gutiérrez' works was considerable, indeed never before attained by an Argentine novelist. The public responded avidly to each novel that left the pen of this famed author. In late 1879 the reader was first introduced to Gutiérrez' novelistic production, when in the pages of *La Patria Argentina* there appeared in serial form the famous *Juan Moreira*. There followed in that same newspaper many other novels by Gutiérrez, which he enthusiastically supplied to the ardent public until 1883. An indication of his great popularity may be seen by noting that during the latter half of 1882 two of his works appeared simultaneously in *La Patria Argentina*: *Don Juan Manuel de Rosas* (December 27, 1881, to December 29, 1882) and *La muerte de Buenos Aires* (June 25 to December 29, 1882). Furthermore, upon a close examination of other important newspapers of Buenos Aires, notably *La Prensa* and *La Nación,* we notice that a large number of booksellers gave considerable attention to the promotion of Gutiérrez' works. All of his novels that originally appeared in serial form in *La Patria Argentina* were shortly afterward published in book form by that same newspaper. Many of these works, in addition to others not first published serially, were also edited by Natalio Tommasi and Luis Maucci, who evinced a great interest in the divulgation of Gutiérrez' fiction.

It is important to note in what light Gutiérrez considered the gaucho, his attitude and feelings toward him, and the interpretation he gave to his particular mode of living. This judgment was significantly evidenced in each of the gaucho novels and marked the frame within which the works were conceived. Gutiérrez loved, respected, and admired the gaucho; he understood truth and naturalness in his simple and unaffected existence; and he staunchly defended his rights and privileges against those who negated them. The author maintained that the gaucho was inherently as good and as honorable as other men; that his propensity toward crime and violence was no greater than that of other groups, but he was frequently compelled by unfortunate circumstances and the very nature of his nomadic and unhampered form of life to defy the authorities and become an outlaw. Persecuted, humiliated, distrusted, and mistreated by those in power who considered him an inferior citizen, he built up an attitude of belligerency and resentment toward all which smacked of law and order. He found himself unjustly accused of all sorts of misdemeanors, harshly punished for minor offenses, and not infrequently the object of attack and vengeance by unscrupulous officials. Wrangles led to heated disputes, disputes led to violence, and violence to bloodshed and murder; and the once honorable and peaceful gaucho was soon a pariah of society, an implacable enemy of authority. When he abandoned his home, leaving behind wife and children, he severed the last link with order and social organization, his life being reduced to one of fleeing and hiding, in truth to a struggle for self-preservation.

Juan Moreira,[10] the first and perhaps the most famous of Gutiérrez' gaucho novels,[11] may be considered as a representative work, one which brings to the fore the gaucho's sad trajectory from respectability to lawlessness. The protagonist of the work vividly lives in the memory of Argentines, who view Moreira's daring exploits with mixed emotions of dread and admiration. The opening chapters of the novel narrate

[10] *Juan Moreira* originally appeared in *La Patria Argentina* from November 28, 1879, to January 8, 1880. We note that the work did not bear Gutiérrez' name until the very last installment. In 1880 the work was published in book form by La Imprenta de La Patria Argentina, and in 1886 N. Tommasi edited the novel.

[11] It is worth while at this point to list the gaucho novels of Gutiérrez, noting the editions of each work.

a. *Juan Cuello,* in *La Patria Argentina,* January 9 to March 19, 1880; B.A., Imprenta de La Patria Argentina, 1880; B.A., N. Tommasi, 1886 and 1888.
b. *Santos Vega,* B.A., Imprenta de La Patria Argentina, 1880 and 1881; B.A., Imprenta de P. Buffet y Cía, 1886; B.A., N. Tommasi, n.d.
c. *Una amistad hasta la muerte*—continuación de *Santos Vega,* B.A., N. Tommasi, n.d.
d. *Hormiga Negra,* in *La Patria Argentina,* October 16 to December 26, 1881; B.A., Imprenta de La Patria Argentina, 1881.
e. *Juan Sin Patria,* B.A., Imprenta de La Patria Argentina, 1881; B.A., 1886; B.A., N. Tommasi, n.d.
f. *Pastor Luna,* B.A., N. Tommasi, 1886.
g. *Los Hermanos Barrientos,* B.A., N. Tommasi, 1886.

the chain of events which leads this well-intentioned but impetuous gaucho to embark upon a life of open conflict with the forces of law. First, the influential and fearsome justice of the peace, often repelled in his improper advances toward Moreira's wife, wreaks his vengeance by imposing innumerable fines on the gaucho for the slightest infraction of local regulations or for spurious charges fabricated by venal officials. Secondly, a merchant to whom Moreira lent a considerable sum of money brazenly refuses to repay the debt, whereupon the infuriated gaucho challenges him to a duel and kills him.

This incident proves the turning point in Moreira's life, for he now feel himself a common outlaw. Hunted on all sides by the unrelenting authorities and consequently obliged to seek food and shelter under the most wretched conditions, Moreira comes into contact with unsavory and vicious individuals, with vagrants, outcasts, and gamblers who in the *pulperías,* on the open pampa, and in the village streets are disposed to quarrel and fight to the death at the slightest provocation. There follow in subsequent pages of the novel numerous episodes in which Moreira is forced to violence, at times in bitter battle with pursuing federal officials, at times in gory affrays to save his honor or his life. As a consequence of constant success in these encounters, in which his valor and sense of fair play are matched by consummate skill and resourcefulness, Moreira's fame as a feared and redoubtable gaucho spreads rapidly throughout the region.

The adventures of Juan Moreira, as well as those of other gaucho protagonists, like Santos Vega and Hormiga Negra, are steeped in violence and brutality of the most shocking sort. Hideous and revolting crimes are narrated with a seeming desire to cause the reader to recoil with horror and disgust. Descriptions of methods of killing, detailed accounts of mental and physical torture, and harsh reports of vicious fights occupy many pages of the gaucho novels and in many cases even recur with monotonous regularity. Moreover, indicative of the lust for cruelty are the colorful and sanguinarily expressive pictures on the cover and inside pages of many of the early editions of the gaucho works, as well as of the *Dramas policiales* and *Dramas del terror*. These pictures, illustrating gruesome scenes taken from the novels, quickly caught the public's eye and presented a most provocative introduction to the contents of the books.

The novelistic production of Eduardo Gutiérrez is vast and includes not only the gaucho novels but other types of fiction as well. He composed a series of four novels that bears the general title of *Dramas del terror*,[12] which bitterly denounce Rosas' tyrannical administration. Another group of novels, called *Dramas militares*,[13] treats of the struggles in the early 1860's between federal troops and a revolutionary band of *montoneros*, headed by the fearless Ángel Vicente Peñaloza, nicknamed El Chacho. The national forces considered El Chacho and his loyal followers as symbolic of the lawless and rebellious gaucho who by his constant repudiation of established authority impeded progress in the country. Yet in the judgment of Gutiérrez, this heroic and formidable *caudillo* —resolutely opposed to the new government at Buenos Aires, which he believed was usurping his domain—died a martyr to the cause of liberty and justice in the province of La Rioja.

The contemporary Argentine scene is treated in the following works: *La muerte de Buenos Aires—epopeya de 1880*[14] is a novelized account of the political and military events during the struggle for power at the close of Avellaneda's administration; *Los siete bravos*[15] pictures the tenseness and anxiety of the province of Corrientes during the early years of the presi-

---

[12] The series *Dramas del terror* includes the following works:
a. *Don Juan Manuel de Rosas*, in *La Patria Argentina*, December 27, 1881 to December 29, 1882; B.A., Imprenta de La Patria Argentina, 1883; B.A., N. Tommasi, 1888.
b. *La mazorca*, B.A., N. Tommasi, 1888; B.A., L. Maucci, 1893.
c. *Una tragedia de doce años*, B.A., N. Tommasi, n.d.
d. *El puñal del terror*, B.A., N. Tommasi, 1888.
[13] The series *Dramas militares* includes the following works:
a. *El Chacho*, B.A., N. Tommasi, 1886.
b. *Los montoneros*, B.A., N. Tommasi, n.d.
c. *El rastreador*, B.A., N. Tommasi, n.d.
d. *La muerte de un héroe*, B.A., Imprenta de M. Moreno, 1892.
[14] *La muerte de Buenos Aires—epopeya de 1880*, in *La Patria Argentina*, June 25 to December 29, 1882; B.A., Imprenta de La Patria Argentina, 1882; B.A., N. Tommasi, 1888; B.A., L. Maucci, 1894.
[15] *Los siete bravos*, B.A., N. Tommasi, n.d.

dency of Julio Roca, against whom it voted in the election of 1880; lastly, *Croquis y siluetas militares*[16] presents interesting portraitures of many important military officials. In an extensive group of novels collectively entitled *Dramas policiales*,[17] Gutiérrez narrates stories of horrible crimes and gory murders, of astute felons and venal public servants, of insidious plans of revenge and treacherous schemes of theft and corruption. Crudeness, vulgarity, atrocities, and lurid details of brutal incidents cover the pages of these works. Yet this is what a

[16] *Croquis y siluetas militares—escenas contemporáneas de nuestros campamentos*, B.A., Igon Hermanos, 1886.

[17] *Dramas policiales* include the following works;

a. *El jorobado*, in *La Patria Argentina*, March 22 to July 30, 1880; B.A., Imprenta de La Patria Argentina, 1880; B.A., Imprenta de P. Buffet, 1886; B.A., N. Tommasi, 1889; ed. Tommasi y Checchi, Milan, and N. Tommasi y Cía, B.A., 1889.

b. *Astucia de una negra*—continuación y fin de *El jorobado*, B.A. N. Tommasi, n.d. This same work appeared under the title *El jorobado se divierte con su gavilla infernal*, ed. Tommasi y Checchi, Milan, and N. Tommasi y Cía, B.A., 1890.

c. *El tigre del Quequén*, in *La Patria Argentina*, August 10 to November 16, 1880; B.A., Imprenta de La Patria Argentina, 1880; B.A., N. Tommasi, 1886.

d. *Los grandes ladrones*, in *La Patria Argentina*, August 4 to October 15, 1881; B.A., Imprenta de La Patria Argentina, 1881; B.A., N. Tommasi, 1886; ed. L. Maucci, B.A., Imprenta de M. Moreno, 1894.

e. *El asesinato de Álvarez*, in *La Patria Argentina*, December 30, 1882, to March 12, 1883, with the title originally appearing as *Los asesinos de Álvarez;* B.A., Imprenta de La Patria Argentina, 1883; B.A., N. Tommasi, 1896.

f. *Enterrados vivos*—continuación de *El asesinato de Álvarez*, in *La Patria Argentina*, March 13 to April 16, 1883.

g. *Amor funesto*, in *La Patria Argentina*, Abril 17 to May 3, 1883; B.A., Imprenta de La Patria Argentina, 1883; B.A., N. Tommasi, 1896.

h. *Nicanora Fernández*, in *La Patria Argentina*, May 4 to May 21, 1883; B.A., N. Tommasi, 1896.

i. *El asesinato de Fiorini*, in *La Patria Argentina*, May 22 to 28, 1883. The work was not completed.

j. *Doña Dominga Rivadavia*, in *La Patria Argentina*, May 29 to September 12, 1883; B.A., N. Tommasi, n.d.; ed. L. Maucci, B.A., Imprenta de M. Moreno, 1892.

k. *Infamias de una madre*—continuación de *Doña Dominga Rivadavia*, B.A., N. Tommasi, n.d.

l. *Ignacio Monges*, ed. N. Tommasi, B.A., Imprenta de El Orden, 1886.

In addition to these forementioned *Dramas policiales*, Gutiérrez wrote other novels which deal with crime, terror, and violence.

a. *Un capitán de ladrones en Buenos Aires*, B.A., Administración de La Patria Argentina, 1879. Subsequently this work appeared under different titles: *Antonio Larrea, o sea un capitán de ladrones en Buenos Aires*, B.A., N. Tommasi, 1886; *Un capitán de ladrones, o sea Antonio Larrea en Buenos Aires*, B.A., N. Tommasi, n.d.

b. *Carlo Lanza*, B.A., Imprenta de P. Buffet, 1886; B.A., N. Tommasi, n.d.

c. *Lanza el gran banquero*—continuación de *Carlo Lanza*, B.A., N. Tommasi, n.d.

d. *Un viaje infernal*, Obras Inéditas, B.A., N. Tommasi, n.d.; B.A., 1899.

e. *Una demanda curiosa*, Obras Inéditas, B.A., N. Tommasi, n.d.; B.A., Schurer-Stolle, 1899.

large segment of the public craved and Gutiérrez did not hesitate to present such material.

As pieces of literary art Gutiérrez' novels hold but meager claim. There is little artistry in the selection of words and phrases, in the formation of sentences, or in the development of paragraphs. The author's vocabulary is extremely limited and employed in such a careless and at times insipid form that the words leave but slight aesthetic impression on the reader. Gutiérrez' harsh and unpolished language, coupled with the rather sickly interest in revealing almost to the point of nausea the details of crime and suffering, has caused many critics and a portion of the public to forget or disregard the important and original contribution that he made to the progress of the Argentine novel.

With his gaucho works Gutiérrez created a type of fiction proudly and distinctively Argentine. Despite their many serious shortcomings, these gaucho pieces furthered to a very marked degree the awakening of a desire to read the national novel. Gutiérrez sought to entertain the popular taste, to capture the attention of a public which avidly searched for material that could be identified with the living fiber of the nation. His stories of violent action and brutally thrilling episodes provided a suitable stimulus for the wide audience to whom he catered. He never imitated foreign models, but created an atmosphere and a host of characters that were undeniably Argentine.

We must consider Gutiérrez not in the light of his artistic accomplishments as a novelist, but as a writer who brought greater recognition and significance to the term Argentine novel; who created the gaucho novel and advanced it to a stage of considerable popularity; and who laid the foundation for the perfection of that gaucho novel by literary figures of superior merit, notably Ricardo Güiraldes and Benito Lynch.

D. Julio Llanos and his Novel *Arturo Sierra*

In the person of Julio Llanos, *La Patria Argentina* encountered a popular successor to Eduardo Gutiérrez as the writer of daily serials. In his brief novels Llanos continued to satisfy the public's taste for exciting and melodramatic stories, filled with sensational and daring episodes. During the seven-month period from September, 1883, to April, 1884, there appeared in almost uninterrupted succession six short novels by Llanos[18] —works which reveal his fertile imagination and power to retain the reader's interest.

Julio Llanos (1858-1933)[19] first studied engineering, then medicine, before embarking upon a career of journalism and fiction writing. In *La Patria Argentina, La Ilustración Argentina, La Prensa, La Revista Nacional,* and other publications Llanos produced a wide variety of stories, anecdotes, historical episodes, articles of literary criticism, and miscellaneous narrations. He also distinguished himself as a legislator and economist; and in 1908 he was commissioned by the Argentine government to undertake a series of studies on rural industries, commerce, and economy of Europe.

Julio Llanos' most popular work is entitled *Arturo Sierra,*[20] a novel set in a rural region and having as protagonist a detestable and vicious gaucho. Originally appearing as a serial of *La Patria Argentina* with the title *Ofelia* (1884), the work was quickly published in book form that same year. In the preface to *Arturo Sierra,* the editor makes this interesting observation concerning the Argentine novel:

> La novela recién empieza a ser cultivada, y en menos del transcurso de un año, varias produc-

---

[18] The following works appeared in *La Patria Argentina*:
a. *El pirata del hogar—Dramas sociales,* September 10 to October 25, 1883.
b. *Un drama conjugal,* January 21 to February 17, 1884.
c. *Agustina de Libarona,* February 18 to February 28, 1884.
d. *El capitán Morillo—últimas víctimas de Rosas,* February 29 to March 12, 1884.
e. *La número 35—Cuadros sociales,* March 13 to April 11, 1884.
f. *Ofelia,* April 12 to May 2, 1884. This work was subsequently published in book form under the title *Arturo Sierra.*
[19] The wife of Julio Llanos was Ema de la Barra, who under the pseudonym of César Duayen issued the popular novel *Stella* (1905).
[20] Julio Llanos, *Arturo Sierra, B.A.,* Emilio de Mársico, 1884. In addition to *Arturo Sierra* and those works of fiction appearing in serial form, Llanos is the author of a long biographical novel entitled *Camila O'Gorman,* B.A., Imprenta de La Patria Argentina, 1883. The work, a bitter attack against the Rosas regime, narrates in excessive detail the events leading to the brutal execution of the protagonist, her lover (a priest named Gutiérrez), and their unborn child.

ciones de ese género han sido escritas y editadas
en Buenos Aires, sino con todo el éxito que fuera
de desear, al menos con resultados que bien pueden llamarse satisfactorios, por el movimiento que
han orijinado en favor de la literatura nacional.

Nos complacemos en agregar una más al número de las que hasta hoy han aparecido.[21]

In the novel there is a bit of the sensational, the melodramatic, the sentimental, with the protagonist playing the role
of the revengeful villain and the heroine representing his defenseless prey. Most of the scenes are laid on a small ranch,
but there is little characterization of the locale. Elements of
gaucho life enter more directly into the novel in the portrayal
of a *pulpería,* where Arturo Sierra spends many hours in idle-
ness and depravity. When this gaucho makes his appearance
in this place of reunion, called the *Chubeada,* the author describes him in these words:

Vestía con poca desenvoltura el pintoresco traje
del gaucho: su chiripá de paño negro, sus altas
botas charoladas, su camiseta de merino llena de
bordados, y su rumboso tirador, anunciaban a un
hombre mimado por la suerte.[22]

---

[21] *Arturo Sierra,* 1884 edition in book form, *op. cit.,* p. 3, editor's note.
[22] *Ibid.,* p. 6.

IX

THE DEVELOPMENT OF REALISM

1. THE REALISTIC NOVEL THROUGHOUT HISPANIC AMERICA

The 1880's, in addition to witnessing the growth of the gaucho novel, saw the full expansion of realism in Argentine fiction. By realism we understand the faithful portraiture of life, the true characterization of events and personages, the careful objective observation and representation of actions and emotions. The realistic novel attempts to reveal with fidelity, in appropriate lights and darks and grays, in true proportion, the general atmosphere of the work and the individuals living in that milieu. In short, not a society looked at through rose-colored glasses, nor defiled by the perverted minds of villains, nor peopled with cherublike creatures and darling heroes and heroines, but a society taken from life's complexity and incomprehensiveness, breathing and exhibiting a combination of good and evil, of beauty and ugliness, justice and iniquity—this is what realism seeks to portray.

Throughout Hispanic America, realism as a dominant current in the field of fiction generally appeared after the energetic impulse of romanticism had passed away. Yet there was no clear line of demarcation that separated the two types of novels, either as regards strict chronology or novelistic technique. We have mentioned before that from the very beginnings the novel frequently exhibited a mixture of romantic and realistic elements—romantic for the expression of emotion and realistic for the true to life portrayal of social types and customs. The *cuadro de costumbres,* a fundamentally realistic mode of expression, thus served paradoxically as one of the directive forces that molded many romantic novels. As the romantic trappings of exaltation, sentimentality, and exaggerated passion gradually faded out of fiction, the *costumbrista* novel, the regional novel, and in general the realistic novel all emerged in full stature as genuine representations of life in America. Clearly discernible Spanish influences in the development of American realism from the *cuadro de costumbres* are the prose writers Larra, Mesonero Romanos and Estébanez Calderón, as well as the two great novelists Pereda and Palacio Valdés.

It would be worth while at this point to indicate briefly the principal writers of the realistic novel in America in the nineteenth century. In Mexico, succeeding the transition figure of Altamirano came Emilio Rabasa, generally recognized as that country's first true realist; Rafael Delgado, author of the noted *Angelina* (1895); and José López Portillo y Rojas, who with *La parcela* (1890) stands as the first genuine cultivator of the Mexican rural novel. In his native Chile and throughout Hispanic America Alberto Blest Gana won fame for his intensely realistic portraiture of life in various ranges of society, as is seen in *Martín Rivas* (1862), *Durante la Reconquista* (1897), and *Los transplantados* (1904).

In Venezuela the realistic novelist is represented best by Vicente Romero García and Gonzalo Picón Febres, both of whom, in their respective works *Peonía* (1890) and *Nieve y lodo* (1895), reveal a keen interest in depicting their country's particular way of life. Colombia, outstanding in its array of *costumbrista* writers, points with pride to Eugenio Díaz' *Manuela* (1866), a splendid example of the realistic novel that has its roots in this same *costumbrista* current. Furthermore, Colombia may signal out as one of the finest prose writers in Hispanic America the figure of Tomás Carrasquilla, who in such novels as *Frutos de mi tierra* (1896), *Entrañas de niño* (1914), and *El Padre Casafús* (1914), magnificently portrays in the *costumbrista* manner the picturesque mountain region of Antioquia. Lastly, we cite the name of Eduardo Acevedo Díaz, considered as the initiator of the national novel in Uruguay with his firmly realistic works *Nativa* (1880), *Ismael* (1888), *Grito de Gloria* (1893), and, the most meritorious, *Soledad* (1894).

With reference to Argentina, it is significant that the development of the realistic novel should coincide with the extraordinary growth and progress which the Republic manifested during the years 1880 to 1900. As this economic and material transformation took place, greatly affecting every facet of the nation's life and bringing about incessant verve and productive activity, eager writers sought to mirror that rapid change and portray the new society that was surging forth. In the next few pages we shall examine the political events and the social and economic conditions of this momentous period in Argentine history.

B. Argentina's Great Progress

It will be recalled that in 1880, at the close of Avellaneda's administration, the federalization of Buenos Aires was effected. This important event may be taken as the point of departure for the radical change undergone by the nation. Julio A. Roca succeeded Avellaneda as president of the Republic in 1880, and during his six-year term of office witnessed such financial prosperity and economic progress as the country had never previously experienced. The national income and foreign commerce increased markedly; immigration continued to supply new blood and fresh vigor to the growing country; and railroads were extended at an unprecedented rate, augmenting the value of the regions they traversed. Agriculture began to develop and play an important role in the nation's economy. To cattle raising and the exporting of hides and wool there was added as a source of wealth the production of wheat, cereals, and grains. The picture of rural life was thus altered, for the farmer now started to replace the traditional gaucho. Moreover, with the subjugation or extermination of the savage Indians, vast expanses of the southern plains became available for pasture and then for cultivation.

The accelerated activity of the Republic necessitated the creation and reorganization of many municipal and national institutions. Roca arranged for the construction of an adequate port of Buenos Aires to handle the greater flow of commerce to and from the capital; he founded the National Mortgage Bank, revamped the police force in Buenos Aires, and drew up sound penal codes; lastly, he set up an effective National Board of Education to strengthen the foundations of the public school system.

In 1886 Miguel Juárez Celman took office as president of the Republic, in the midst of the prosperity and progress initiated by the Roca administration. To a large measure foreign capital helped to produce this state of wealth, as European bankers and businessmen poured a constant stream of money into the Argentine market. Railroads and other public works and services were financed on a huge scale by foreign investments; the land itself, a potent spring of wealth, was bought and sold by European capitalists; and business transactions, the stock exchange, and the tenor of the economy in general strongly felt the powerful force of these foreign interests.

The economic boom was phenomenal. As in Roca's administration, trade, railroads, immigration, and agriculture increased at a dizzy rate. Business never enjoyed such profitable years, and many banks, corporations, and other commercial organizations were formed throughout the capital. The government, large business houses, and private individuals entered into an orgy of reckless spending and foolhardy investment, never preoccupied with their financial position, always confident that funds would be readily available. Transactions on the stock exchange reached a fever pitch, as multitudes of people, caught in the vertiginous frenzy of speculation and swept along by its cogent force, traded in millions of pesos. Banks extended easy credit and their deposits reached soaring figures. To be sure, these were golden years of prosperity.

Such added wealth stimulated construction of all types. Of fundamental importance for the nation was the opening of the port of Buenos Aires in the early part of 1889, by virtue of the building of docks and basins and the dredging of an entrance channel. Shipping was thus greatly facilitated, as

large vessels could enter the harbor and discharge their cargo
or passengers. Moreover, Buenos Aires, under the leadership
of its energetic mayor, Torcuato Alvear, sought to rival in
beauty and splendor the glorious cities of Europe. The magnificent Avenida de Mayo, with its continental architecture
and atmosphere, cut across the central part of the capital. For
the rising elite, the fashionable Jockey Club, boasting a costly
staircase and elaborately furnished salons, was constructed on
the principal commercial artery, Calle Florida. Work began
on new hospitals, a medical school, and a central post office;
and shops, dwellings, hotels, and restaurants rose swiftly
throughout the capital. Furthermore, other cities of the nation
—Entre Ríos, Corrientes, Córdoba—although not suffering
such a marked change as Buenos Aires, did construct many
public works and government buildings.

The culminating point of this period of prosperity was
reached in 1889, but during the second half of that same year
there was already observed the beginning of a financial crisis
and economic decline which were to sweep destructively across
the nation in 1890. The wealth and fortune that had favored
the country and had spiraled upward and upward in the years
1880-1890 came plunging down with equal vigor and rapidity.
An important factor which brought about this economic devas-
tation was the devaluation of paper money, a condition that
started in 1884 and carried the Republic to bankruptcy in 1890.
Inflation gripped the country and wreaked havoc on its economy. The value of stocks, bonds, and certificates suffered a sudden drop. Even the land itself, as well as the basic products of
Argentine consumption and exportation descended in value.
Credit became restricted, purchases of land and buildings were
reduced, domestic and foreign commercial activity diminished
considerably, and transactions of private and government securities underwent a decided cut. Financial paralysis set in. A
large number of concerns suspended payment. Many banks
found themselves helpless in stemming the tide of economic
disaster and were on the verge of complete ruin. In 1889 Argentina suffered an unfavorable balance of trade and its na-

tional debt increased. Late that year the Republic became insolvent, unable to meet its obligations at home or to fulfill its commitments abroad.

Juárez Celman supported the wealthy landowners, influential businessmen, and foreign investors; and once the financial crisis took root, it was to the defense of these groups that he first turned his attention, to the neglect of the interests of the country as a whole. In 1890 the economic structure of the nation grew weaker and weaker and finally collapsed completely. The people were desperate and sought aid and protection from somewhere, somehow. Amid the discontent and confusion there was organized a strong political group called the *Unión Cívica,* which angrily condemned Celman's extravagance and recklessness and determined to overthrow his government by force of arms. The head of this radical party was Leandro Alem, whose vigorous personality and resoluteness of purpose caused the masses to seek in him the leadership they so urgently needed. In July, 1890, the *Unión Cívica* began a military uprising in Buenos Aires, but it was suppressed after several days of combat. Yet despite his victory over the rebels, Celman recognized the futility of attempting to save the economic situation, and on August 6, 1890 resigned his office.

Carlos Pellegrini, who had been vice-president, now assumed the presidency. Although a *porteño*—the first one in thirty years to be head of the nation—he felt secure in the support of the provinces. During the brief period he remained in office, 1890-1892, Argentina's financial and economic condition improved greatly, but a return to normalcy was not accomplished until several years later. In December, 1891, the Bank of the Argentine Nation was founded, which was instrumental in reaffirming the soundness of government finances. An able and sincere statesman, Pellegrini succeeded in restoring the confidence of the people and freeing the nation from political unrest.

During these years Argentina emerged as a strong, wealthy, and resolute nation. Her character came to be well defined, distinctive, of a savor peculiarly her own. These two decades provided writers with engaging and significant material for their realistic novels. The economic boom, increased business and trade, the fever of speculation, the rapid rise of a well-to-do class, and the influx of immigrants—of all this novelists availed themselves, desirous of depicting vividly and truthfully this period of utmost importance.

With reference to the cultural and intellectual life of the Republic during this era, it is necessary to mention the *generación del '80,* an appellation commonly given to a group of prose writers, among whom may be cited Miguel Cané (son), Eduardo Wilde, José S. Álvarez, Lucio V. Mansilla, Santiago Estrada, José M. Cantilo, and Bartolomé Mitre y Vedia. Rather than the novel, most of them preferred the short story, the *cuadro de costumbres,* the essay, the sketch, and the voyage narration. These *prosistas fragmentarios,* as they are frequently called, wrote in a light, gracious, and picturesque fashion, achieving a wide popularity among Argentine readers.

Scholars, historians, orators, statesmen, and men of letters, of the caliber of Alberto Navarro Viola, Ernesto Quesada and Paul Groussac, continued to define and analyze the nation's pattern of culture, but in a more original and subjective manner than was exhibited in preceding decades. Literary and intellectual societies, books, newspapers and periodicals, *tertulias* and *salones,* all served as able instruments to implement the passion for culture. Magazines such as *La Revista Argentina* (1880), *La Nueva Revista de Buenos Aires* (1881), and *La Biblioteca* (1896), the newspapers *El Diario, La Nación* and *La Prensa,* as well as the enterprising publishing houses of Casavalle, Coni, and Lajouane, prodigiously disseminated the varied artistic labor of persevering authors, journalists, critics, and other men of learning.

Although these prose writers formed one of the most original and distinctive groups of literary artists of the period, poetry and the drama also produced important authors. Rafael Obligado (1851-1920) evinced in his poems a genuine feeling for the reality that is America, and with his collection *Tradiciones argentinas* represented at its best gaucho poetry in cultured language; Calixto Oyuela (1857-1935) reverted to the neo-classical art in poetry; while the controversial figure of Pedro Bonifacio Palacios (1847-1917), more familiarly known as Almafuerte, sought in his verses to strengthen an almost fanatical individualism. The drama, not developed with outstanding merit until the twentieth century in the persons of Florencio Sánchez and Robert Payró, nevertheless was expressed in such works as *Juan Moreira* (1886), by José J. Podestá, and *Calandria* (1896), by Martiniano Leguizamón, as well as in minor plays by Martín Coronado (1850-1919) and Nicolás Granada (1840-1915).

3. La gran aldea

The first novel to portray realistically the changing Buenos Aires of the 1880's was *La gran aldea* (1884),[1] by Lucio Vicente López (1848-1894). Appearing originally from May 20 to July 2, 1884, as a serial of the popular newspaper *Sud-América,* the novel was published in book form that same year and since then has gone through many editions.[2] Readers received the work with hearty enthusiasm; in it they saw reflected the past and present of their own lives. In it they recognized something vitally Argentine, something with which they could identify themselves. The novel belonged to them; it "struck home," for the very *gran aldea* which flashed before their eyes was the setting for their personal drama of life. Contemporary reviews of the novel were numerous and for the most part favorable, especially in consideration of its value in defining a concrete period in Argentine's history.

[1] Lucio Vicente López, *La gran aldea—costumbres bonaerenses,* B.A., Imprenta de M. Biedma, 1884. In 1880, four years before *La gran aldea* appeared, José María Cantilo (1840-1891) came out with a short novel entitled *La familia Quillango.* The work, which presents the story of a young man who seeks fortune through marriage, is set vaguely in the Buenos Aires of 1880, but touches only rudimentarily on life in the capital. The novel first appeared serially in *El Correo del Domingo,* from January 4 to February 29, 1880, under the pseudonym Sísifo. It was then published in a volume by Cantilo entitled *Un libro más,* ed. F. Lajouane, B.A. and Ch. Bouret, Paris, B.A., 1887, pp. 9-93.

[2] Among the later editions of *La gran aldea* may be mentioned: Biblioteca de la Nación, 1903, Vol. 71; Grandes Escritores Argentinos, 1928, Vol. VIII; Claridad, 1939; Biblioteca Mundial Sopena, 1939; Tor. 1939; Editorial Calomino, 1944; Clásicos Americanos, 1945; Colección Ángel Estrada, 1948, Vol. 57.

Son of Vicente Fidel López, Lucio Vicente was born in Montevideo in 1848 and received his primary education in that city. At the age of fifteen he arrived in Buenos Aires, where he began the study of law and was awarded the degree of Doctor of Law in 1873. He took a vigorous part in the politics of the day, served his country with distinction in several important official positions, taught history and law at the University of Buenos Aires, and exercised assiduously his legal profession. In addition, Lucio López engaged in serious literary pursuits which earned for him a solid reputation as an interesting and gifted writer. In his youthful years he collaborated on *La Revista del Río de la Plata* and *La Revista de Buenos Aires.* He wrote numerous articles in *El Nacional* and *Sud-América,* particularly during the years 1877-1884. In 1881 he published an extremely popular work entitled *Recuerdos de viaje,*[3] which narrates his journey through Europe; and following the example of his father he wrote *Lecciones de historia argentina*[4] and several volumes on law.

La gran aldea vividly describes two stages in the social evolution of Buenos Aires. The protagonist's reminiscences of his youthful years date back to the early 1860's, to a Buenos Aires, as the author states, "patriota, sencillo, semitendero, semicurial y semialdea."[5] The capital of that period he compares with contemporary Buenos Aires of 1883, "con un pueblo con grandes pretensiones europeas, que perdía su tiempo en planear en las calles."[6] It is significant that the subtitle of the novel reads *Costumbres bonaerenses,* for to a large measure the work is composed of a series of impressions revealing customs and manners of the Argentine capital. Around these recollections and observations the plot is drawn. The protagonist's life is brought forth in scattered instances and at great intervals of time, a condition which causes individual scenes to be far more engrossing and artistically presented than the completed picture.

[3] Lucio Vicente López, *Recuerdos de viaje,* B.A., Imprenta de El Nacional, 1881.
[4] Lucio Vicente López, *Lecciones de historia argentina,* ed. Carlos Casavalle, B.A., 1878.
[5] *La gran aldea,* 1884 edition in book form, *op. cit.,* p. 144.
[6] *Loc. cit.*

Julio (the protagonist) looks back with nostalgic remembrance on the old Buenos Aires of his adolescence. He recalls with tender sympathy the simple yet charming stores, the affable shopkeepers, and in general the wholesome and friendly commercial spirit pervading the streets of the capital. His thoughts return with happy emotion to the older generation of politicians and men of letters, many of whom he observed with youthful eagerness at his uncle's home. Julio relates the tremendous enthusiasm of the *porteños* upon learning of the victory at Pavón in 1861. He tells briefly of the feminine taste in literature and the fashions of the period. At the same time he contemplates the capital of the 1880's, the Buenos Aires now surrounding him. The emotion he feels is light-hearted displeasure at the modernity and Europeanization of the capital, at its shameful ostentation of wealth and luxury, its ebullient activity for material purposes.

With lively grace and a frequent touch of veiled humor, Lucio López brings to light salient traits of the capital during the 1880's. The frenzied fever of speculation is personified in the astute and ambitious executive for whom the protagonist worked in his youth; descriptions of the busy streets and shops, the picturesque dances and gay societies, like the important Club del Progreso, lend much local color; and styles, modes of social behavior, and manner of speech are likewise charmingly revealed. By way of example we cite the following paragraphs which picture the famous Teatro Colón:

> Se daba Semíramis aquella noche, y el Colón estaba en gala; los palcos, ocupados por las más lindas y conocidas mujeres de la gran sociedad, presentaban un aspecto deslumbrador. Se había cantado el primer acto; la Borghi y la Scalchi electrizaban al público y en la sala no se escuchaba sino un eco del entusiasmo y de los elogios.

> Una noche clásica de ópera en el Colón reúne todo lo más selecto que tiene Buenos Aires en hombres y mujeres. Basta echar una visual al semicírculo de la sala; presidente, ministros, capitalistas, abogados y leones, todos están allí; aquello es la feria de las vanidades, en la cual no faltan

sus incongruencias de aldea: el vigilante de quepis
encasquetado en medio de la sala; la empresa, en
menage, instalada en uno de los mejores palcos
del teatro, el humo de los cigarros obscureciendo
la sala entera.[7]

4. *Fruto vedado*

A few months after the appearance of *La gran aldea* in *Sud-América,* there was issued in that same newspaper another realistic novel, *Fruto vedado*[8] by Paul Groussac (1848-1929). The work met with immediate success, was quickly published in book form,[9] and became the subject of numerous articles of criticism in newspapers and magazines. The novel carried the subtitle *Costumbres argentinas,* as if to announce that the public's desire to read about national customs, types, and ideas was to be satisfied. The success which Paul Groussac achieved in Argentina as an author and historian is all the more to be admired upon considering that it was not until the age of eighteen that he emigrated from his native France and came to Buenos Aires. His knowledge of Spanish at his arrival was practically nil, but within a relatively short period of time he acquired an almost complete mastery of the language. After fulfilling teaching assignments in the Colegio Nacional of Buenos Aires and of Tucumán, and holding other offices in education in the latter city, Groussac was appointed in 1885 director of the Biblioteca Nacional, a position he maintained for forty-four years until his death in 1929.

To a keen and discerning mind he added a seriousness of purpose and an indefatigable capacity for scholarly investigation, qualities manifested in the numerous works he composed on Argentine culture. Literary criticism, historical essays, biographical studies, and voyage narrations—all these writings are evidence of the contribution made by Groussac to the exami-

---

[7] *Ibid.,* pp. 237-238.
[8] The work appeared in *Sud-América* from August 4 to October 4, 1884.
[9] Paul Groussac, *Fruto vedado—costumbres argentinas,* B.A., Imprenta de M. Biedma, 1884.

nation, analysis, and divulgation of Argentine civilization. Yet his academic discipline did not preclude the cultivation of imaginative literature. In addition to the novel *Fruto vedado*, Groussac is the author of a notable historical drama entitled *La divisa punzó* (1923) and a collection of stories called *Relatos argentinos* (1922).

Fruto vedado is divided into two distinct parts: the first occurs in Argentina during the middle 1870's and presents realistic scenes of Argentine life, especially in the city of San José; the second part takes place exclusively in Paris. It is not surprising that Argentina and France should thus constitute the twofold setting of *Fruto vedado*, for Groussac, although adopting Argentina as his country and dedicating himself to its cultural advancement, always remembered dearly the land of his birth.

The success of the novel can be attributed in a large measure to its rather frank treatment of the love and passion motives in life. In its barest outline, *Fruto vedado* narrates the story of an adulterous relationship between an enterprising engineer and a sensual young woman whose marriage of convenience to a noble blind youth proves a complete failure. The doubtful pleasures of "forbidden fruit" seem far more important for both than the sweet contentment that comes from licit affairs. The clever protagonist is portrayed as a basically decent and upright person, torn between his love for two sisters—women who exhibit diametrically opposed natures, but who satisfy, each in her own way, the inner desires of the ambitious engineer. He vacillates, turns from one love to another, not as a licentious and insincere man, but as a man unable to comprehend his true feelings, as a man lost in the complexities of his own emotions. In the adulteress he loves the ceaseless vitality, the invigorating companionship, the fervent passion; while in her innocent sister he loves the proud virtue, the unaffected manner, the warmness of heart, and the passiveness of approach. "Quería a Rosita como el condenado arrepentido quiere la virtud y el honor; sin esperanza posible de levantarse hasta esas estrellas de la vida."[10] This generous girl is admirably

[10] *Fruto vedado*, 1884 edition in book form, *op. cit.*, pp. 353-354.

drawn and arouses our deepest compassion, as we see her tossed about by the inconstant protagonist. Her ingenuousness and simplicity stand in painful contrast to her sister's daring and immodesty.

Picturesque San José, the setting for many of the scenes in the first part of *Fruto vedado,* is portrayed well, with marked descriptive force and power of observation. Quite opposed to the agitated and haughty Buenos Aires, the city of San José maintained a subdued and easygoing provincial spirit. The weekly arrival of the stagecoach from Córdoba was always heralded as a signal event, for then there came passengers from all walks of life to offer comment and information on the national scene, as well as to provide a change in the routine affairs of the city.

Like the capital, but on a much smaller scale, San José also indicated definite processes of growth during the middle 1870's. Speculation in land, encouraged by convenient facilities for obtaining credit, began to interest venturesome citizens. The young engineer, in particular, bought and sold each week huge lots and fields in the hope of realizing sizable profits. Furthermore, important agricultural and industrial improvements could be observed in San José. The diligent don Tiburcio, father of the two sisters in the novel, contributed greatly to this progress. "Él tuvo las primeras grandes praderas artificiales, introdujo las mejoras en el ganado caballar y vacuno, hizo progresar el plantío de la caña dulce."[11] With pride of accomplishment, Tiburcio boasts: "......he sido el primero en poner el trapiche de acero con rueda hidráulica, tengo aquí las turbinas más antiguas de la Provincia; y seré el primero también en tirar de un puntapié esos tachos salvajes, y colocar aquí una maquinaria moderna, un tren completo de triple efecto, molino de vapor y alambique perfeccionado."[12] Tiburcio also expresses the belief that the rapid increase in European investments, although instrumental in effecting economic progress, will eventually place the Republic in the hands of foreigners, who will exploit the people and turn their productive labor to personal advantage.

[11] *Ibid.,* p. 123.   [12] *Ibid.,* p. 131.

5. Novels of the Financial Crisis of 1890

The fever of speculation and the concomitant financial crisis of 1890 provided a stirring theme for several realistic novels. All published within a few years after the events and conditions portrayed, these works proved very significant for the many Argentines whose lives were deeply affected by the changing economic situation of the country. Here was subject matter vitally national—exactly what the public eagerly sought— and writers were quick to interpret that material in fiction.[13] Ernesto Quesada, noted Argentine critic of that era, stated in reference to two novels of this group:

> Esos libros (*La bolsa* and *Quilito*) quedarán, pues, porque han tomado a la sociedad argentina en un momento psicológico de su evolución y han fotografiado instantáneamente su fisonomía moral en aquel instante.[14]

La bolsa. The most distinguished novel in this group, as well as the most famous, is *La bolsa*,[15] by José María Miró, published in 1891 under the pseudonym of Julián Martel. The *bolsa,* or stock exchange, is symbolic of the impetuous and materialistic period from 1880 to 1890, when many lives formerly peaceful and regulated were precipitously caught in the maelstrom of financial fervor. One of the most significant

---

[13] In 1890, one year before the famous *La bolsa* appeared, Eugenio M. Auzón (1857-1936) published a novel entitled *Conflicto entre dos amores,* B.A., Imprenta Sud-Americana, 1890, which, although not treating principally with the economic boom of this period, does deal in selected portions with the fever of speculation, the abuse of easy credit, and the sudden rise of corporations. Auzón, born in France, came to Argentina as a young man and distinguished himself as an art critic, journalist, author, and public functionary. In addition to *Conflicto entre dos amores,* Auzón wrote a deeply touching novel entitled *Severina,* B.A., Imprenta de M. Biedma, 1887, in which a young girl's intellectual and social inferiority deters her paramour from proposing marriage.

[14] Ernesto Quesada, *Dos novelas sociológicas,* B.A., La Plata, Rosario, 1892, p. 176.

[15] The novel first appeared serially in *La Nación,* from August 24 to October 4, 1891. Then in book form that same year: Julián Martel, *La bolsa—estudio social,* B.A., Imprenta de la Nación, 1891. The second edition carried the author's real name: José Miró, *La bolsa,* B.A., Imprenta Buenos Aires, 1898. Among later editions may be mentioned: Biblioteca de la Nación, 1905, Vol. 175; Grandes Escritores Argentinos, 1938 and 1944, Vol. 21; Biblioteca Clásica Americana, 1942, Vol. I; Tor, 1942; Editorial Emecé, 1943; Biblioteca de Clásicos Argentinos, 1946, Vol. XXI.

facts in the life of José Miró (1867-1896) is its brevity, for the literary merits of his only novel, *La bolsa,* evince a skillful talent unfortunately nipped by a premature death. From early manhood Miró dedicated himself diligently to journalism, composing varied articles and narrations for *La Nación, La Patria,* and other publications of the capital. With the appearance of *La bolsa* in 1891 he acquired an esteemed literary reputation, but death claimed him a few years afterward, on December 9, 1896.

In *La bolsa* the compelling force of the stock exchange envelops in its current the very ethical and conscientious attorney, Dr. Glow. Largely as a result of the fraudulent dealings of two unsavory gamblers who manage to stay just within the pale of the law, Dr. Glow loses immense sums of money that he invested in securities. Constant and intense worry, coupled with a bitter resentment against his former associates who deserted him in time of financial need, undermines his health and destroys his reasoning. At the termination of the novel, the good attorney is found in the throes of complete dementia. In the tragedy of Dr. Glow there is exemplified the dire consequences that may befall those who plunge headlong into the whirlpool of speculation. The final words of the novel, "Soy la Bolsa," which the protagonist in his delirium imagines to be uttered by some hideous monster, bring out well the intensity and impact of the misfortune, and the strange, overwhelming influence wielded by the stock exchange.

La bolsa stands as one of the most notable novels of the nineteenth century. Its literary excellence serves to mark José Miró as a writer of distinction, of fine artistic accomplishment. The work is written well, skillfully constructed and adeptly executed, revealing Miró's estimable verbal expression and sure novelistic technique. His language is picturesque, lively, and highly evocative. A fine sense of proportion and balance in sentence structure and a vital expressiveness are particular merits which render his prose forceful and effective. What is outstanding in *La bolsa* is the power of the written word to bring out and sustain the turbulent, nervous atmosphere of

Buenos Aires—an atmosphere determined to a large measure
by the ceaseless and vigorous activity of the stock exchange.

A través de las grandes y majestuosas arcadas
que unen al salón central con los laterales, se veía
moverse una muchedumbre compacta, numerosa,
inquieta. Notábase mucha agitación en los diver-
sos grupos por entre los cuales se deslizaban de
vez en cuando esas figuras pálidas, trémulas, ner-
viosas, que sólo se ven en la Bolsa en los últimos
días de cada mes; figuras que suelen representar a
los protagonistas de tragedias íntimas, espantosas,
no sospechadas. El doctor se abrió paso como pu-
do, hasta que consiguió llegar a la reja que limita
el recinto destinado a las operaciones, vulgo rueda.

Agolpábase a aquella reja una multitud ansiosa,
estremecida por corrientes eléctricas. Se veían pes-
cuezos estirados en angustiosa expectativa, con la
rigidez propia del jugador que espera la salida de
la carta que ha de decidir la partida; ojos desme-
suradamente abiertos, siguiendo con fijeza hipnó-
tica los movimientos de la mano del apuntador, el
cual, subido sobre su tarima, anotaba las operaciones en las pizarras que, negras, cuadradas, sinies-
tras, se dibujaban como sombras en la pared del
fondo.

En medio de ella se destacaba la blanca esfera
del reloj, sereno e imperturbable como el ojo vigilante del destino; la esfera de aquel reloj que era
lo único que permanecía inalterable en aquel lu-
gar donde la tranquilidad y la estabilidad de las
cosas están desterradas para siempre; la esfera de
aquel reloj que había señalado tantas horas gratas
y tantas amargas, y que ahora miraba al doctor
como diciéndole: ya veremos, amigo mío, ya veremos.

La rueda estaba muy animada. Salía de ella un
estrepitoso vocerío, una algarabía de mil demo-
nios: voces atipladas, roncas, sonoras, de tenor, de
bajo, de barítono, voces de todos los volúmenes y
de todos los metales. Los corredores parecían unos

> energúmenos; más tenían el aire de hombres en-
> redados en una discusión de taberna, que el de co-
> merciantes en el momento de realizar sus opera-
> ciones. Y no sólo gritaban como unos locos, sino
> que también gesticulaban y accionaban como si
> estuviesen por darse de bofetadas.[16]

The stock market engulfs the lives of a host of secondary
personages, all of whom are swiftly carried along in its eddy.
There appear brokers, bankers, titled foreigners, and wealthy
immigrants, as well as usurers, gamblers, and wastrels. Their
activities at the exchange involve all sorts of financial entangle-
ments, speculative inveiglements, deception, and sheer dis-
honesty. Lifelong dreams of power, riches, and security sud-
denly come alive with each stock quotation. Ambitions, illusions, and happiness are all seen as dependent upon fluctua-
tions of the market and the whims of the speculators.

Yet Miró's personal sympathies were not with the turbulent
and agitated atmosphere of Buenos Aires, and he looked with
disfavor at the welter of financial transactions and its many
nefarious consequences. A sensitive, serious-minded, and
scholarly person, Miró viewed with misgiving and aversion
the tendency to place undue importance on the acquisition of
wealth. Without denying that the *bolsa* was in many respects
the very nucleus of economic progress, Miró understood that
at the same time it represented an enigmatical force of life,
capable of turning men into defenseless victims of an intense
passion.

The Financial Crisis Revealed in Other Novels. In 1891,
Segundo I. Villafañe (1860-1937)[17] published *Horas de fiebre,*[18]
a noteworthy novel now forgotten by the Argentine public,

---

[16] *La bolsa,* edition of Biblioteca de Clásicos Argentinos, *op. cit.,* pp. 14-15.

[17] Segundo I. Villafañe, besides pursuing a literary career, held many important municipal offices, the outstanding being that of general secretary of the
Post Office department in Buenos Aires. His literary production includes many
articles, stories, and poems published in newspapers and magazines of the
capital, especially in *La Nación* and *La quincena.* Besides *Horas de fiebre,*
Villafañe is the author of two other novels: *Don Lino Velázquez,* ed, F. Lajouane, B.A., Libraire Générale, 1886, treats of domestic problems among
members of a modest Argentine family; and *Emilio Love,* ed. F. Lajouane,
B.A., Imprenta de Mackern y McLean, 1888, deals with a degenerate and
evil youth.

[18] Segundo I. Villafañe, *Horas de fiebre,* B.A., Imprenta de Juan A. Alsina,
1891.

but which deserves an honored place alongside *La bolsa* as a convincing interpretation of the decade of economic and material growth. In this work a youth of modest family becomes the tragic victim of the stock market craze. He rises rapidly from an obscure bank employee to a wealthy and influential member of society; but then when fortune no longer smiles and he loses his investments, he commits suicide.

Villafañe draws an excellent realistic picture of this period, describing concretely manifestations of the pomp, luxury, and desire for speculation then prevalent in the busy capital. Horse racing, auction sales, fashionable residences, elegant *confiterías,* showy tea salons—these are all indicative of the prosperous *porteño* environment into which the protagonist, by virtue of his acquired riches and social position, happily enters. Concerning this ostentation in Buenos Aires, the author states:

> En la fiebre de ostentación que consumía a todos, no bastaban tampoco los ricos mueblajes y las tapicerías más valiosas que ofrecían las fábricas o depósitos del país a la prodigalidad de los millonarios, y era necesario encargarlos a Europa para que tuvieran sanción plena: los carruajes debían de tener en la taza de sus ruedas la firma del fabricante extranjero que acusase su procedencia europea, los caballos y los troncos de yeguas soberbias debían de ser forzosamente importados y costear sendos miles de oro.[19]

One of the most sharply realistic characterizations is that of the father of the protagonist's childhood sweetheart. A poor but dignified and proud office worker, he refuses to gain advancement and additional money by false flattery, appropriate gifts to his superiors, or even mildly unscrupulous dealings with co-workers. This ethical and self-respecting conduct under all conditions is skillfully revealed by many touching scenes, while the irksome pettiness and flagrant injustices of the business world may be viewed in the light of his routine activities at work. Moreover, his humble character stands out amid the arrogant and artificial tone that generally pervades the materialistic capital.

[19] *Ibid.,* p. 214.

In the same year 1891, when both *La bolsa* and *Horas de fie-bre* appeared, there was published in Paris the novel *Quilito,*[20] which interweaves the lives of several people who are seized with the passion to play the market. We may gauge the magnetism of the financial theme in the Argentine novel by noting that the author of *Quilito,* Carlos María Ocantos (1860-1949),[21] resided abroad during much of the period depicted, but sufficiently felt the verve of his country's contemporary affairs to translate his secondhand impressions to the pages of fiction. Another praiseworthy work dealing with the financial crisis came from the pen of Alberto del Solar (1860-1921), distinguished Chilean-born writer who resided many years in Argentina, becoming closely associated with its culture and earning the esteem of a wide public. This novel, *Contra la marea* (1894),[22] is a carefully written and well-developed work in which a young man engages in speculation and other financial operations to gain a woman's affection. In the end he loses his money, kills his rival in anger, and is sent to prison.

A wife's inordinate desire for wealth and social prestige is the theme of the novel *Grandezas* (1896),[23] by Pedro G. Morante.[24] Domineering, haughty, and selfish, she is presented as a product of the materialistic period of the 1880's; while her husband is content to lead a quiet and simple life, fulfilling his duties as an obscure clerk. In this divergence of basic philosophy lies the principal conflict of the novel. The work is noteworthy not only for its rich and faithful depiction of the economic boom, but also for its apt portrayal of the protagonists. The wife, envious of socially prominent women who spend their afternoons leisurely shopping in expensive shops

---

[20] Carlos María Ocantos, *Quilito,* Paris, Librería Española de Garnier Hermanos, 1891. The work was also published in Biblioteca de la Nación, 1913, Vol. 548; and in Biblioteca Sopena, Barcelona, 1917, Vol. 26.

We may note as well that Émile Zola's *L'Argent,* dealing with the Parisian stock market, appeared also in 1891; and that in 1903 appeared Frank Norris's *The Pit,* a novel which treats of speculation in wheat in Chicago.

[21] We shall treat this author more fully in a subsequent chapter.

[22] Alberto del Solar, *Contra la marea,* ed. F. Lajouane, B.A., 1894. Del Solar is also the author of *Rastaquouère,* ed. F. Lajouane, B.A., 1890, a novel which describes the adventures of a wealthy South American family in Paris.

[23] Pedro G. Morante, *Grandezas,* ed. F. Lajouane, B.A., 1896. The work was republished the following year, edited by Ivaldi and Checchi, B.A., 1897.

[24] Morante, journalist by profession, is also the author of *Música, amor y vino*—zarzuela en un acto y en prosa, B.A., La Joven Minerva, 1893.

and their evenings entertaining guests in their fashionable homes, sharply rebukes her mate for his want of ambition, and so incessantly prods him that he lives constantly under a painful emotional strain. The husband, weak and submissive, is dragged against his will and better judgment into financial dealings for which he has little ability. He finally achieves short-lived success, which enables his wife to boast that her husband has scaled important rungs in the social ladder. Yet too late does this woman realize that wealth and splendor are only superficial, for the false friends she made by virtue of her spouse's brief period of prosperity vanish as soon as her funds are depleted and she can no longer use her husband's social prestige to her own advantage.

6. Other Novels Depicting Buenos Aires

Many other novels revealing realistic scenes of Buenos Aires were published in the last two decades of the nineteenth century.[25] We need not enter into a detailed analysis of these works, but we shall merely cite them and offer a few essential words of comment. The vast majority of these novels reveal little originality or distinctiveness in literary style, the prose being no more than adequate in its power of description and beauty of word or phrase. The important and redeeming feature of these works lies in their faithful portrayal of selected characteristics of the changing capital.

[25] After Eduardo Gutiérrez and Julio Llanos discontinued writing novels for *La Patria Argentina*, that newspaper kept on satisfying the public demand for national fiction; and during the period 1884-1885 it published the following novels in serial form:
a. Luis A. Mohr (1844-1929), *Alberto Trejo—¿castigo del cielo, o justicia de la tierra?*, March 15 to April 16, 1884.
b. Rafael Barreda (1847-1927), *Magistrados que matan*, July 28 to August 20, 1884.
c. Rafael Barreda, *La pera envenenada*, August 21 to September 28, 1884.
d. Juan de Lóriga, *Canuto Bochín—la comedia política*, October 1 to October 12, 1884.
e. Miguel Lucas, *La reconquista de mi novia—cuadros sociales*, April 4 to April 17, 1885.
f. Miguel Lucas, *Los descamisados—entre bastidores*, April 18 to May 4, 1885.
g. Miguel Lucas, *La carta—cuadros sociales*, May 5 to May 19, 1885.
h. Juan Lussich (1860-1885), *El crimen de Barracas—la mujer embarrilada*, October 10 to November 10, 1885.
i. Eduardo Pimentel and Matilde Guardiola, *Los amantes del Pergamino*, December 1 to December 15, 1885.

Student life in Buenos Aires is the theme of a carefully developed realistic novel entitled *Amar al vuelo* (1884),[26] by Enrique E. Rivarola (1862-1931).[27] In well-motivated and clearly defined scenes there are presented the loves, frivolities, and ideas of a young provincial Argentine residing in the capital to study engineering. The author captures well the atmosphere of the boarding house where the protagonist and other students lodge. *Clelia* (1886),[28] by Karl Lehardy, narrates the story of an adulterous love between an unhappily married woman and a sensitive youth. The novel, set in the progressive Buenos Aires of 1880, exhibits a strong consciousness of the changing social life of the capital. Specifically, picturesque scenes in the Club del Progreso and the Teatro Colón, as well as in the resort area of Palermo, provide the narration with much local color.

Enrique Ortega (1847-1912) is the author of two short novels which are included under the general title of *Vida porteña* (1886).[29] One work, *Un drama íntimo*, explains the pernicious effects that journalistic misrepresentation may produce on the life of an unsuspecting married couple. The opening chapter

---

[26] The work first appeared serially in *La Patria Argentina*, from June 29 to July 27, 1884, with the title *El arma de Werther—escenas de vida estudiantil*. The novel was then published in book form with the title *Amar al vuelo—costumbres estudiantiles*, ed. E. de Mársico, B.A. and La Plata, Librería de Los Estudiantes, n.d. By virtue of a notice in *Sud-América*, April 18, 1885, p. 3, we learn that the date of publication was 1885.

[27] Rivarola was a distinguished jurist and legislator who served particularly the province of Buenos Aires. His literary production includes articles, narrations, stories, and poems. Besides *Amar al vuelo*, Rivarola is the author of *Mandinga*, ed. Leopoldo López, B.A., 1895, a novel in which a doctor believes that his impure lover is possessed of an evil spirit which she in turn passes on to him; and *La novela de una joven maestra*, B.A., Imprenta de Coni Hermanos, 1917, a melodramatic novel of tragic love, set in the city of La Plata.

[28] Karl Lehardy, *Clelia*, ed. F. Lajouane, B.A., Libraire Générale—51-53 Calle Perú, 1886. Lehardy is a pseudonym; despite careful investigation we have been unable to ascertain the real identity of the author. However, from an article in *Sud-América*, July 21, 1886, p. 2, we learn that Lehardy belonged to a distinguished Argentine family and was employed in the Colegio Nacional of Buenos Aires in 1886.

[29] Enrique Ortega, *Vida porteña—Un drama íntimo y La familia H*, B.A., La Plata, Imprenta de J. Peuser, 1886. Ortega, born in Spain, resided in Uruguay for a short time before settling definitely in Argentina about 1875, where he pursued with enthusiasm a journalistic career. Besides *Vida porteña*, Ortega is the author of three other novels: *Una hora menguada*, B.A., Imprenta de J. Peuser, 1886, treats of a dissolute Argentine youth who abandons his lover and their small child; *Los casamientos del diablo*, Paris, Librería Española de Garnier Hermanos, 1889, is a complicated romantic story set in the Buenos Aires of 1880; and *Justos y pecadores*, Paris, Librería de Garnier Hermanos, 1889, is a melodramatic work set in Spain.

describes the incessant movement of workers, the noise of trolley cars, the chatter of newspaper boys, the daily activities of store clerks, and the colorful promenades along the crowded Calle Florida. The other work, *La familia H,* portrays daily life among members of a modest Argentine family which has its share of foolish arguments, petty problems, and troubles with relatives. Social customs are revealed with charm. In one account the author tells of three sites for the Sunday or holiday stroll, each one frequented for the most part by people of a distinct economic class.

The highly popular novel, *León Zaldívar* (1888),[30] by Carlos María Ocantos, presents a happy combination of romantic and realistic elements. The romantic plot centers around a young girl's marriage of convenience to a false French baron, who she later discovers is really a notorious thief. When León Zaldívar, deeply in love with this heroine, learns of the matrimony, he falls sick of grief. The baron flees to France, abandoning his bride. Zaldívar, realizing how frivolous and insincere she truly is, marries a humble orphan girl. Around this story, narrated with charming simplicity and warmth of emotion, Ocantos offers realistic descriptions of family life and customs of Buenos Aires. With delicacy, grace, humor, and at times effective irony the author depicts such things as a family excursion on the much frequented Tigre River, the streets of the capital during the carnival season, preparations for a wedding, and the activities of the *círculo,* or social club.

In *Tierra y cielo* (1888),[31] by Antonio B. Massioti, a young student at the University of Córdoba spends some leisure time in Buenos Aires to seek enjoyment and easy fortune. Through his affairs there are portrayed, among other features, the Teatro Colón, the stock exchange, the Boca del Riachuelo (the neighborhood where immigrants settle), and elegant shops

[30] Carlos María Ocantos, *León Saldívar,* Madrid, Imprenta de Fortanet, 1888. In this first edition, the second word of the title begins with an "S," while in subsequent editions there is a "Z." The work appeared in serial form in *La Patria Argentina,* from March 6 to April 20, 1888. It was also published in Biblioteca de la Nación, 1911, Vol. 478; and in Biblioteca Sopena, Barcelona, 1916, Vol. 11.

[31] Antonio B. Massioti, *Tierra y cielo—estudio social bonaerense,* ed. F. Lajouane, B.A., Imprenta de M. Biedma, 1888.

and luxurious mansions. *La liga* (1893),[32] by Gervasio Marques, has for its object that of exposing and ridiculing abnormal jealousy in women, which, the author claims, is a manifestation of the smart, arrogant, and devilish society of the period. Finally, the novel *Quimera* (1899),[33] by José Luis Cantilo (1871-1944),[34] treats of a humble country youth who, aided by his uncle, is accepted into the "high life" of the capital. Nevertheless, the falseness and frivolity of his new surroundings cause him to experience an immense sadness and inquietude, and he returns to his small village a disillusioned and wretched person.

7. THE IMMIGRANT REVEALED IN THE REALISTIC NOVEL

One of the serious problems confronting the nation since the independence has been that of populating its vast territory. In several early novels, such as *Peregrinación de Luz del Día,* this need is briefly mentioned in an incidental fashion. The years 1870 to 1900 witnessed a tremendous influx of foreign peoples to Argentine shores, and these persons played an important role in the development of the Republic. Constituting a vital national element, the immigrant in Argentina provided excellent material for a realistic portrayal of life and formed the theme of three novels published in the 1890's. In each of

[32] Gervasio Marques, *La liga,* B.A., Imprenta de la Nación, 1893. According to an article by Segundo I. Villafañe, appearing in *La Nación* on March 6, 1893, p. 2, the name Gervasio Marques is a pseudonym, the real identity of the novelist being unknown. Marques also wrote a novel called *En la sierra,* ed. Ángel Estrada y Cía, B.A., Imprenta de Juan A. Alsina, 1896, in which a licentious youth achieves spiritual regeneration in a mountain retreat of Córdoba.

[33] José Luis Cantilo, *Quimera—boceto de costumbres,* B.A., Librería Bredahl, 1899. The first two chapters of the novel appeared in *La Revista Moderna* (which Cantilo himself edited), May, 1897, pp. 115-121.

[34] José Luis Cantilo achieved fame as a legislator and diplomat, holding important positions in the government, among which may be mentioned that of governor of the province of Buenos Aires in 1922 and that of national congressman from 1940 to 1944.

We may cite two other novels depicting selected aspects of Buenos Aires: Marcos F. Arredondo, *Carmen, o batallas de la vida,* B.A., Imprenta Rápida, 1890, a short work which treats the theme of money versus love in the materialistic society of Buenos Aires; and Un antiguo comisario de policía (sic), *El descuartizador—historia íntima de un asesino,* B.A., 1894, deals with the investigation and solution of a brutal murder in the streets of the capital, revealing pertinent antecedents of the crime and the background of the assassin.

these works the multifold problems connected with immigrant life were treated with sympathy and understanding. The dreams and hopes of immigrants to achieve a modicum of success and recognition, as well as the long and arduous task frequently necessary for this accomplishment, embraced stories of human struggle from which novelists drew their inspiration.

Bianchetto (1896),[35] by the noted historian and diplomat Adolfo Saldías (1854-1914), follows the progress of an Italian youth in Argentina. We see him first in his native Genoa as a lonely musician; then in Buenos Aires as a diligent newspaper vendor; then as a worker on a ranch, tending sheep and doing odd jobs; and finally as the entrusted manager of this same ranch. In depicting the radical change in the personality of Bianchetto—from a poor and humble youth to a prosperous and proud man—the author symbolically portrays the economic and social transformation of Argentina itself.

In *Teodoro Foronda* (1896),[36] by the Spanish-born Francisco Grandmontagne (1866-1936),[37] an industrious Spanish immigrant realizes his dream of becoming a successful and esteemed merchant; yet he takes his own life upon failing to command the respect and admiration of his children, who foolishly disdain their father's humble birth and undistinguished social position. As the author indicates, the progress of the protagonist attests to the limitless opportunities in Argentina for the persevering immigrant, who may proudly forge ahead merely by dint of his own toil.

In the charming and inspiring novel entitled *Promisión* (1897),[38] Carlos María Ocantos envisages Argentina as a great melting pot of nationalities, where Spaniards, Italians, Eng-

[35] Adolfo Saldías, *Bianchetto—la patria del trabajo,* ed. F. Lajouane, B.A., 1896.

[36] Francisco Grandmontagne, *Teodoro Foronda—evoluciones de la sociedad argentina,* B.A., Tipografía La Vasconia, 1896, 2 vols.

[37] Grandmontagne came to Argentina as an adolescent and by virtue of varied jobs, ranging from peon to journalist, became intimately acquainted with the Republic's traditions and ways of life. He returned to his native Spain in 1903, where he lived the rest of his life. In addition to *Teodoro Foronda,* Grandmontagne is the author of the novel *La maldonada,* B.A., Imprenta Artística, 1898, in which a young girl, raised by foster parents, dies of grief after her lover loses his life in the revolution of July, 1890.

[38] Carlos María Ocantos, *Promisión,* Madrid, Establecimiento tipográfico de I. Moreno, 1897. The work was also published in Biblioteca Sopena, Barcelona, 1918, Vol. 47.

lishmen, Frenchmen, Germans, and others may achieve their goals of happiness and economic security. The central plot revolves around the adjustment, problems, and ambitions of a French family of immigrants. The husband, enterprising and energetic, rises from an obscure sawmill employee to owner of the company; while the son, whose mischievous and improper conduct seriously besets his parents, becomes a useful and upright citizen, gainfully employed and the proud owner of some land. The concerns of other recently arrived people—a family from Cádiz, a German amiably referred to as "el cachorro de Bismark," and an industrious and sympathetic English capitalist—enhance the picture of immigrant life in Argentina and provide the novel with an interesting variety of incidents and characters.

8. General Considerations of the Argentine Novel of the Last Two Decades of the Nineteenth Century

During the 1880's and 1890's the novel in Argentina flourished to an extent hitherto not even closely attained in the preceding periods. Just as socially and economically the Republic achieved unprecedented progress from 1880 until the end of the century, so too the novel in this era emerged vigorously in great numbers and reached a considerable degree of literary merit. The huge volume of fiction that appeared in these two decades may be understood better by noting a comparison with former periods. Taking *Amalia* as the starting point, twenty-two novels were published from the year 1851 to 1859, while seventeen appeared from 1860 to 1869, and only twelve from 1870 to 1879. Then came the boom in fiction writing. The number of novels issued during the ten-year span from 1880 to 1889 reached the extraordinary figure of one hundred and one;[39] and the decade of the 'nineties, although not nearly so prolific as the preceding one, did produce the very sizable number of forty-eight. Granted this abundance of fiction of the 1880's and 1890's,

---

[39] We refer to novels issued both in book form and serially.

it is well to note the several principal types of novels that appeared. First, the realistic current which developed and flourished during these two fertile decades had as its most original and genuine expression the faithful depiction of the energetic and materialistic capital. Secondly, at the same time these years witnessed the introduction and growth of naturalism, a study of which we shall undertake subsequently. Also, as we have noticed in preceding chapters, Eduardo Gutiérrez issued his very popular gaucho novels in the 1880's, Eduardo L. Holmberg published his scientific and supernatural works in the 1890's, while the indigenous element in the novel received attention during both decades. In addition, it will be recalled that romanticism continued to have expression in the 1880's and 1890's, even after realism and naturalism had made their way into fiction. Lastly, our investigation of the novel reveals a host of secondary works that disconnectedly covered the rich field of fiction during these last two decades. These minor novels treated such varied subject matter as seduction and women's immoderate passion, as in *Estela* (1880);[40] a middle-aged man's sudden awakening to the need for an education, as in *El ex-abrupto de don Cándido* (1886);[41] the horrifying experiments of an insane and misanthropic medical scientist, as in *El doctor Jacobo* (1891);[42] the inner thoughts and emotions involved in amorous relationships, as in *Mi amigo Luis*

---

[40] Jorge Alberto, *Estela,* B.A., 1880. In *Anuario bibliográfico de la República Argentina,* B.A., Imprenta del Mercurio, 1880, pp. 294-295, there appears this comment concerning the novel *Estela:* "El carácter íntimo que asume esta narración por la participación del autor en los últimos sucesos que cuenta, me veda entregar al público su nombre conocido."

It is convenient to point out here that this *Anuario bibliográfico,* edited by Alberto Navarro Viola from 1879 to 1884 and by Enrique Navarro Viola from 1885 to 1887, cites a few novels which we have not been able to locate:
a. Guillermo Quiroga, *Una sanjuanina, o sea Carolina,* San Juan, Imprenta de La Unión, 1881. The *Anuario* refers to this work as a "novela de costumbres."
b. José Oteza Bustamante, *Un acontecimiento en Tucumán,* B.A., Imprenta de R. M. Cañaberas, 1883. This work is called a historical novel.
c. Luis A. Mohr, *Verdad y ficción,* B.A., Imprenta de El Censor, 1886. Navarro Viola describes this work as a"crítica de vida social y política."
d. Pastor M. Carballido, *Días sombríos,* ed. Llambías y Pardo, B.A., 1887.
[41] C., *El ex-abrupto de don Cándido,* B.A., Imprenta de J. Peuser, 1886. The unknown author, whose name was indicated only by "C," also wrote *Los celos y la electricidad,* B.A., Imprenta de J. Peuser, 1886, which treats in a light vein of a husband's unfounded suspicions concerning his wife's fidelity.
[42] Carlos Blomberg, *El doctor Jacobo—estudio social,* ed. Ignacio Mosquera, B.A., 1891.

(1895);[43] and a white girl's love for a mulatto youth, as in *La casta* (1898).[44]

We may discern from the pages of this chapter that for the most part the raw material of the realistic novel was Argentina itself in the process of growth. The development of realism reflected graphically the enormous strides which the nation made in the last two decades of the nineteenth century. By virtue of this progress and prosperity, the people awakened to the importance of their country and came to admire and respect more fully the way of life that was peculiarly their own. It is difficult to conceive of a more inspired endeavor or a greater steadfastness of purpose than that evinced by the vast number of Argentine novelists who realistically sought to capture the nation's pattern of existence.

[43] Hernán Prins, *Mi amigo Luis,* B.A., Imprenta Elzeviriana, 1895. Prins is a pseudonym; the author's real name is Carlos Octavio Bunge (1875-1918), distinguished sociologist and philosopher. Being a mere youth when the novel appeared, Bunge assumed the pseudonym to avoid shocking his family, inasmuch as the book was quite frank in discussing intimate affairs of the heart. We received this information in an interview (B.A., January 12, 1953) with Manuel Gálvez, whose wife Delfina Bunge was related to Carlos Octavio.

[44] José María Vélez, *La casta,* Córdoba, Tipografía La Minerva de Alfonso Aveta, 1898. Of a well-known Cordovan family, Vélez achieved fame as the literary painter of the beautiful mountains around Córdoba. He composed, among his descriptive works, *Perlas rotas,* B.A., Casa de J. Peuser, 1908.

Other minor novels of this period are the following:

a. Pedro S. Lamas, *Silvia—episodios de la Guerra de la Independencia Americana,* Paris, Charaire e hijo, 1884. The work was subsequently published in Biblioteca Popular, 1898, Vol. IV. Son of the illustrious Uruguayan historian Andrés Lamas, Pedro (1847-1922) distinguished himself in journalism and public service.

b. Bachiller Churruca, *Políticos del día—tipos y escenas electorales,* B.A., 1886. The novel portrays the absorbing role that politics plays in the lives of so many Argentines.

c. Fabio Monroy, *El ángel de la virtud,* B.A., Imprenta Rápida, 1890. In this novel, a jealous girl seeks revenge on her rival by attempting to force her into prostitution.

d. Guillermo Stock, *El valor de la vida,* B.A., 1896. This work, in which an understanding wife forgives her unfaithful husband, first appeared serially in *La Quincena,* June 1, 1895 to March 1, 1896. Stock (1896-1944) is the author of many volumes of verse, among them *Ave, duce,* 1935, and *Bandera soñada,* 1939.

e. Isaac R. Pearson, *Patria,* B.A., Imprenta La Revista, 1896. The work is a loosely constructed historical novel of the pre-independence period in Argentina. Pearson (1872-1945) wrote several volumes on national and world history, among them *Las gloriosas jornadas de 1806-1807 en Buenos Aires,* 1939. He was also active in journalism, politics, and teaching.

f. Isaac R. Pearson, *El triunfo del siglo,* B.A., Imprenta La Revista, 1899. This work treats the trite theme of the failure of scientific and material advancement to bring happiness and peace of mind.

X

NATURALISM IN THE ARGENTINE
NOVEL

The cult of Zola and the vogue of naturalism entered into the literature of Hispanic America during the years 1880-1885. Through translations and original French editions brought over from the Continent, Zola quickly captured the attention of the public. Naturalism, as pronounced by Zola in his *Roman expérimental* and cultivated by him and his disciples, represents the application to the novel of the principles of scientific experimentation, with its insistence upon suitable selection and accurate documentation of subject matter, detailed observation, minute analysis, and careful recording of conclusions. With this scientific approach, the lives of individuals are much the same as chemical elements in a test tube; that is, given certain qualities and conditions, an inevitable result will follow. Thus, heredity and environment play primordial roles in the naturalistic novel.

For his characters Zola deliberately chose for the most part degenerates, alcoholics, prostitutes, and people of similar low station in society; for the milieu he selected the dirty and crowded avenues of industry, the factory and mine, the putrid city street, the squalid home, and the house of ill repute. Zola penetrated with scientific detachment and complete objectivity into the baseness and depravity of life, observing the tenets of determinism and fatalism wreak their unyielding destruction on floundering and hopeless mankind.

To the Argentine Eugenio Cambaceres (1843-1888) belongs the distinction of being the first to apply the principles of Zola to the Hispanic-American novel. From 1882 to 1887, Cambaceres shocked and at the same time interested the Argentine public with a series of four novels patently revealing Zola's sweeping influence. Of this author, as well as of other Argentine naturalists, we shall treat presently. Succeeding Cambaceres, writers in other Hispanic-American countries produced novels which also followed the current of naturalism. Among these novelists we may cite the following: Mercedes Cabello de Carbonera, Peruvian, author of *Blanca Sol* (1889); Federico Gamboa, Mexican, who wrote *Apariencias* (1892), *Suprema ley* (1896), *Metamorfosis* (1899), and *Santa* (1903); Mateo Magariños Solsona, Uruguayan, author of *Las hermanas Flamaris* (1893); Carlos Reyles, Uruguayan, who wrote *Beba* (1894), *La raza de Caín* (1900), and *El terruño* (1916); and Augusto D'Halmar, Chilean, famous for his *Juana Lucero* (1902).

1. THE WORK OF EUGENIO CAMBACERES

Eugenio Cambaceres was born in Buenos Aires in 1843, of a French father and Argentine mother. After graduation from the law school of the University of Buenos Aires, he practiced his profession and at the same time entered into politics. A man of the world, distinguished, personable, and forceful, Cambaceres fitted comfortably in all circles of society and thus acquired a wide field of experience and knowledge which served him well in his novels.

Two important events in his short political career help to define the daring and unconventional character which Cambaceres evinced in his naturalistic works. In 1871, in the capacity of delegate to the convention of the province of Buenos Aires, he audaciously proposed the separation of Church and State, a suggestion for which he was angrily rebuked. Secondly, as a member of Congress he brazenly exposed the elections of 1874 as an outrageous fraud. Not experiencing much success in politics, he abandoned that career and dedicated himself to literature, but his years as a writer were truncated by death in Paris in 1888.

Pot-pourri. Cambaceres' first novel, *Pot-pourri,*[1] appeared anonymously in Buenos Aires in 1882. The work aroused the scorn and resentment of the critics and public alike, who read in its pages the unwholesome philosophy of an inveterate pessimist and vituperative censor of contemporary Argentine society. Viewing the deceitful, hypocritical, and immodest individuals about him from his self-made tower of cynicism and misanthropy, Cambaceres presents a veritable potpourri of corruption and vice in the great capital. Concerning the novel, one contemporary writer stated:

> Es un libro de un espíritu enfermo, y sus páginas están saturadas de hiel...... Es la deforme imitación de esa literatura francesa de que Zolá es el iniciador, escuela realista que vive del retrato al natural...... No hay en este libro una ráfaga de luz.[2]

Pot-pourri, lacking a sustained and well-delineated plot, vaguely tells the story, amid ceaseless interruptions and extraneous material, of a sordid adulterous love. The narration is carried out in the first person by the author himself, who rambles at length about politics, society's foibles, women, love, and the significance of life in general. There are monologues, lively conversations, miscellaneous anecdotes, all written in a loose and unorganized prose, charged with bitter satire, contemptuous ridicule and derisive wit. Furthermore, French words and phrases, pithy sayings, and clever remarks are frequently interspersed in the novel, producing an effect similar to that attained by a glib and haughty speaker who wishes to impress with his ingenuity and worldliness.

Música sentimental. Cambaceres' second novel, *Música sentimental,*[3] was published in Paris in 1884. It deals with a young

[1] Anon., *Pot-pourri—silbidos de un vago,* B.A., Imprenta de M. Biedma, 1882. Subsequent editions, which carried Cambaceres' name, are the following: Imprenta de M. Biedma, 2nd edition of 1882; ed. E. Denné, Paris, 1883; Editorial Minerva, 1924; Editorial Beybe, 1945.

[2] Anon., "Pot-pourri—silbidos de un vago," in bibliographical section of *La Nueva Revista de Buenos Aires,* Año II, B.A., Imprenta de E. Quesada, 1882, V, 570-571.

[3] Eugenio Cambaceres, *Música sentimental—silbidos de un vago,* ed. E. Denné, Paris, Imprenta Hispano-Americana, 1884. Subsequent editions include Minerva, 1924, and Editorial Beybe, 1945.

Argentine in that French capital who dissipates his money and undermines his health in a life of frivolity and vice. The work reveals the same acrimonious cynicism and sarcastic vision of life that is observed in *Pot-pourri*. A friend of the protagonist, ostensibly Cambaceres himself, narrates the story in a fresh, lively and very personal fashion, injecting bitter comments on society's failings and inconsistencies, and philosophizing bluntly on the events and personages of the novel. The language is always free-flowing, animated, and expressed with apparent effortless facility.

Clearly discernible are the many naturalistic features of *Música sentimental*—the portraiture of the protagonist's vulgar passions and his numerous illicit, even adulterous relationships; the consideration given to the wretched environment of his most constant paramour; the presenting of her life of vice and degradation, and the revealing of the force of circumstances which prevents her from extricating herself from the grip of sin. Unforgettable is the characterization of this pathetic and downtrodden heroine, who, having fallen, wishes to be redeemed in the eyes of the world. Her intense and true love for the unstable and licentious protagonist awakens in her soul a sense of shame, repentance, and bitter grief; yet she wonders whether society will forgive her past sins and permit her to live decently.

Sin rumbo. With *Sin rumbo* (1885)[4] Cambaceres reached the pinnacle of his literary career, composing a novel which stands as the most noteworthy work of Argentine naturalistic fiction in the nineteenth century. In this novel the author achieved the artistic maturity that was not fully developed in *Pot-pourri* or *Música sentimental*. *Sin rumbo* presents the tragic fate of an insolent and morally offensive youth who gains temporary emotional and spiritual rejuvenation by virtue of a great love for his natural daughter. Through a series of ardently realistic scenes, each one of short extension but com-

---

[4] Eugenio Cambaceres, *Sin rumbo—estudio,* ed. F. Lajouane, B.A., Imprenta de M. Biedma, 1885. The second and third editions were also published in 1885 by M. Biedma. Subsequent editions include the following: Joyas Literarias, 1922, No. I; Editorial Minerva, 1924; Biblioteca Pluma de Oro, 1939; Editorial Beybe, 1944; Grandes Escritores Argentinos, 1944 and 1947, Vol. XI; Biblioteca de Clásicos Argentinos, 1949, Vol. 21.

pact and intensely vivid, there is revealed the painful story of the protagonist's life—his despicable attitude toward mankind, his purely sensual relationship with women, his strange attachment to his daughter, and his suicide when that girl dies.

The characterization of the dissolute and misanthropic youth (Andrés) is a carefully studied and graphically developed piece of novelistic art. There is obviously a bit of the autobiographical in Cambaceres' portrayal of this protagonist, for the deeply implanted traits of skepticism and independence found in Andrés can be equally applied to the author himself. Andrés represents a solitary and cold spirit of unyielding pessimism, a tragic figure of wicked temperament, seeing in the world nothing but the blackness and stupidity of his own perverted mind. For him there are no noble sentiments or actions, no uplifting values or lofty principles, for his haughtiness and insolence do not permit him to see beyond his own coarseness and iniquity. Love he calls "un torpe llamado de los sentidos," friendship "una ruin explotación," patriotism "un oficio, o un rezago de barbarie," and generosity and abnegation he designates as "una quimera o un desamor monstruoso."[5] Hostile to everything which makes for harmony, order, and beneficial restraint, he rebels against society, marriage, a home, and the acquisition of knowledge. Thus he states: "Saber es sufrir; ignorar, comer, dormir y no pensar, la solución exacta del problema, la única dicha de vivir."[6]

With this vile disposition toward mankind Andrés lives from year to year, until the moment he finds out he is a father. Then he becomes a changed man, for he welcomes his daughter joyously and exhilaratingly into his heart and unselfishly places her happiness before his own. Experiencing perhaps for the first time a noble emotion, he comes to cherish and love his infant daughter, who fills a void in his life and apparently causes all his former cynicism and wickedness to vanish. "Se sentía como purificado... capaz de todas las virtudes, accesible a la bondad, inclinado a la indulgencia."[7] However, in this child's untimely and horrible death a few years later, Andrés

[5] *Sin rumbo,* first edition, 1885, *op. cit.,* pp. 25-26.
[6] *Ibid.,* p. 39.
[7] *Loc. cit.*

can only understand the work of some cruel force that has succeeded in depriving him of his one object of love, as if in retaliation for his past misdeeds. Society and life itself, which he has so relentlessly mocked, now claim their vengeance, believes Andrés. His scorn and bitterness return just as intensely as ever; and in a final expression of contempt for life he kills himself in a brutal, maniacal fashion. Indicative of his venom are his final words, frantically uttered after he mutilates himself and impatiently awaits a slow death: "Vida perra, puta.... yo te he de arrancar de cuajo."[8] And at this he shoots himself dead.

In assigning the terrible pathetic fate to Andrés' daughter, Cambaceres follows the doctrine of determinism. Given her inferior parentage, her meager environment and her poor physical condition, her destiny would necessarily be sad.

> Pero, ¿dependía de él (Andrés) que así no fuera, estaba en su mano el evitarlo, la educación, el ejemplo algo importaban, el tierno y solícito interés, la prédica amorosa y constante de los padres, tenían virtud bastante a contrariar la influencia misteriosa de leyes eternas y fatales?[9]

Cambaceres continues, bitterly opposing the tenet of free will:

> ¿De dónde, pues, esas teorías brutales y monstruosas, esa titulada moral del libre arbitrio, esa pretendida traición de la mujer a una fe que no había debido, que no había podido jurar; ¿cómo, con qué sombra o apariencia de razón declararla responsable de culpas que no eran tales y que, aun cuando lo fuesen, no eran suyas, por qué hacerla igual al hombre, ¿por qué atribuirle derechos que no era apta a ejercitar, por qué imponerle obligaciones cuya carga la agobiaban?
>
> La limitación estrecha de sus facultades, los escasos alcances de su inteligencia incapaz de penetrar en el dominio profundo de la ciencia, rebelde a las concepciones sublimes de altas nociones de justicia y de deber, el aspecto mismo de su cuerpo, su falta de nervio y de vigor, la molicie de sus for-

[8] *Ibid.*, p. 295.
[9] *Ibid.*, pp. 235-236.

mas, la delicadeza de sus líneas, la suavidad de su
piel, la morbidez de su carne, ¿no revelaban cla-
ramente su destino, la misión que la naturaleza le
había dado, no estaban diciendo a gritos que era
un ser consagrado al amor esencialmente, casi un
simple instrumento de placer, creado en vista de
la propagación sucesiva y creciente de la especie?[10]

Meriting detailed consideration in our study of *Sin rumbo*
is its language. What stands out most in Cambaceres' prose
technique is the naturalness and spontaneity of narration. The
author demonstrates a notable gift of writing in a smooth,
limpid, unlabored style, yet replete with strength and vitality.
Of defiant and unconforming temperament, Cambaceres exhibits in his prose an almost complete disregard of literary artifice
and verbal glitter, composing simply and directly at all times.
Like the characters and situations he creates, his language is
real and palpitating, a reflection of life itself.

Cambaceres' descriptions, whether of the physical environment or the mental states of the characters, possess a quickly
noticeable element of terseness and compactness. His sentences
are rapid and succinct, at times suggesting and motivating
rather than forming a completed picture of the scene, object,
or emotion portrayed. This conciseness of expression may be
seen in the paragraphs that follow, which describe a festival
in a small rural town:

En las pulperías, los "mamaos" quemaban grue-
sas de cohetes.

Los muchachos, en ronda, agarrados de las manos, saltaban gritando.

Los caballos, atados a los postes de las veredas,
asustados, se sentaban, reventaban los cabestros,
las riendas.

De vez en cuando, un carricoche pasaba sonan-
do con un ruido de matraca. Lo envolvía una nu-
be de polvo.[11]

Notice in the following lines how Cambaceres achieves the
effect of succinctness by the omission of several verbs and by
the appropriate use of prepositional phrases:

[10] *Ibid.*, pp. 236-237.
[11] *Ibid.*, p. 32.

> A la izquierda, en ángulo recto, una ramada
> servía de cocina. A la derecha, un cuadro cercado
> de cañas: el jardín. En frente, entre altos de viz-
> naga, un pozo con brocal de adobe y tres palos de
> acacio, en horca, sujetando la roldana y la huasca
> del balde. Más lejos, protegido por la sombra de
> dos sauces, el palenque.
> Bajo el alero del rancho, colgando de la última
> lata del techo, unas botas de potro se veían. Tira-
> das por el suelo, acá y allá contra la pared, pren-
> das viejas: un freno con cabezada, una bajera, una
> cincha zurcida arrastrando su correa.[12]

Another important observation concerning Cambaceres'
prose is the following: the subject and verb are frequently
placed at the very end of the sentence; and leading up to them
are many descriptive clauses, prepositional phrases, ablative
absolute constructions, past participles, and gerunds. Here, for
example, is the manner in which the author introduces the
protagonist:

> En el balcón abierto de su cuarto, largo a largo
> tendido sobre un sillón de hamaca, alto, rubio, la
> frente fugitiva, surcada por un profundo pliegue
> vertical en medio de las cejas, los ojos azules, dul-
> ces, pegajosos, de ésos que es imposible mirar sin
> sufrir la atracción misteriosa y profunda de sus
> pupilas, la barba redonda y larga, poblada ya de
> pelo blanco no obstante haber pasado apenas el
> promedio de la vida, estaba un hombre: Andrés.[13]

In the following paragraph notice the accumulation of vivid,
expressive words and phrases which serve as the object of the
verb form *había seguido*:

> Al vaivén tumultuoso de la hacienda, a los rui-
> dos del tendal, al humear de los fogones, el haci-
> namiento de bestias y de gente, de perros, de ga-
> tos, de hombres y mujeres, viviendo y durmiendo
> juntos, echados en montón, al sereno, en la cocina,
> en los galpones, a toda esa confusión, esa vida, ese

---

[12] *Ibid.*, p. 17.
[13] *Ibid.*, p. 9.

bullicio de las estancias en la esquila, un silencio
de desierto había seguido.[14]

In his narrative passages, descriptions, and dialogue Cambaceres often avails himself of terms and phraseology which are
peculiarly Argentine. Interestingly used are the colloquial and
slang expressions of the rural element, which lend an autochthonous savor to the work. We may cite the following: *bicha-
ban, autero, se cortaban solos,* and *oh, y si no.*[15] Moreover, in
addition to rural locutions, the author employs the common,
everyday pattern of speech of the great mass of *porteños.* Referring to Cambaceres' language, the respected critic and
author Martín García Merou makes this comment:

> Es el verdadero *slang* porteño. Las locuciones
> más familiares, los términos corrientes de nuestra
> conversación, la jerga de los paisanos como el ar-
> got semi-francés, semi-indígena de la clase eleva-
> da, son los retazos que forman la trama de ese len-
> guaje pintoresco, hábilmente manejado, genuina-
> mente nacional.[16]

Sin rumbo is not only an excellent naturalistic work, but an
enduring national novel as well. Although a firm adherent of
Zola's naturalism, Cambaceres is no servile imitator of that
notable French writer. The colorful descriptions of rural life,
the protagonist's discontent with Argentine society, and the
effective use of the national idiom clearly show that *Sin rumbo*
is inspired in the life and spirit of Argentina itself.

En la sangre. The last of Cambaceres' novels, *En la sangre,*
appeared originally as a serial of *Sud-América* from September
12 to October 14, 1887, and that same year was published in
book form.[17] The protagonist (Genaro), of humble Italian
parents, dreams of making something of himself, of achieving
success and position in society, but he is preoccupied with the

---

[14] *Ibid.,* pp. 8-9.

[15] *bichar* - to spy, to watch; *autero* - adjective describing the sound of the *tero,*
a bird; *cortarse solos* - to withdraw from the rest; *oh, y si no* -Why not?

[16] Martín García Merou, "La novela en el Plata—Pot-pourri, Música sentimental, Sin rumbo," *Sud-América,* December 7, 1885, p. 3.

[17] Eugenio Cambaceres, *En la sangre,* B.A., Imprenta de Sud-América, 1887.
The novel was subsequently published by Porter Hermanos, 1924, and Editorial
Minerva, 1924.

thought that his obscure origin may act as a severe handicap. Presented as a vicious and inherently vile youth, he exhibits his depravity on many occasions throughout the novel. He forces into marriage a girl of wealth and standing, and thus envisages in her the fulfillment of his ambitious plans. Then he uses his wife's money for his own pleasure and squanders her father's huge inheritance as well. When she finally summons up enough courage to refuse his requests for further funds, Genaro becomes infuriated, beats her terribly, and threatens her life. With his words "Te he de matar, un día de éstos, si te descuidas," the novel is brought to a close.

The effect of heredity and environment on Genaro's way of life is carefully brought out. Born of unloving parents, amid wretched poverty, he spent a most unwholesome infancy and early childhood, suffering pathetically from rickets, malnutrition, and anemia. Mistreated and neglected, at the age of five he began to roam the streets with a mischievous eye and became initiated into a life of petty thievery and immorality. With neither parental control nor guidance of any sort, Genaro fell prey to the nefarious elements in his squalid environment. As he grew older he gained a bitter awareness of his meager station in life and determined to rise above his "inferior" hereditary traits and unfavorable surroundings. In this respect Cambaceres states:

> ¿Por qué había sido arrojado al mundo marcado de antemano por el dedo de la fatalidad, condenado a ser menos que los demás? ......¿Le sería dado acaso quitarse alguna vez de encima esa mancha, borrar el recuerdo del pasado?[18]

That his actions are wicked and his sentiments base, Genaro knows full well. Although many times he endeavors to lay aside the past and lead an upright and worthwhile life, inherent traits of cruelty and evil, made worse and clearly brought to the fore by the cogent influence of a poor environment, prevent him from correcting his ways. In regard to this point we note the following paragraph, in which Cambaceres explains the title *En la Sangre* and sets forth the doctrine of determinism:

[18] *En la sangre,* 1887 edition, *op. cit.,* p. 62.

(Genaro wished) inspirarse, retemplarse, redimirse en el ejemplo de lo bueno, de lo puro, de lo noble, que en torno suyo veía, resistir, sobreponerse a esa ingénita tendencia que lo impulsaba al mal. . . . . . estaba en su sangre eso, constitucional, inveterado, le venía de casta como el color de la piel, le había sido transmitido por herencia, de padre a hijo, como de padres a hijos se transmite el virus venenoso de la sífilis.[19]

. . .

The importance of Cambaceres in the over-all story of the Argentine novel cannot be underestimated. Writing in a most significant period in the Republic's history, he enabled the novel to acquire a status and recognition which it had previously hoped for but never attained. Just as the social, economic, and material progress of the years 1880 to 1890 afforded Argentina tremendous prestige and respect, so the efforts of Cambaceres in his four works gave to the novel a more profound meaning and more enduring credit than it had possessed before.

The world that Cambaceres presented was not a noble or dignified one. It was cruel, sordid, and unrewarding, peopled with many selfish, wicked, and depraved individuals who were incapable of adjusting normally to life or achieving any measure of inner contentment. The author contemplated with despair man's futile endeavors, his bungling, ineffectual actions, and his disastrous moral weakness. It was a world of misery and suffering, of low passions and base conduct, of distorted minds and perverted emotions; but it was a world which naturalistic writers, like Cambaceres, intentionally sought to reveal in fiction.

2. *Inocentes o culpables*

In 1884 there appeared the important naturalistic novel entitled *Inocentes o culpables,*[20] by Juan Antonio Argerich (1862-

---

[19] *Ibid.,* p. 112.
[20] Antonio Argerich, *Inocentes o culpables,* B.A., Imprenta del Courrier de la Plata, 1884. Subsequently the work was published in Biblioteca La Tradición Argentina, 1933, Vol. XXXVI, bearing the slightly changed title of *Inocente o culpable.*

1924).[21] Two years prior to the publication of this work, the author read before a literary circle a dissertation entitled *Naturalismo*.[22] In it he defends wholeheartedly Zola's scientific and documental approach to fiction, and criticizes just as vigorously those who see in naturalism only a dirty, vulgar art. Furthermore, he observes that naturalism, since it presents humanity in the raw, stripped of all conventional ideas of nobility and sweetness, necessarily is obliged to paint the dark and ugly path through which man travels. Yet he notes also that such a portrayal of vice and corruption may very well serve a didactic purpose and act as a possible deterrent for wayward and perverse youths.

As indicated in the author's prologue, *Inocentes o culpables* purports to study a family of "inferior" Italian immigrants and show the tragic end which comes to its members. Argerich fully recognized the importance of immigration to Argentina's future progress and prosperity, but at the same time he steadfastly opposed the influx of what he called the "low-class" European immigrant. Populating the land with such people of "inferior" mentality and physical development, stated the author, could only bring complex problems and general social disorder. Argerich further affirmed that immigration of this sort, instead of creating a stronger Argentina, would demoralize the nation and impede normal advancement. "¿Cómo, pues, de padres mal conformados y de frente deprimida, puede surgir una generación inteligente y apta para la libertad?"[23] The full import of this interrogation is sensed as the novel progresses and we find one of the principal characters, the son of "inferior" immigrant parents, held in the clutches of vice and degradation.

Inocentes o culpables is written in a cold and almost mathematical fashion, as if all artistic sensibility and aesthetic delight were removed from the author's pen by virtue of the very somberness of the theme. The language is matter-of-fact, dry,

---

[21] Argerich distinguished himself as a legislator and jurisconsult.

[22] Antonio Argerich, *Naturalismo*—disertación leída en Politeama, con motivo de la velada literaria a beneficio de Gervasio Méndez, B.A., Imprenta de Ostwald, 1882.

[23] *Inocentes o culpables*, 1884 edition, *op. cit.*, prologue, p. IV.

unimpressive, with a noticeable absence of picturesque words and colorful phrases. The importance of the novel, therefore, lies not in its literary merit, but in the fact that it represents one of the most determined efforts to apply Zola's novelistic principles to Argentine fiction.

In *Inocentes o culpables* the action centers first on the ruinous marital affairs in the Dagiore household, and secondly on the wretched and depraved life led by the offspring of this unhappy union. The husband, a crude and uncultured man, emigrated from his native Italy to Argentina to seek economic security, and in a period of years managed to progress from shoe-shine boy, to brick layer, to owner of an inn. His wife, also of Italian descent, soon shrinks with aversion from her mate's coarseness, becomes dissatisfied with her modest way of life, and enters into an adulterous relationship with a gallant army officer. Of equal importance is the fact that she loses interest in the care of her son and neglects his moral and social training.

The remainder of the story is then developed with particular reference to the son. Neglected and unloved in childhood, he exhibits a mean, sullen, and displeasing disposition in early manhood. His life becomes errant and useless. Indolent, depraved and cynical, he wanders the streets aimlessly, associating with all sorts of miscreants and sinking deeply into moral degradation. Yet into this confused life the author injects a ray of hope in the person of a wholesome and sincere girl. Happiness for this youth, however, is short-lived, since Argerich can not permit him to veer from his already determined path toward ultimate tragedy. The fateful end is hastened when he contracts a venereal disease; not being able to face the world and in particular his sweetheart, he sees no other exit but suicide.

Of prime importance with respect to Argerich's naturalism is the portrayal of this youth in the light of his heredity and environment. Granted the limited mental capacities of his parents on the one hand and parental neglect on the other, it follows, insists the author, that the son would find it difficult to avoid the road to vice and depravity. Concerning hereditary influences Argerich states:

> Todo se produce por eslabones graduales. Por eso, un cretino nunca procreará un ser inteligente. ....En la familia de José no existía hábito del pensamiento, y para que nuestro joven hubiera podido entrar sin peligro en ciertas especulaciones del saber humano, era menester que varias generaciones de los Dagiore hubieran pensado, ejercitando sus facultades intelectuales.[24]

The bad seed—heredity—grows in equally poor soil—environment. Accordingly, the son is pictured first as an unhappy child, then as a rebellious adolescent, and finally a debased youth who falls an easy victim to the viciousness and immorality of the modern city. Referring to this character's formative years, Argerich notes:

> Ni una vez siquiera lo habían sacado al campo, no había visto ni un pedazo vivo de la naturaleza: todo lo que tenía ante sus ojos era falsificado. .....La vida de invernáculo de la ciudad moderna tendía ya la traidora tela de su influencia, engañando sus sentidos con nociones falsas, que más tarde turbarían su criterio y lo harían vagar en un mundo de convención.[25]

At the close of the novel, after the son's suicide, the author poses the provocative question: "¿Inocente o culpable?" Argerich, in accord with the tenet of determinism, would have us believe that he is innocent of the foolish and wasteful life he led since childhood. Poor heredity and environment were factors too potent to overcome, and he tragically succumbed to their influence.

3. FURTHER DEVELOPMENTS IN THE ARGENTINE NATURALISTIC NOVEL

Not only did Argentina produce the first naturalistic novelist in Hispanic America in the figure of Cambaceres, but that

[24] *Ibid.*, pp. 246-247.
[25] *Ibid.*, p. 63.

country displayed as well the greatest over-all development of the naturalistic current in the nineteenth century. The tremendous material advancement, the great influx of immigrants, the changing social pattern, and the growing industrialization of the Republic—all these things writers used to advantage in applying the tenets of Zola to Argentine fiction. We have already seen the manifestations of naturalism as revealed in the works of Cambaceres and Argerich; it remains for us now to note in what manner several other writers expressed their adherence to that naturalistic current.

The noted critic and diplomat Martín García Merou (1862-1905) tried his hand at novel writing and produced a well-constructed and rapidly moving naturalistic work entitled *Ley social* (1885).[26] The scene is set for the most part in Madrid, where, we may observe, García Merou served as secretary of the Argentine embassy in 1882. *Ley social* concerns the lascivious life of a young Argentine diplomat who finally awakens, but too late, to a realization of the emptiness and wastefulness of his persistent transgressions. The influence of preceding generations on the formation of his moral character is clearly pointed out:

> Llevaba sobre sus hombros el peso de la herencia de varias generaciones envilecidas; y en su sangre se reunían fatalmente los detritus y la escoria de esta pobre y lastimosa especie rebajada por siglos y siglos de vicios y de crímenes, transmitidos de padres a hijos, como los malos humores de un organismo morboso.[27]

Through the protagonist's final act the author gives meaning to the title *Ley social*. When this libertine is engaged in a duel with his lover's husband, he willingly allows himself to be killed, accepting the inevitable fate resulting from his sinful ways. It would appear that "la ley debía cumplirse sin piedad: talión inexorable, martirio cruento, ley social, que lo condenaba a sufrimiento eterno."[28]

[26] Martín García Merou, *Ley social,* ed. F. Lajouane, B.A., Imprenta de M. Biedma, 1885. The novel originally appeared in serial form in *Sud-América,* from April 25 to May 12, 1885, under the title *Marcos.*

[27] *Ley social,* 1885 edition in book form, *op. cit.,* p. 208.

[28] *Ibid.,* p. 211.

García Merou's naturalistic development of character is further revealed in the portrayal of one of the protagonist's paramours, a young hussy who captures the love denied to her in childhood by entering into numerous illicit relationships. The author narrates the tragic story of her early years in order to show how her poor environment left its devastating mark on her future way of life. Surrounded by abject poverty, deprived of a mother's love and pitifully abused by a drunken father, she was brought up in an atmosphere of vulgarity and baseness, with no one to afford her guiding moral inspiration or to satisfy her craving for recognition and affection.

In the novel *Emilio Love* (1888),[29] by Segundo I. Villafañe, the protagonist is a degenerate and evil person who, despite efforts to redeem him, continues his immoral conduct and is finally sent to prison, where he dies shortly afterward. The work reveals the progressive stages, from childhood to maturity, in his life of waywardness and depravity, vices which eventually bring about his premature death. That the reader may at once perceive the important role that heredity played in the formation of the protagonist's character, seems to be of deep concern for the author; and he wastes no time in conveying this idea, as in the prologue he sets forth these words:

> Esta es la historia de una vida desordenada, lanzada sin quicio y sin objeto a rodar por el mundo, solicitada por fuerzas distintas y contrarias, juguete del azar y las pasiones. La historia de un rico heredero en que se habían acumulado las herencias de sus antecedores maternos y paternos y en el cual se cumple una ley de atavismo fatal e inexorable. Sólo así se explicarían ciertos caracteres extraños, ciertos neurópatas que no podrían figurar sin embargo en las listas de un manicomio.[30]

A carefully elaborated consideration of the unyielding influence of heredity appears in *Irresponsable* (1889)[31] by Manuel

---

[29] Segundo I. Villafañe, *Emilio Love,* ed. F. Lajouane, B.A., Imprenta de Mackern y Mc. Lean, 1888.

[30] *Ibid.,* p. 5.

[31] Manuel T. Podestá, *Irresponsable,* B.A., Imprenta de La Tribuna Nacional, 1889. The novel was also published in Biblioteca de la Nación, 1903, Vol. 100, and in Editorial Minerva, 1924. Podestá is also the author of the

T. Podestá (1853-1920). Significantly enough, this author was a notable physician and professor of medicine, whose field of specialization was mental diseases. In his work Podestá studies the steady process of moral decomposition of one tragic individual, called the *hombre de los imanes*. This protagonist suffers from a sick and degenerate mind, to a large measure transmitted to him through heredity. Just as Argerich in *Inocentes o culpables* declares the son innocent of the way of life he led, so Podestá absolves the *hombre de los imanes* from any responsibility for the acts and states of mind which are the result of hereditary influences. One of the protagonist's friends tells him: "...eres un desgraciado, uno de tantos, en los que se cumple fatalmente una ley de herencia, de la que pocos pueden sustraerse."[32]

The novel assumes the form of a series of vivid episodes revealing the distraught and unbalanced character of the *hombre de los imanes*. He falls hopelessly in love with a harlot and accepts her as his mistress, with all her vulgarity and ignorance. Pusillanimous and indecisive, he continues to live with her despite his conviction that he is doing wrong and harming himself. Moreover, he becomes addicted to alcohol, which undermines his health and leaves its scar on his mind. His judgment twisted and his sense of reasoning shaken, he finds himself a misfit in society, a man without faith, hope, or aim in life, a worthless and abulic individual. Yet, keenly realizing his deficiencies and vices, he sincerely desires to change his mode of living and to begin leading a normal life. He undertakes a career in politics; and on one occasion he becomes unduly aroused at a political meeting, speaks his mind too candidly, and is finally led away in a fit of epilepsy. Subsequently he is made the object of public laughter, is scoffed at as a drunk, and condemned as a thief. The novel closes with the death of the *hombre de los imanes* in a mental institution.

An interest in abnormal personalities and mental aberrations

novel *Alma de niña*, B.A., Imprenta de P. Coni e hijos, 1892, a moving story of unrequited love, in which a young girl tortures her soul with the thought of her sweetheart's perfidy. *Alma de niña* was subsequently published in Biblioteca de la Nación, 1903, Vol. 100, in the same volume containing *Irresponsable*.
[32] *Irresponsable*, 1889 edition, *op. cit.*, p. 205.

is evinced in the voluminous naturalistic work entitled *Libro extraño*,[33] consisting of five interrelated sections which appeared separately from 1894 to 1902. The author, Francisco A. Sicardi (1856-1927),[34] was a distinguished doctor and professor, who in much the same manner as Podestá availed himself of his wide clinical experience to gather material for his novel. *El libro extraño* is a vast social study of a group of families and other individual characters, many of whom reveal some sort of psychopathic behavior pattern or disclose a propensity toward vice. Sicardi traces mental diseases and moral depravation from one generation to the next, in this way concretely expounding a form of fatalism to which naturalistic writers adhere.

There are examined in the novel the lives of individuals suffering from such disorders as megalomania, abulia, delirium tremens, persecution complex, and epilepsy. Furthermore, playing important roles are a family of suicides, a hereditary alcoholic, a homicidal maniac, and a score of unhappy, emotionally unstable persons constantly in conflict with themselves and the world about them. The setting in which these confused and irrational people act is the contemporary heterogeneous and complex capital, where passions, jealousies, ambitions, and desires are mingled to present the spirit and verve of the progressing nation.

There are brazenly realistic scenes of prostitution, alcoholism, viciousness, and sundry forms of social misbehavior, which Sicardi understands as resulting in part from underprivileged environments and the rapid material growth of the Republic. It is interesting to note, concerning Sicardi's frank portrayal of the uglier aspects of life, the comment made by Manuel Gálvez, whose naturalistic works of the twentieth century won for him fame and success as a novelist:

---

[33] We have not been able to locate the originally published individual books, which bear the titles *Libro extraño*, 1894, *Genaro*, 1896, *Don Manuel de Paloche*, 1899, *Méndez*, 1900, and *Hacia la justicia*, 1902. The edition we consulted, consisting of two volumes that contain the five sections listed above, is the following: Francisco A. Sicardi, *Libro extraño*, ed. F. Granada y Cía, Barcelona, Tipografía El Anuario, n.d. 2 vols.

[34] Sicardi is also the author of *Perdida*, B.A., J. Roldán, 1911, a loosely constructed novel about a blind young woman who keeps her dignity and self-respect amid the vulgarity of the people surrounding her.

Yo declaro que en los libros de Sicardi aprendí
a ver el colorido y la tristeza del bajo fondo de
Buenos Aires; y no sé si habría escrito *Nacha Regules* e *Historia de arrabal* en el caso de no existir
los libros de Sicardi.[35]

4. MINOR NOVELS REVEALING NATURALISTIC INFLUENCES

Several other Argentine novels show naturalistic influences,
although they are not fully conceived in the mold of true naturalistic works. In general, what is lacking is the well-de-
fined manifestation of the doctrine of determinism, the clear
presentation of the interplay of heredity and environment, and
the objective exposition of successive stages leading inexorably
to the protagonist's sorrowful fate. Following these novels in
chronological order, we first come upon the works of Silverio
Domínguez (1852- ?),[36] who often wrote under the pseudonym of Ceferino de la Calle.[37] The naturalistic influence
in Domínguez lies almost exclusively in the candidness and
crudeness with which he treats lascivious themes. *Perfiles y
medallones* (1886)[38] revolves around the illicit love affairs of
the author and several of his companions. Appearing in the
novel are scenes in houses of ill repute, episodes of adultery
and promiscuity, accusations of paternity, and a description of
bathing in the nude in mixed company. Besides this Zolaesque
influence,[39] the novel is rich in vivid realistic descriptions of

---

[35] Manuel Gálvez, *Amigos y maestros de mi juventud—recuerdos de la vida
literaria, 1900-1910,* B.A., Editorial G. Kraft, 1944, p. 115. *Nacha Regules,*
1919, and *Historia de arrabal,* 1922, mentioned in the paragraph cited, are
two of Gálvez' naturalistic works.

[36] Domínguez, born in Spain in 1852, arrived in Argentina at the age of
twenty-two, having just received a medical degree. In Buenos Aires he enjoyed
a brilliant career as a professor and bacteriologist, distinguishing himself particularly in the study of tuberculosis. Domínguez published many scientific
works in Buenos Aires, among them *Apuntes de bacteriología para uso de los
alumnos de anatomía patológica,* ed. A. Núñez, B.A., 1887.

[37] We learned of the author's real name in the following manner. In a rare
collection in the Biblioteca de San Fernando in Argentina, we found a copy of
his novel *Palomas y gavilanes,* published with his pseudonym Ceferino de la
Calle. On the inside cover of this work there appears the author's written dedication to Lucio N. Mansilla—signed "Silverio Domínguez, el 30 de mayo de
1890."

[38] Ceferino de la Calle, *Perfiles y medallones—panorama bonaerense, salón
reservado,* B.A., Establecimiento tipográfico de Moreno y Núñez, 1886.

[39] In the prologue to *Perfiles y medallones,* p. III, the author states: "Entonces
al leer lo que había escrito, me encontré un discípulo de Zolá, no en cuanto
a carácter literario, sino en la prosecución de escenas reales tan descarnadas y
tan de verdad que a mí mismo me asustaron."

social customs in Buenos Aires. In an easy, intimate style, Domínguez tells of the Teatro Colón, the fashionable shops and restaurants, the *cafés cantantes,* and the Paseo de la Recoleta, all of which no doubt imparted pleasant and familiar sensations to the contemporary reader of the capital. In *Palomas y gavilanes* (1886),[40] a malicious and artful procuress lures several girls into prostitution. The climax of the story occurs when a retired man of leisure encounters his own daughter in one of the brothels that he frequently visits.

Another writer who painted man's desires with complete lack of restraint was Antonio Babuglia (1865-1929).[41] Journalist and instructor of mathematics and physics, he published two novels under the anagramatic pseudonym of Abul-Bagi. The first work, entitled *Nenna* (1887),[42] we have not succeeded in locating, but it appears cited by Enrique Navarro Viola in his *Anuario bibliográfico* (1887),[43] with the qualification "una imitación de Zolá." The second novel, *Wanda,*[44] tells the story of an erotic young man whose insatiable sexual passion causes him to abandon his loving wife and seek pleasure in the arms of a harlot.

That crime is frequently induced by unfavorable environmental conditions is the thesis sustained in the novel *Castruccio* (1889),[45] by Ventura Aguilar. The author understands that the great capital—nervous and undisciplined in its commercial

---

[40] Ceferino de la Calle, *Palomas y gavilanes,* ed. F. Lajouane, B.A., Libraire Générale, 1886. We may add that under his real name Domínguez published a short novel entitled *Perfiles de una llaga social,* B.A., Imprenta de Pablo Coni, 1881, which treats of a man who finally cures himself of a pernicious gambling habit.

[41] From a telephone conversation held with Babuglia's sister in Buenos Aires on January 19, 1953, we learned that the author was born June 5, 1865, and died November 28, 1929.

[42] Babuglia (Abul-Bagi), *Nenna,* ed. Emilio de Mársico, B.A., 1887. In an article by Félix Leo, appearing in *La Patria,* May 28, 1887, p. 2, we learn that *Nenna* treats of the seduction of a young girl and her subsequent life of prostitution.

[43] Enrique Navarro Viola, *Anuario bibliográfico de la República Argentina,* B.A., Imprenta del Mercurio, 1887, p. 247.

[44] Abul-Bagi, *Wanda,* ed. Emilio de Mársico, B.A., 1888.

[45] Ventura Aguilar, *Castruccio—episodio novelesco de actualidad,* B.A., Imprenta de Buffet y Bosch, 1889. Aguilar is the author of two other novels: *Otilia—episodio de la guerra de Cuba,* ed. Emilio de Mársico, B.A., 1887, uses the Cuban independence movement as the background for a trite love story; *Noche penal,* B.A., Imprenta de Buffet y Bosch, 1888, is a ridiculous story of a sinful clergyman.

and social activities, absorbed in material progress to the sorrowful neglect of moral and spiritual considerations—acts as a breeding place for depravity and criminal behavior. The protagonist of the novel is a youthful Italian immigrant who lives aimlessly from day to day in the unwholesome surroundings of bars, cheap cafes, and sinful sidewalks. The vulgarity of this environment, coupled with disillusion in love and dissatisfaction with his meager job, sets him on the path of cynicism and crime. He conceives an ingenious and diabolical scheme to collect the insurance of a man he contrives to murder. Without conscience he effects the hideous killing, but within a short time he is apprehended and placed in prison.

. . .

It will be recalled that the realistic novel in Argentina attained full stature in the 1880's. Naturalism, being an outgrowth and continuation of realism, did not supplant that literary current, but developed side by side with it. While in 1884 there appeared the very realistic novels *La gran aldea* and *Fruto vedado,* there also was published the decidedly naturalistic work *Inocentes o culpables;* and throughout the decades of the 1880's and 1890's, alongside realistic novelists like Miró, Ocantos, Villafañe, and Rivarola, there may be cited such naturalistic writers as Cambaceres, Podestá, and Sicardi.

Naturalism corresponded to the same period in Argentina's development as realism. That period, as we have seen, represented the years of economic and social progress of the 1880's and 1890's, when Argentina began to assert itself as an important nation. Both the realistic and naturalistic writers strove to portray faithfully the Argentina of that time, but the latter group sought in particular to depict the more sordid and vulgar features of life, to expose the ugly and wretched forms of humanity. For these naturalists, the economic progress, material growth, and incipient industrialization in Argentina brought about a vast network of social evils and unhealthy, distorted attitudes and modes of behavior. This mass of vice and corruption, of sick and degenerate persons, understood and interpreted in relation to the social setting, was poignantly revealed in the naturalistic novels.

We have seen that naturalistic fiction in Argentina began with the appearance of Cambaceres' first books in the early 1880's, and lasted until a few years beyond the close of the century with the publication of the final section of *El libro extraño* in 1902. Yet some years later the naturalistic novel was to reappear in Argentine fiction with the works of Manuel Gálvez. In his novels *El mal metafísico* (1916), *Nacha Regules* (1919), and *Historia de arrabal* (1922), this author presents the tragic fate of several weak individuals who are led onto the road of moral degradation by the unrelenting social forces of contemporary Argentina.

XI

TRANSITION TO THE TWENTIETH
CENTURY—CONCLUSION

1. The Work and Significance of Carlos María Ocantos

On a few occasions in the chapter on realism we made brief mention of selected works of Carlos María Ocantos. It is appropriate at this time to consider the author more fully, both as a national novelist of notable merit and an important figure in the transition to the present century. Spanning both the nineteenth and twentieth centuries with a vast and significant production, Ocantos holds a distinguished place in the history of the Argentine novel.

Of an aristocratic Argentine family, Ocantos was born in Buenos Aires on May 20, 1860. After earning a law degree at the University of Buenos Aires, he embarked on a diplomatic career, which for long years was to form a most important part of his life. In 1886, he secured a position in Madrid as first secretary of the legation and charge d'affaires, and from that date until 1910 (with the exception of a stay in Paris from 1890 to 1891 and four years' residence in Buenos Aires from 1891 to 1895), he continued in the diplomatic service in the Spanish capital. During these years the author was busily engaged in composing the long series of novels which we shall presently consider. From 1910 to 1918, Ocantos held various official posts in Denmark and Norway, after which period he retired from diplomacy and settled again in Madrid to continue his literary tasks. The author passed away in that city on August 30, 1949.

Ocantos' initial work, entitled *La cruz de la falta* (1883),[1] is

---

[1] Carlos María Ocantos, *La cruz de la falta,* B.A., Imprenta de Pablo E. Coni, 1883.

a typically romantic novel of overplayed emotions and exaggerated sentiment, replete with jealousy, unrequited love, duels, and repentance. Its chronological significance far outweighs its literary merit, yet critics were quick to notice in this unknown author a rich imagination, an embryonic talent for colorful descriptions, and a facility for vivid dialogue.[2]

During Ocantos' initial years in Madrid he published his second work, the famous *León Zaldívar* (1888),[3] which was favorably received both in Spain and Argentina and did much to establish the author's reputation as a novelist of merit. It forms the first of the *Novelas argentinas,* a long series of novels portraying contemporary Argentine life in its multifold manifestations. Romantic in plot and characterization of protagonists, yet intensely realistic as regards descriptive detail and depiction of manners and customs, *León Zaldívar* represents an important work of transition toward the more fully developed novels which Ocantos composed in subsequent years.

In Ocantos' next novel, *Quilito* (1891),[4] there are clearly shown a more mature novelistic skill and an originality of style. *Quilito,* a novel of the stock market craze, forms the second volume of *Novelas argentinas* and was published in Paris while the author briefly resided in that city. During the years 1891-1895, a period in which he was in Argentina on a leave of absence from his diplomatic post in Madrid, Ocantos published three of his most accomplished works—*Entre dos luces* (1892),[5] *El candidato* (1893),[6] and *La Ginesa* (1894).[7] Political intrigue and unrest, passion for control and power, and corruption among important government officials are the themes

---

[2] Among the reviews of this novel we cite the following: Anon., "La cruz de la falta," *La Nueva Revista de Buenos Aires,* 1883, VIII, 659-668; Calixto Oyuela, "La cruz de la falta," *Revista Científica y Literaria,* B.A., 1883, I, 62-64.

[3] See Chap. IX, p. 157, for further information regarding this work.

[4] See Chap. IX, p. 154, for further information regarding this work.

[5] Carlos María Ocantos, *Entre dos luces,* B.A., La Plata, and Rosario, Imprenta de J. Peuser, 1892. The work was also published in Biblioteca de la Nación, 1912, Vol. 522, and in Biblioteca Sopena, Barcelona, 1914, Vol. 28.

[6] Carlos María Ocantos, *El candidato*—segunda parte de *Entre dos luces,* B.A., La Plata, and Rosario, Imprenta de J. Peuser, 1893. The work was also published in Biblioteca de la Nación, 1912, Vol. 523, and in Biblioteca Sopena, Barcelona, 1917, Vol. 32.

[7] Carlos María Ocantos, *La Ginesa, B.A.,* Imprenta de Pablo E. Coni e hijos, 1894. The work was also published in Biblioteca de la Nación, 1913, Vol. 565, and in Biblioteca Sopena, Barcelona, 1916, Vol. 2.

of the novels *Entre dos luces* and *El candidato*. Here Ocantos reveals with singular acumen the whole electoral organization both in a small town and in the capital, presenting in sharp relief sundry types of politicians and staunch party adherents, as well as the machinations and deceit used to gain their ends. In *La Ginesa,* a weak and timid youth, overprotected by his stepsister, spurns an arranged marriage to an innocent girl and falls hopelessly in love with a hussy. The work presents interesting feminine types and studies the position of women in Argentine society.

Having returned to Madrid in 1896, Ocantos continued to compose work after work in the series *Novelas argentinas.* *Tobi* (1896)[8] treats of the disillusion of a young idealistic sculptor who comes face to face with the cruel and unsympathetic materialistic society of the capital. In the struggle of this sensitive youth for public recognition and appreciation, there is epitomized the struggle of all diligent and sincere creative artists who find in the hectic and commercialized Buenos Aires an atmosphere unsuited for the proper cultivation of their talents. *Promisión* (1897)[9] encarnates the spirit of a vigorous and industrious Argentina, presenting the lives of several groups of immigrants who adjust favorably to the Republic's way of life and contribute in their own small way to progress and prosperity. In *Misia Jeromita* (1898),[10] a complacent middle-class family of the province of Catamarca receives a severe jolt upon learning that its boarder has deceived one of the daughters. This young rascal makes love to Jeromita, arranges a sham marriage, takes her savings, and promptly flees.

The novel *Pequeñas miserias* (1900)[11] delves into the well-to-do class and exposes the sad consequences of a marriage of convenience. For his next work, *Don Perfecto* (1902),[12] the

[8] Carlos María Ocantos, *Tobi*, Madrid, Imprenta del Sucursal de J. Cruzado, a cargo de F. Márquez, 1896. The work was also published in Biblioteca Sopena, Barcelona, 1917, Vol. 41.

[9] See Chap. IX, pp. 159-160, for further information about this novel.

[10] Carlos María Ocantos, *Misia Jeromita,* Madrid, Establecimiento tipográfico de I. Moreno, 1898. The work was also published in Biblioteca Sopena, Barcelona, 1919, Vol. 74.

[11] Carlos María Ocantos, *Pequeñas miserias,* Madrid, 1900. Also published in Biblioteca de la Nación, 1915, Vol. 651.

[12] Carlos María Ocantos, *Don Perfecto,* Barcelona, Montaner y Simón, 1902. Also published in Biblioteca de la Nación, 1915, Vol. 672.

author goes back to the middle of the nineteenth century, and around episodes in the life of a gentleman possessing exaggerated notions of virtue and kindness, draws a colorful picture of the social life of the capital. In *Nebulosa* (1904),[13] Ocantos shifts his scene to the fashionable seaside resort of Mar del Plata and presents the problems of an unmarried woman who is denied independent financial security.

We mentioned that in 1910 Ocantos left Spain and spent the following eight years in Scandinavian countries on diplomatic missions. During that period he wrote *Fru Jenny* (1915),[14] a collection of short novels reflecting life in Denmark, as well as two additional works of *Novelas argentinas* entitled *El peligro*[15] (1911) and *Riquez* (1914).[16] After Ocantos terminated his diplomatic career in 1918 and again took up residence in Madrid, he published *El camión* (1922),[17] a volume of short novels portraying Spanish life, that stands as a noble tribute to the nation with which he so closely identified himself. In addition, he worked assiduously and completed the remaining volumes of *Novelas argentinas*, composing seven novels from 1922 to 1929.[18]

The comprehensiveness of *Novelas argentinas* lies in many directions. Ocantos portrays the urban region and the rural one, the wealthy city dwelling and the huge country estate, the modest house in the capital and the tidy home on a small ranch. He depicts the quiet, subdued atmosphere of a provincial town and the clamor and hustle of Buenos Aires; and he

[13] Carlos María Ocantos, *Nebulosa*, Madrid, Establecimiento tipográfico de I. Moreno, 1904.
[14] Carlos María Ocantos, *Fru Jenny*—seis novelas danesas, Paris, B.A., Casa Editorial Hispano-Americana, 1915. The work was also published in Madrid, Tipografía de la Revista de Archivos, Bibliotecas y Museos, 1923.
[15] Carlos María Ocantos, *El peligro*, Madrid, Imprenta de V. Tordesillas, 1911. The work was also published in Biblioteca de la Nación, 1916, Vol. 719.
[16] Carlos María Ocantos, *Riquez*—memorias de un viejo verde, Madrid, Imprenta de V. Tordesillas, 1914. Also published in Biblioteca de la Nación, 1917, Vol. 738.
[17] Carlos María Ocantos, *El camión*—seis novelas españolas, Madrid, Tipografía de la Revista de Archivos, Bibliotecas y Museos, 1922.
[18] Ocantos' remaining novels are the following: *Victoria*, Madrid, Impr. de la Revista de Archivos, ... 1922; *La cola de paja*, Madrid, Tip. de la Revista de Archivos, ..., 1923; *La ola*, Madrid, Tip. de la Revista de Archivos, ..., 1925; *El secreto del doctor Barbado*, Madrid, Impr. G. Hernández y G. Sáez, 1926; *Tulia*, Madrid, Impr. G. Hernández y G. Sáez, 1927; *El emboscado*, Madrid, Impr. G. Hernández y G. Sáez, 1928; *Fray Judas*, Madrid, Impr. G. Hernández y G. Sáez, 1929.

reveals the wide, vacant expanse of the pampa and the busy, crowded streets of the commercial metropolis. In the matter of selection of characters, Ocantos chooses from all strata of society: the obscure city dweller and the lowly peasant, the urban workman and the modest rancher, the merchant, the small landed proprietor and the middle class in general, the wealthy landholder and the opulent aristocracy. Furthermore, appearing in the novels in appropriate setting and characterization are gauchos, immigrants, wastrels, fortune hunters, scions of distinguished stock, gossipy women of leisure, dowagers, and young maidens with enviable dowries.

This heterogeneous group of individuals naturally becomes involved in a variety of problems, which Ocantos realistically sets forth as a reflection of Argentina's pattern of life. Underlying many of the conflicts is the incessant and vigorous struggle of the young Republic to progress healthily from year to year, and to achieve a measure of stability and prosperity. Among the many significant aspects of life revealed in the *Novelas argentinas* may be cited the following: the political scene, with its petty wrangling and fraudulent dealings; family affairs, with the attendant problems of courtship, marriage, filial obligations and responsibilities, parental control, inheritance, and ancestral pride; the breaking down of those traditional social conventions which no longer serve a useful purpose and are considered a barrier to fruitful living and happiness; economic and financial concerns, understood in the main in relation to a materialistic society; and the fervent desire for cultural expression, which the ill tides of an unresponsive audience batter down and mercilessly destroy.

A frequently employed technique of Ocantos, which quickly brings to mind the works of Galdós and Balzac, is that of placing in more than one novel the same character or relatives of that character. In such a lengthy series as the *Novelas argentinas,* this recurrence and interrelationship of personages serve to link more closely the various novels and enhance the effect of a realistically conceived and developed group of works.

One of the most significant items that we encounter in the study of Ocantos is the duality of his life—a duality that ex-

presses itself in his twofold success as writer and diplomat; in
his almost lifelong residence in Spain as an Argentine citizen;
in his composition and publication in Spain of novels thoroughly Argentine; and in his sincere love and admiration for
Spanish tradition and culture alongside an intense patriotic
feeling toward his native land. Furthermore, this duality is
clearly carried over into Ocantos' works; that is, while the
subject matter and personages of his novels are distinctly Argentine, the style and language employed are more characteristic of pure Spanish. Residing in Madrid when the great masters of the Spanish novel were enjoying a splendid reputation,
Ocantos undoubtedly fell under their influence as regards the
writing of a pure, classical prose. Ocantos is *castizo;* he writes
in correct Castillian Spanish, devoid of gallicisms, regionalisms,
and peculiar Argentine phrases and turns of speech. The
author maintains that the constant use of such foreign elements
tends to vitiate and weaken the language, turning its purity
into a dissonant medley of several national tongues. In the
novel *El peligro,* which treats precisely this linguistic question,
there appears the following paragraph:

> Pues, si de un mismo tronco proceden (refer-
> ring to all the Spanish-speaking nations), hoy que
> en el concierto universal procuran todos enten-
> derse, ¿por qué levantar una barrera tal como la
> del idioma? ¿No es mejor cuidar de que no se
> adultere, de no mancharlo, siendo hermoso y ex-
> presivo más que ninguno? Y no que yo me opon-
> ga a la admisión de voces nuevas, necesarias, por-
> que señalan cosas que en nuestra España no exis-
> ten ni se conocen, o porque resuciten palabras
> muertas del tiempo de la Conquista. No. En este
> sentido, mi manga es muy ancha. Yo no predico
> el estacionamiento, la cristalización. Lo que yo
> predico es la higiene del lenguaje. Contra lo que
> yo peleo es contra los atentados a la Gramática,
> contra la invasión de bárbaros en nuestro Dic-
> cionario.[19]

What quickly strikes the reader upon examining the pages

[19] *El peligro,* edition of Biblioteca de la Nación, *op. cit.,* pp. 51-52.

of Ocantos' novels is the genial informality and gracious intimacy of narration. There is warmth, sympathy, and closeness between writer and public, a relationship which grows out of the author's sincere interest in his material and his zeal and enjoyment in relating it. Unlimited is Ocantos' enthusiasm, radiated to the reader in the form of a rapid, fluid, and spontaneous prose. The author nimbly spins his story as if he were speaking to us personally and observing our emotional reaction. His prose is full, well-rounded, expansive, containing many interpolative phrases, exclamatory utterances, happy turns of speech, and other informal and lighthearted remarks. Ocantos seems to write exactly as he thinks, so that in the construction of a paragraph he transcribes freely every related thought and emotion that runs through his mind. In this way he goes on for pages and pages in an amiable, relaxed fashion, until he fairly exhausts the particular matter under consideration. The following paragraph, taken from *Entre dos luces,* describes one of the many politicians who figure prominently in the novel:

> Es tiempo de decir la verdad acerca del doctor don Francisco de Paula Trujillo, que aquí aparece como una personalidad eminente de la política argentina, y la verdad es bien sencilla y fácil de decir: el doctor Trujillo no pasaba de ser un pobre diablo, y si yo le he aplicado calificativos rimbombantes, que en apariencia lo enaltecen, ha sido contagiado por el mal ejemplo de *El Noticiero Ombúense* y otros periódicos adictos a la causa eneísta, que gastaban en su honor el incienso a toneladas, envolviéndole en nube tan espesa, que no había ya quien lo conociera. Pero, yo, que lo conozco como a mis manos, rasgaré sin temor el velo, con que sus partidarios se empeñan en cubrirlo, y lo presentaré a ustedes como un abogado ramplón, que había subido precisamente por la razón física que la escoria sale a la superficie y la barra de oro cae al fondo. Otra razón, no científica pero humana, explicará mejor la causa de su rápida carrera: y era la simpatía que de toda su

persona trascendía, aquella sonrisa de miel con
que engolosinaba a los extraños, el don de los án-
geles, en fin, que parecía ser su patrimonio exclu-
sivo; afectado de optimismo crónico, lo negro y lo
blanco eran igualmente gratos a sus ojos; pensaba
como todo el mundo y se encontraba bien en todas partes. Todos decían: —¡Pero qué hombre
más simpático es este doctor Trujillo! Empezó
borroneando sueltos políticos en un periódico, y
sus amigos dieron en decir que tenía talento y en
letras de molde lo repitieron tantas y tantas veces,
que el público se acostumbró a oírlo y lo creyó,
y la capacidad intelectual de Trujillo quedó con-
sagrada por *los chicos de la prensa,* como donosa-
mente los llamó Pereda a estos repartidores de la
fama por entregas. Era entonces Trujillo un po-
brecito huérfano, mal vestido y peor comido, pero
muy listo para introducirse por el ojo de la llave
donde encontrar pudiera algo que mascar o de
provecho; se hizo abogado no sé cómo y estuvo
de pasante mucho tiempo en un bufete de crédito,
que le dió más acopio de relaciones que dinero, y
pasó luego con un cargo oficial de poca monta, y
como no salía de las antesalas de los poderosos, a
los que se agarraba como la lapa a la peña, y sus
amigos no daban paz al bombo, nuestro hombre
sacaba siempre mendrugo: le hicieron secretario
particular de un alto personaje y después diputado
y después... no sé cuántas cosas, porque, como era
abogado, servía para todo.[20]

In the *Novelas argentinas* the dialogue, copiously employed
and effectively handled, assumes the same lively and spontaneous form as the narration itself. Characters frequently speak
at length and with decided emphasis in what appears to be a
monologue, disclosing their innermost thoughts and feelings
with complete lack of inhibition. Moreover, there is an effective blending of narration, dialogue, and actual monologue,
which results in a marked fluidity of composition and sustained vigor of presentation. The ensuing paragraph, selected
from *Tobi,* is the answer given to the protagonist when he

[20] *Entre dos luces,* edition of Biblioteca Sopena, *op. cit.,* pp. 120-121.

idealistically announces his intention of becoming a sculptor:

> ¡Conque el señorito quería ser escultor! ¿Qué es eso? ¿Estos cacharreros que hacen muñecos de yeso y voceándolos van por las esquinas? Muy bien, carrera más lucida... ¡Ah! pero no tenía él la culpa, sino su señor tío, que le hacía creer que los burros vuelan. ¡Qué esculturas ni qué demonches! Ya lo dijo el otro, «que oficio que no da de comer, no vale dos habas»; y en estas tierras no hay más arte que dé fruto que el de teatro, y para eso ha de ser de extrangis. Aquello de embadurnarse los dedos y amasar monigotes, era un gusto como otro cualquiera, y parecíale preferible a más peligrosos pasatiempos; lo inadmisible, lo estúpido, lo descabellado, era querer hacer de eso una carrera seria y provechosa.[21]

In reviewing the *Novelas argentinas* in their totality we note several important features: 1) a keen sense of the dramatic pervades many parts of each novel—the narrative passages, the dialogue, and the descriptive selections. At all times there is the impression of movement and vividness; 2) Ocantos reveals a good-natured and genial humor, a wholesome and zestful attitude toward life, a spirit of imbibing enjoyment and happiness from all that surrounds him. He feels life's problems deeply, but he is never despairing, pessimistic, or bitter; 3) there is light satire of society's foibles, but it is always tempered with gracious benevolence and human understanding; 4) Ocantos, in exposing and criticizing Argentina's weaknesses and defects, is guided more by his patriotic feelings than by a desire to set himself up as a public censor. He recognizes the limitations of his country, but he has unswerving faith in its future.

The series *Novelas argentinas* marks an epoch in the history of the Argentine novel, for it represents the initial endeavor to reveal through a group of varied works a comprehensive picture of contemporary Argentina. Others before Ocantos portrayed well particular elements or specific aspects of the nation, whether it was in one work as in the cases of Lucio Vicente López and Miró, or in a series as with Eduardo Gutié-

[21] *Tobi*, 1896 edition, *op. cit.*, p. 66.

rrez and Cambaceres. Yet it remained for Ocantos to possess the broadness of vision and fullness of scope to portray the whole of the nation, to paint the complete scene in its many and complex phases. Just as Balzac in *La comédie humaine* studied almost every facet of French life and Galdós in *Novelas españolas* interpreted fully the problems of contemporary Spain, so Ocantos in *Novelas argentinas* set his pen to the entire intense drama occurring in his own land. Arduous indeed was the task that Ocantos proposed for himself upon initiating the group of *Novelas argentinas* in 1888, yet he faced it bravely and upon completion of the series forty-one years later, in 1929, he looked with pride and dignity at the fruit of his labor. The accomplishment is all the more to be admired when it is recalled that he composed most of the novels while in Spain. Despite his protracted absence from Argentina, Ocantos never disassociated himself from the cultural, political, or social life of the nation, but constantly kept abreast of the times and felt the pulse of his country as strongly as if he were within its borders.

2. TWENTIETH-CENTURY TRENDS IN ARGENTINE FICTION

Our analysis of the work of Ocantos has taken us through nearly three decades of the twentieth century, until 1929, when the series *Novelas argentinas* was concluded with the publication of *Fray Judas*. While Ocantos was thus producing novels in Madrid during these years of the present century, in Argentina itself several other distinguished authors made their appearance on the scene of fiction and composed novels which have given fame and glory to Argentine letters. It is important, therefore, to place ourselves at the turn of the century and view briefly the principal works composed during that period.

During the closing years of the past cenutry and the early years of the present, there was witnessed in Hispanic America the manifestation in fiction of the current of modernism. In Colombia, José A. Silva composed the novel *De sobremesa* (1887-1896). In Mexico, Manuel Gutiérrez Nájera revealed an exquisite prose in *Cuentos frágiles* and *Cuentos color de humo* (1898-1903). In Venezuela, Manuel Díaz Rodríguez showed himself a lover of pure artistic expression in his two modernistic novels, *Ídolos rotos* (1901) and *Sangre patricia* (1902). Also natives of Venezuela, Pedro Emilio Coll, in *El castillo de Elsinoro* (1896), and Pedro César Dominici, in *La tristeza voluptuosa* (1899) and *Dionysos* (1906), both displayed the brilliant and sensitive prose of modernism.

In Argentina, Ángel de Estrada (1872-1923) and Enrique Larreta (1875-   ) revealed in their modernistic novels a refined artistic sensibility and a delicate appreciation of the exotic and the classical. In these works Argentina itself plays no role, in sharp contrast to the novels of the 1880's and 1890's. Wishing to shun what they considered the crude materialism and uninspiring commonplaceness of contemporary Argentine society, these fastidious writers took spiritual refuge among the peoples and objects of foreign lands, far from the humdrum realism of their own existence.

Estrada, a figure of universal culture who sought beauty and delight in the artistic monuments of past civilizations, is the author of *Redención* (1907) and *Las Tres Gracias* (1916). In *Redención,* Estrada leads us through the beauty and elegance of classical Italy and Greece, presenting in a polished but cold prose his artistic sensations as he contemplates with ecstatic pleasure the glories and truths of a bygone age. For the setting of *Las Tres Gracias* the author takes us to early sixteenth-century Italy, to the era of Michelangelo and Raphael, in whose masterpieces Estrada sees eternal loveliness and rapturous inspiration.

With Larreta's modernistic work *La gloria de don Ramiro* (1908), Argentina acquired a distinguished piece of fiction. In a rich and carefully polished prose Larreta paints the Spanish city of Ávila during the reign of Philip II. The action of the novel, centering around an abulic and dissatisfied Spaniard of noble lineage, appears as a mere pretext for descriptions of beauty. A veritable museum of color and luxury, of refined taste and elegant display, of artistic impressions and sensuous imagery, the work reveals the temperament of a pure artist, one who understands poetic expression not only in verse, but in prose as well.[22]

About the same time that Estrada and Larreta were composing modernistic novels of sheer aesthetic delight, another important writer, Roberto J. Payró (1867-1928), continued the current of sharp realism developed in the 1880's and 1890's. Payró started fiction writing as a mere youth, publishing three works which revealed a keen observation and rich imagination—*Antígona* (1885),[23] a novel, and *Scripta* (1887)[24] and *Novelas y fantasías* (1888),[25] collections of short novels and stories.

In 1906 there appeared the very original work, *El casamiento de Laucha,* which relates in a manner recalling the Spanish picaresque novel the adventures of a roguish youth who, to acquire money, contrives a sham marriage to the owner of a rural store. For its ingenious presentation of plot, its skillful characterization of the worthless and mean, yet at times, charming protagonist, its effective use of popular speech, and its gracious flow of narration, *El casamiento de Laucha* stands as one of the most popular and meritorious novels of the twentieth century.

From an early age Payró demonstrated an eager interest in journalism and for long years practiced that profession with vigorous devotion. For this reason his novels frequently indicate the reporter's rapid, hurried, and somewhat careless style. As a journalist Payró was particularly concerned with Argentina's progress, as well as with the deficiencies and defects that it was striving to overcome. In 1908, Payró published two volumes of stories, *Pago Chico* and *Violines y toneles,* in which he depicts with a decidedly critical intention and a fine sense of irony the inefficient social and political organization

---

[22] Larreta is also the author of *Zogoibí,* 1926, a novel of gaucho life which reveals the same cult of beauty as that displayed in *La gloria de don Ramiro.*
[23] Roberto J. Payró, *Antígona,* B.A., Imprenta Sud-América, 1885. This novel, a highly complex story of youthful love, clearly shows the beginning of Payró's great talent for creating roguish and deceitful characters—a talent that was to be most artistically revealed in *El casamiento de Laucha.*
[24] Roberto J. Payró, *Scripta,* B.A., La Plata, Imprenta de J. Peuser, 1887.
[25] Roberto J. Payró, *Novelas y fantasías*—segunda serie de *Scripta,* B.A., La Plata, Imprenta de J. Peuser, 1888.

of the fictitious Pago Chico, in reality the then expanding town of Bahía Blanca.

Payró further revealed his preoccupation with national problems in his estimable realistic novel *Divertidas aventuras del nieto de Juan Moreira* (1910), which satirically portrays a vain, unscrupulous, and maliciously ingenious professional politician. This novel and the stories of *Pago Chico* have notable nineteenth-century antecedents in such works as *La gran aldea* and *Entre dos luces*, where may be observed the same critical yet patriotic spirit as that evinced by Payró.[26]

The first decade of the present century saw the initial works of Gustavo Martínez Zuviría (1883-   ), known more familiarly to thousands of readers as Hugo Wast. Publishing his first novel, *Alegre*, in 1905, and his second, *Novia de vacaciones*, in 1907, Wast has steadily built up a phenomenal literary popularity, unequaled in the annals of Hispanic-American fiction. His novels have not only attained an extraordinary success in Argentina and throughout America, but have reached a vast public in Spain and several non-Spanish-speaking countries as well. Furthermore, among his readers Wast numbers not only the professional class, but the myriad people working in offices, shops, restaurants, and in domestic service, including countless girls and women who have found in his novels a source of pleasure and interest.

A spontaneous and vivid narrator, Wast composes a type of novel which proves exceptionally agreeable and entertaining to the masses. His stories, full of charm and genuineness of feeling, succeed in moving the reader simply yet effectively, in touching his emotions with the happiness and sorrow of the characters. Never affected, vulgar, or sensational, the novels of Wast interest the public by virtue of their intrinsic human value, sincerity of expression, and geniality of presentation. The author spins an engrossing story, scrupulously planned and executed, full of exciting happenings and episodes of rapid action. The scope of Wast's thirty-odd works is extremely vast: simple and ingenious novels of Argentine cus-

[26] Payró is also the author of three novels of historical background: *El falso inca*, 1905, *El capitán Vergara*, 1925, and *El Mar Dulce*, 1927.

toms, as in *Flor de durazno* (1911); novels of country setting, as in *Valle negro* (1918) and *Desierto de piedra* (1925); novels of adventure and intrigue, exemplified in *La casa de los cuervos* (1916) and *El camino de las llamas* (1930); and novels which evoke Argentina's past history, as in the trilogy *Myriam la conspiradora* (1926), *El jinete de fuego* (1926), and *Tierra de jaguares* (1927).

In Hugo Wast Argentina gains a novelist whose primary and almost exclusive function is to entertain and delight, to form simple and gratifying literature. No pretense has he of being a social reformer, a moralist, or psychologist, nor does he strive to be recognized as a consummate artistic novelist or a profound interpreter of national problems. Wast's sole purpose is to lead the reader into an emotionally pleasing and stimulating experience in fiction. Within this limitation he has succeeded well.

Although not reaching quite so vast and varied a public as the works of Hugo Wast, the novelistic production of Manuel Gálvez (1882-   ) is considered of more significant and deeper artistic value. Gálvez' career as a novelist began in 1914 with the publication of *La maestra normal,* a masterly portrayal of life in the provincial city of La Rioja. Since that date Gálvez has produced some twenty-five novels, which in their totality have earned for him one of the most distinguished places in Argentine fiction.

In many of his novels the author evinces a strong preoccupation with the complex social problems of city life. This interest is shown in his naturalistic works *El mal metafísico* (1916), *Nacha Regules* (1919), and *Historia de arrabal* (1922); and in vividly realistic works such as *La sombra del convento* (1917), *Tragedia de un hombre fuerte* (1922), and *Hombres en Soledad* (1938). Forming another essential part of Gálvez' work are two series of historical novels. In *Escenas de la guerra del Paraguay* (1928-1929) and *Escenas de la época de Rosas* (1931-1932), Gálvez reconstructs important periods in Argentina's history, combining with excellent skill fictional and historical elements.

Gálvez composes his works with the sureness and knowledge of one who has studied the great masters of fiction and has dedicated himself most earnestly to the writing of novels. He is a complete novelist, possessing an admirable technical skill, a keen mind, and an acute awareness of the daily drama of life about him. He narrates events with great vigor, describes objects and scenes colorfully, and analyzes character and motives of conduct with sharp psychological and sociological perspicacity. Gálvez is a serious writer with a serious mission in fiction. He wishes his novels to serve as an effective medium for understanding and interpreting life as it really is, in particular those aspects relating to the social structure of Argentina's great capital. The problems he lays bare and examines are reflections of his country's mode of living and evidence of its imperfections as well.

. . .

For its traditional significance, its picturesqueness, and its distinctively national characteristics, rural life in Argentina has always held a peculiar fascination for both writer and public. The pampa, the gaucho, rural customs, the struggle between "civilization and barbarism"—all these things elicit a strong emotional response from the Argentine people and serve to define a truly genuine and deeply rooted component of the nation's character.

From this interest in rural Argentina was born the *novela criolla,* or novel of the land, the formation of which we have already traced in *El hogar en la pampa, Aventuras de un centauro de la América meridional,* and above all in the gaucho novels of Eduardo Gutiérrez. This type of fiction, however, was far overshadowed in the nineteenth century by the novel of urban life, in particular the portrayal of the busy capital. Very naturally did Buenos Aires form the predominant note in fiction during the last two decades of the century, when writers wished to mirror the vast growth and progress of the nation. On the other hand, the *novela criolla,* with the exception of Gutiérrez' works, played a decidedly inferior role as realism and naturalism were developing during these years. Then in the early twentieth century we note the reappearance and perfection of the *novela criolla,* which now stands side by side with the novel of the city as an important manifestation of Argentine fiction.

True it is that the great capital is the social, political, and economic head of the nation, and the pampa can hold no claim to representing twentieth-century Argentina. Yet a novelistic expression of this rural element occupies the attention of such distinguished writers as Benito Lynch (1885-1952) and Ricardo Güiraldes (1886-1927), who have made of this type of fiction a consummate art and an enduring tribute to the sturdy men of the pampa. Lynch succeeds well in painting a complete realistic picture of the gaucho and the surroundings in which he moves. His portrait of rural life is convincing and natural, for he wishes neither to clothe the gaucho with false virtues and greatness, nor to assign to him modes of action and ways of thinking which are not in harmony with his true character. In novels such as *Los caranchos de la Florida* (1916), *El inglés de los güesos* (1924), and *El romance de un gaucho* (1930), the vast majority of gauchos are humble, artless people, living poorly and without enlightenment in their rustic world and preoccupied for the most part with their daily tasks and domestic problems.

Güiraldes, author of the crowning glory of gaucho fiction, *Don Segundo Sombra* (1926), was born of an illustrious family of the capital, but was intimately acquainted with rural life. In his masterpiece Güiraldes brings to view a completely literary and artistic type of gaucho, a lyrical and idealized concept of what the gaucho represents to his poetic temperament. The protagonist of the novel thus appears as a synthesis of virtue and heroism, of stalwart manliness and sympathetic understanding. The author portrays the rural scene with admirable descriptive touches and a fine power of evocation. Güiraldes is a stylist; he writes in a prose full of color, imagery, and poetic sensitiveness. With this rich and picturesque language, he creates the unforgettable character of Segundo Sombra, who although a mere shadow and memory and wishful ideal, seems a real and palpitating figure in the hearts of Argentines.

3. Conclusion of Study

The Argentine novel truly emerged only after political freedom and relative stability had been established with the defeat
of Rosas in 1852. It emerged in the form of bitter attacks
against the tyrannical regime which had just been destroyed.
Amalia and the several novels of similar mold that immediately succeeded it were born of firm political motives, of an intense feeling of antagonism against a brutal system of government. The Argentine novel did not spring from a literary
moment, but arose by virtue of opportune conditions in the
nation. It is understandable, therefore, that *Amalia* and the
other works dealing with the Rosas theme did not strictly follow one sole literary current, but selected elements from both
romanticism and realism and fused them appropriately. The
authors of these novels adhered to romanticism to weave the
plot and paint the character of the protagonists, but owing to
their personal and painful experiences during the Tyranny,
they turned to realism to depict the historical background.

With *Amalia* the public recognized that it had its first real
novel—a vivid combination of romantic and realistic traits.
Yet during the years immediately following its publication,
there appeared a group of writers who observed strictly the
romanticism brought over from France and then in vogue in
Hispanic America. Their novels of exaggerated sentiment and
overplayed emotion were for the most part mediocre works,
yet they not only represented the important initial efforts at
fiction writing, but by their adherence to French romanticism
indicated the path that the novel was to follow in subsequent
years. In truth, the various stages in the development of the
Argentine novel—romanticism, realism, naturalism, and modernism—derived from nineteenth-century currents in French
fiction. It must be pointed out, however, that owing to social
and political factors, the currents of romanticism and realism,
as well as modernism, were late in reaching Argentine shores.
All these literary currents were in many instances superim-
posed one upon the other, with no neat, clear-cut division be-

tween any two. Romantic novels were still being written when realism and naturalism were flourishing; realistic and naturalistic works appeared simultaneously; and the modernistic novels *Redención* and *La gloria de don Ramiro* were published about the same time that Payró's thoroughly realistic works made their appearance.

The story of the Argentine novel is that of a proud country evincing a dogged determination and unyielding vigor to reveal its identity in the field of fiction. Through its history, traditions, social customs, and distinguished citizens, Argentina has made known to its own people and the entire world its essential characteristics and enduring values. For writers, critics, and the vast public the novel has served a similar function. Besides, it has acted as an effective agent for propagating a sense of national consciousness and for furthering the spirit of literary accomplishment. In this respect the growth of the Argentine novel may be viewed from the following three points: 1) the formation of a distinctively national type of novel; 2) the acquiring of a wide reading public; 3) the appearance of the full-fledged novelist, the professional novelist. A consideration of these points would enable us to arrive at basic conclusions concerning the nineteenth-century novel.

With reference to the first point..... The majority of early writers manifested at least an attempt, feeble as it might have been, to reveal in their novels some aspect of Argentine life. At times the author's prologue would announce such a desire, as if it were primordial in his mind, but the contents of the work frequently belied his intent. Even in some of the early romantic novels which in general are lacking in Argentine elements, there may be found a shy mention of some Argentine type, social custom, or particular street. Many of these early writers recognized the necessity of portraying Argentine life, but lacked the ability or stimulus to define the national atmosphere and delineate characteristic types and institutions. Furthermore, it is interesting to note in this regard that the critics and publishers, in their eagerness to promote a national novel, would frequently single out in a work isolated and rather faint national elements, stressing the vital significance they had in the growth of Argentine fiction. As the nation matured and took on a more distinctive character, writers began to observe Argentina with increased interest and care, and they reflected that attention in their novels. The land, people, customs, politics, and society in general they looked at with more penetrating eyes and a more discerning mind. Argentina became a subject for study, analysis, and interpretation. The national novel thus came into being, first in sporadic attempts, as in *La familia de Sconner* and *El hogar en la pampa,* then rather unartistically with the blood-curdling novels of Eduardo Gutiérrez, and finally in full blush with Cambaceres, Groussac, Lucio López, Miró, Ocantos, and other realistic and naturalistic novelists.

With reference to the second point..... During the initial years of the Argentine novel the public turned to foreign artists for much of its reading in fiction. When Argentine authors began to turn out their highly romantic novels during the 1850's and 1860's, the public responded to these works with interest and curiosity, for it was eager to savor the first fruits of fiction written by its own countrymen. A more decided increase in the reading public was noticed as writers started to portray Argentine life and the national novel acquired a firm footing. Gutiérrez satisfied the tastes of the less fastidious reader; Cambaceres caused unprecedented scandal with his naturalistic works; Lucio López left an indelible impression on thousands of readers with his *Gran aldea;* and Ocantos interested thousands more with his charming *León Zaldívar* and other genial novels. Then in the twentieth century, with the highly successful novels of Hugo Wast and Manuel Gálvez, the Argentine public was finally won.

With reference to the third point...... From the brief biographical data we have furnished, it is noticed that the authors of the vast majority of nineteenth-century novels were men who did not make an exclusive career of fiction writing. They were men of versatile ability, who although earning their livelihood as journalists, lawyers, politicians, teachers, or public functionaries, at the same time cultivated the novel with talent and sincere interest. Many, enjoying a distinguished national reputation or excelling in particular fields of endeavor, published only one or two novels, but highly important ones in the history of that genre. During the early romantic period many novels came from the pen of young, obscure writers, who after their initial works dropped completely from the scene of fiction. Other romantic novels were written by feminine authors who, possessing general literary skill and considerable fame in artistic circles, attempted these works in part as an expression of their versatility. Finally, we make mention of the host of minor figures, of diverse fields of interest, who, endowed with a modicum of literary competency, tried their hand at novel writing in a somewhat haphazard and artificial fashion, as a literary exercise or avocation.

Only Cambaceres and Ocantos even approached the status of professional novelists. Nineteenth-century Argentine society was not ready to receive that type of writer, for it was virtually impossible for an author, however talented he might have been, to sustain himself exclusively on the proceeds of his novels. Owing to this condition, it is safe to assume that much novelistic talent remained undeveloped and even untested; yet, considering all, the number of writers who at least tried their fortune at fiction writing was truly impressive. It was not before the twentieth century, nevertheless, in the persons of Wast and Gálvez, that the true professional and full-fledged novelists appeared.

. . .

The development of the nineteenth-century Argentine novel was the result of the labor of a relatively large number of authors, each contributing one or two important works, rather than that of a few outstanding figures who monopolized the scene of fiction. In a cursory examination only the more worthy and popular novelists receive due attention, but in a comprehensive study such as ours the complete gamut of writers who shared in the story of the novel can be considered in their appropriate significance. In the 1850's and 1860's romanticism was sustained by such celebrated figures as Mármol, Cané, and Gorriti, by other national figures like Eduarda

Mansilla, Juana Manso, and Pedro Echagüe, and just as assiduously by many lesser known writers like Ángel J. Blanco,
Laurindo Lapuente, and Bernabé Demaría. It is in the growth
of realism that we most sharply see that the nineteenth-century
novel was in the main an aggregate product of many writers.
Alongside the noted Lucio López, Groussac, Ocantos, and
Miró, there stands an array of creditable but rather obscure
writers like Morante, Villafañe, Rivarola, Ortega, and Auzón,
all of whom took part in developing various manifestations
of the current of realism.   As an illustration we may consider
for a moment the novels of the financial crisis.   Here, one
novelist—José Miró—deservedly towers above the rest, and
his work *La bolsa* is the only novel of the group that has received wide recognition and acclaim. Yet the four other works
in the same group are worthy novels which, although not
equaling *La bolsa* in literary value, represent important realistic pieces and contribute significantly to the portrayal of a
most colorful period in the nation's history.

The naturalistic current in Argentina also reveals the aggregate nature of the novel in the nineteenth century. The
mention of the term Argentine naturalism generally brings to
mind the one figure of Cambaceres, almost to the exclusion of
other important writers. Yet significant as he is, Cambaceres
does not represent by himself the entire picture of naturalism.
For this complete portrayal it is necessary to consider, in addition to Cambaceres, the other novelists who wrote naturalistic
works and even those who only slightly revealed the influence
of naturalism.

Furthermore, in viewing the nineteenth-century novel in its
totality, we must not overlook the several types of novels that
remain in a somewhat isolated position, apart from the more
numerous works reflecting the currents of romanticism, realism, or naturalism. Thus, the novels portraying the indigenous
element, like *Painé* and *El cacique blanco,* mirrored a subject
of vital interest to the nation; Holmberg's novels of science
and the supernatural manifested the desire to understand the
universe; and the novels of criminal investigation of Luis V.

Varela revealed the concern of the author with legal ana social problems. Moreover, standing as an unusual and original piece of fiction is the allegorical satire on Hispanic-American civilization, *Peregrinación de Luz del Día*. All these novels, the themes of which are closely related to the authors' professional or special interests, indicate the variety of types of novels cultivated in the nineteenth century.

Varied and richly expressive of the Republic's pride in its national distinctiveness and fundamental worth, the Argentine novel of the nineteenth century may be understood in its totality as a meritorious literary record of the country in the vital process of development. It stands as the significant and noteworthy opening chapters in the continuously advancing story of Argentine fiction.

BIBLIOGRAPHY

I. Chronological List of Argentine Novels of the Nineteenth Century (including other pertinent works of early prose fiction).

ESTEBAN ECHEVERRÍA, *El matadero* (written about the year 1838). First published in *La Revista del Río de la Plata*, B.A., Imprenta de Mayo, 1871, I, 563-585.

JUAN MARÍA GUTIÉRREZ, *El hombre hormiga, artículo sobre costumbres de Buenos Aires en 1838*, in *El Iniciador de Montevideo*, Montevideo, June, 1838.

MARCOS SASTRE, *Cartas a Genuaria*, B.A., 1840.

JUAN MARÍA GUTIÉRREZ, *El capitán de Patricios* (written in 1843). First published in *El Correo del Domingo*, B.A., April 3 to April 17, 1864.

JUAN BAUTISTA ALBERDI, *Tobías, o la cárcel a la vela* (written in April, 1844). First published in *El Mercurio*, Valparaíso, 1851.

JUANA MANUELA GORRITI, *La quena*, in *La Revista de Lima*, Lima, 1845.

JUANA MANSO DE NORONHA, *Los misterios del Plata* (written in 1846). First available edition, B.A., Imprenta Los Mellizos, 1899.

BARTOLOMÉ MITRE, *Soledad*, La Paz, Imprenta de la Época, 1847.

BARTOLOMÉ MITRE, *Memorias de un botón de rosa*, Valparaíso, 1848.

JOSÉ MÁRMOL, *Amalia*, Montevideo, 1851, Vol. I.

MIGUEL CANÉ, *Esther* (concluded in May, 1851). First published in Biblioteca Americana, ed. Magariños Cervantes, B.A., Imprenta de Mayo, 1858, IV, 25-105.

MIGUEL CANÉ, *Una noche de boda* (written in September, 1854). First published in Biblioteca Americana, ed. Magariños Cervantes, B.A., Imprenta de Mayo, 1858, III, 215-256.

VICENTE FIDEL LÓPEZ, *La novia del hereje, o la Inquisición de Lima*, B.A., Imprenta de Mayo, 1854.

JUANA MANSO DE NORONHA, *La familia del comendador*, B.A., Imprenta de J. A. Bernheim, 1854.

JOSÉ MÁRMOL, *Amalia*, B.A., Imprenta Americana, 1855, Vols. I and II.

ÁNGEL JULIO BLANCO, *Una venganza funesta*, B.A., Imprenta Americana, 1856.

ESTANISLAO DEL CAMPO, *Camila, o la virtud triunfante*, B.A., Imprenta de la Revista, 1856.

FRANCISCO LÓPEZ TORRES, *La huérfana de Pago Largo*, B.A., Imprenta del Plata, 1856.

FEDERICO BARBARÁ, *El prisionero de Santos Lugares*, B.A., Imprenta de Las Artes, 1857.

ÁNGEL JULIO BLANCO, *Emeterio de Leao*—continuación de *Una venganza funesta*, B.A., Imprenta Americana, 1857.

LAURINDO LAPUENTE, *El Herminio de la Nueva Troya*, B.A., Imprenta de la Reforma Pacífica, 1857.

MARGARITA RUFINA OCHAGAVIA, *Un ángel y un demonio, o el valor de un juramento*, B.A., Imprenta de Mayo, 1857.

CARLOS L. PAZ, *Santa y mártir de veinte años*, B.A., Imprenta de la Reforma, 1857.

JOSÉ V. ROCHA, *Un drama de la vida*, B.A., 1857.

MANUEL ROMANO, *El isleño—episodio de la guerra de la independencia,* B.A., Imprenta Americana, 1857.

TORIBIO ARAUZ, *Aurora y Enrique, o sea La Guerra Civil,* B.A., Imprenta de Mayo, 1858.

MIGUEL CANÉ, *La familia de Sconner,* in Biblioteca Americana, ed. Magariños Cervantes, B.A., Imprenta de Mayo, 1858, IV, 106-219.

TOMÁS GUTIÉRREZ, *Carlota, o la hija del pescador,* in *La Tribuna,* B.A., April 20 to April 28, 1858.

LAURINDO LAPUENTE, *Virtud y amor hasta la tumba,* B.A., Imprenta de la Reforma, 1858.

FRANCISCO LÓPEZ TORRES, *La virgen de Lima,* B.A., 1858.

ÁNGEL JULIO BLANCO, *Luis y Estevan,* in *Museo Literario,* B.A., January 20, 1859.

EUSEBIO F. GÓMEZ, *Angélica, o una víctima de sus amores,* Paraná, Imprenta de El Nacional Argentino, 1859.

TOMÁS N. GIRÁLDEZ, *Vengador y suicida,* B.A., Imprenta de Pedro Gautier, 1860.

ROSA GUERRA, *Lucía Miranda,* B.A., Imprenta Americana, 1860.

ERNESTO O. LOISEAU, *Hojas de mirto,* B.A., Imprenta de la Reforma, 1860.

EDUARDA MANSILLA DE GARCÍA, *Lucía Miranda,* in *La Tribuna,* B.A., May 10 to July 4, 1860.

EDUARDA MANSILLA DE GARCÍA, *El médico de San Luis,* B.A., Imprenta de La Paz, 1860.

MERCEDES ROSAS DE RIVERA, *María de Montiel,* B.A., Imprenta de la Revista, 1861.

RAMÓN MACHALI, *Emilia, o los efectos del coquetismo,* B.A., Imprenta de la Bolsa, 1862.

CORIOLANO MÁRQUEZ, *El pirata, o la familia de los condes de Osorno,* novela histórica, escrita en la cárcel pública de Buenos Aires, en el calabozo No. 5, en octubre de 1862, B.A., Imprenta de la Bolsa, 1863.

PEDRO ECHAGÜE, *Elvira, o el temple de alma de una sanjuanina,* San Juan, 1865. The novel was subsequently entitled *La Rinconada.*

JUANA MANUELA GORRITI, *El ángel caído,* in *Sueños y realidades,* B.A., Imprenta de Mayo, 1865, II, 3-86.

JUANA MANUELA GORRITI, *El guante negro,* in *Sueños y realidades,* B.A., Imprenta de Mayo, 1865, I, 69-106.

JUANA MANUELA GORRITI, *Gubi-Amaya,* in *Sueños y realidades,* B.A., Imprenta de Mayo, 1865, I, 107-200.

JUANA MANUELA GORRITI, *El tesoro de los incas,* in *Sueños y realidades,* B.A., Imprenta de Mayo, 1865, II, 87-133.

SANTIAGO ESTRADA, *El hogar en la pampa,* B.A., Imprenta del Siglo, 1866.

JOSÉ JOAQUÍN DE VEDIA, *Aventuras de un centauro de la América meridional,* ed. Santiago R. Pilotto, B.A., Imprenta del Orden, 1868.

BERNABÉ DEMARÍA, *Revelaciones de un manuscrito,* B.A., Imprenta Argentina de El Nacional, 1869.

ENRIQUE LÓPEZ, *El indicador positivista, o la novela enciclopédica,* B.A., Imprenta Española, 1869.

FORTUNATO A. SÁNCHEZ, *El ciego Rafael,* B.A., Imprenta tipográfica de Pablo E. Coni, 1870.

HÉCTOR F. VARELA, *Elisa Lynch,* B.A., Imprenta de La Tribuna, 1870.

JUAN BAUTISTA ALBERDI, *Peregrinación de Luz del Día, o viaje y aventuras de la Verdad en el Nuevo Mundo,* B.A., 1871.

NICANOR LARRAIN, *El alma de Jesús Pérez, o la justicia del terror,* San Juan, Imprenta de D. A. Luna, 1871.

EDUARDO L. HOLMBERG, *Viaje maravilloso del Sr. Nic-Nac al planeta Marte*, B.A., 1875.

JOSEFINA PELLIZA DE SAGASTA, *Margarita*, B.A., Establecimiento tipográfico de El Orden de W. Muntaner y Cía., 1875.

JUANA MANUELA GORRITI, *Juez y verdugo*, in *Panoramas de la vida*, B.A., Imprenta de Mayo, 1876, I, 239-347.

JUANA MANUELA GORRITI, *Peregrinaciones de una alma triste*, in *Panoramas de la vida*, B.A., Imprenta de Mayo, 1876, I, 17-238.

JUANA MANUELA GORRITI, *El pozo del Yocci*, in *Panoramas de la vida*, B.A., Imprenta de Mayo, 1876, I, 349-450.

EDUARDO L. HOLMBERG, *La pipa de Hoffmann*, in *El Plata Literario*, B.A., June 15 to September 15, 1876.

JOSEFINA PELLIZA DE SAGASTA, *La chiriguana*, in *Novelas Americanas*, B.A., Imprenta y administración, Santiago del Estero 176, 1877, pp. 3-32.

LUIS V. VARELA, *La huella del crimen*, in Biblioteca Económica de Autores Nacionales, B.A., Imprenta de Mayo, 1877.

LUIS V. VARELA, *Clemencia*—continuación de *La huella del crimen*, in Biblioteca de Autores Nacionales, B.A., Imprenta de Mayo, 1877.

LUIS J. ALBERT, *Lía*, B.A., Tipografía Borghese, 1879.

EDUARDO GUTIÉRREZ, *Juan Moreira*, in *La Patria Argentina*, November 28, 1879, to January 8, 1880.

EDUARDO GUTIÉRREZ, *Un capitán de ladrones en Buenos Aires*, B.A., Administración de La Patria Argentina, 1879.

EDUARDO L. HOLMBERG, *Horacio Kalibang, o los autómatas*, B.A., Imprenta de El Album del Hogar, 1879.

MALAQUÍAS MÉNDEZ, *Lucía*, Santa Fe, Imprenta El Santafesino, 1879.

ÁQUILES SIOEN, *Buenos Aires en el año 2080*, ed. Igon Hermanos, B.A., Librería del Colejio, 1879.

JORJE ALBERTO, *Estela*, B.A., 1880.

JOSÉ VICTORIANO CABRAL, *Lina Montalbán, o el terremoto que destruyó el Callao y la ciudad de Lima en 1746*, B.A., Imprenta del Porvenir, 1880.

JOSÉ MARÍA CANTILO, *La familia Quillango*, in *El Correo del Domingo*, B.A., January 4 to February 29, 1880.

EDUARDO GUTIÉRREZ, *Juan Cuello*, in *La Patria Argentina*, January 9 to March 19, 1880.

EDUARDO GUTIÉRREZ, *El jorobado*, in *La Patria Argentina*, March 22 to July 30, 1880.

EDUARDO GUTIÉRREZ, *Astucia de una negra*—continuación y fin de *El jorobado*, B.A., c. 1880.

EDUARDO GUTIÉRREZ, *Santos Vega*, B.A., Imprenta de La Patria Argentina, 1880.

EDUARDO GUTIÉRREZ, *Una amistad hasta la muerte*—continuación de *Santos Vega*, B.A., c. 1880.

EDUARDO GUTIÉRREZ, *El tigre del Quequén*, in *La Patria Argentina*, August 10 to November 16, 1880.

RICARDO GUTIÉRREZ, *Cristián*, B.A., Imprenta de La Patria Argentina, 1880.

LUIS V. VARELA, *El doctor Whüntz*, ed. Carlos Casavalle, B.A., 1880.

EDUARDO GUTIÉRREZ, *Los grandes ladrones*, in *La Patria Argentina*, August 4 to October 15, 1881.

EDUARDO GUTIÉRREZ, *Hormiga Negra*, in *La Patria Argentina*, October 16 to December 26, 1881.

EDUARDO GUTIÉRREZ, *Don Juan Manuel de Rosas*, in *La Patria Argentina*, December 27, 1881, to December 29, 1882.

EDUARDO GUTIÉRREZ, *Juan Sin Patria*, B.A., Imprenta de La Patria Argentina, 1881.

GUILLERMO QUIROGA, *Una sanjuanina, o sea Carolina*, San Juan, Imprenta de la Unión, 1881.

EUGENIO CAMBACERES, *Pot-pourri—silbidos de un vago*, B.A., Imprenta de M. Biedma, 1882.

LOLA LARROSA DE ANSALDO, *Las obras de misericordia*, B.A., Imprenta Ostwald, 1882.

EDUARDO GUTIÉRREZ, *La muerte de Buenos Aires—epopeya de 1880*, in *La Patria Argentina*, June 25 to December 29, 1882.

EDUARDO GUTIÉRREZ, *El asesinato de Álvarez*, in *La Patria Argentina*, December 30, 1882, to March 12, 1883.

EDUARDO GUTIÉRREZ, *Enterrados vivos*—continuación de *El asesinato de Álvarez*, in *La Patria Argentina*, March 13 to April 16, 1883.

EDUARDO GUTIÉRREZ, *Amor funesto*, in *La Patria Argentina*, April 17 to May 3, 1883.

EDUARDO GUTIÉRREZ, *Nicanora Fernández*, in *La Patria Argentina*, May 4 to May 21, 1883.

EDUARDO GUTIÉRREZ, *Doña Dominga Rivadavia*, in *La Patria Argentina*, May 29 to September 12, 1883.

EDUARDO GUTIÉRREZ, *Infamias de una madre*—continuación de *Doña Dominga Rivadavia*, B.A., c. 1883.

JULIO LLANOS, *Camila O'Gorman*, B.A., Imprenta de La Patria Argentina, 1883.

JULIO LLANOS, *El pirata del hogar—dramas sociales*, in *La Patria Argentina*, September 10 to October 25, 1883.

CARLOS MARÍA OCANTOS, *La cruz de la falta*, B.A., Imprenta de Pablo E. Coni, 1883.

JOSÉ OTEZA BUSTAMANTE, *Un acontecimiento en Tucumán*, B.A., Imprenta de R. M. Cañaberas, 1883.

JUAN ANTONIO ARGERICH, *Inocentes o culpables*, B.A., Imprenta del Courrier de la Plata, 1884.

EUGENIO CAMBACERES, *Música sentimental—silbidos de un vago*, ed. E. Denné, Paris, Imprenta Hispano-Americana, 1884.

PEDRO ECHAGÜE, La Chapanay, San Juan, Sanda y Yofré, 1884.

PEDRO S. LAMAS, *Silvia—episodios de la Guerra de la Independencia Americana*, Paris, Charaire e hijo, 1884.

JULIO LLANOS, *Un drama conjugal*, in *La Patria Argentina*, January 21 to February 17, 1884.

JULIO LLANOS, *Agustina de Libarona*, in *La Patria Argentina*, February 18 to February 28, 1884.

JULIO LLANOS, *El capitán Morillo—últimas víctimas de Rosas*, in *La Patria Argentina*, February 29 to March 12, 1884.

JULIO LLANOS, *La número 35—cuadros sociales*, in *La Patria Argentina*, March 13 to April 11, 1884.

LUIS A. MOHR, *Alberto Trejo—¿castigo del cielo o justicia de la tierra?*, in *La Patria Argentina*, March 15 to April 16, 1884.

JULIO LLANOS, *Ofelia*, in *La Patria Argentina*, April 12 to May 2, 1884. Subsequently the novel was entitled *Arturo Sierra*.

LUCIO VICENTE LÓPEZ, *La gran aldea*, in Sud-América, May 20 to July 2, 1884.

ENRIQUE E. RIVAROLA, *El arma de Werther—escenas de vida estudiantil*, in *La Patria Argentina*, June 29 to July 27, 1884. Subsequently the novel was entitled *Amar al vuelo*.

RAFAEL BARREDA, *Magistrados que matan*, in *La Patria Argentina*, July 28 to August 20, 1884.

PAUL GROUSSAC, *Fruto vedado*, in *Sud-América*, August 4 to October 4, 1884.

RAFAEL BARREDA, *La pera envenenada*, in *La Patria Argentina*, August 21 to September 28, 1884.

JUAN DE LÓRIGA, *Canuto Bochín—la comedia política*, in *La Patria Argentina*, October 1 to October 12, 1884.

EUGENIO CAMBACERES, *Sin rumbo*, ed. F. Lajouane, B.A., Imprenta de M. Biedma, 1885.

EDUARDO GUTIÉRREZ, *Los siete bravos*, B.A., c. 1885.

EDUARDA MANSILLA DE GARCÍA, *Un amor*, B.A., Imprenta de El Diario, 1885.

ROBERTO J. PAYRÓ, *Antígona*, B.A., Imprenta Sud-Americana, 1885.

MIGUEL LUCAS, *La reconquista de mi novia—cuadros sociales*, in *La Patria Argentina*, April 4 to April 17, 1885.

MIGUEL LUCAS, *Los descamisados—entre bastidores*, in *La Patria Argentina*, April 18 to May 4, 1885.

MARTÍN GARCÍA MEROU, *Marcos*, in *Sud-América*, April 25 to May 12, 1885. The novel was subsequently entitled *Ley social*.

MIGUEL LUCAS, *La carta—cuadros sociales*, in *La Patria Argentina*, May 5 to May 19, 1885.

JUAN LUSSICH, *El crimen de Barracas—la mujer embarrilada*, in *La Patria Argentina*, October 10 to November 10, 1885.

EDUARDO PIMENTEL AND MATILDE GUARDIOLA, *Los amantes del Pergamino*, in *La Patria Argentina*, December 1 to December 15, 1885.

C., *El ex-abrupto de don Cándido*, B.A., Imprenta de J. Peuser, 1886.

C., *Los celos y la electricidad*, B.A., Imprenta de J. Peuser, 1886.

BACHILLER CHURRUCA, *Políticos del día—tipos y escenas electorales*, B.A., 1886.

SILVERIO DOMÍNGUEZ, *Perfiles y medallones—panorama bonaerense, salón reservado*, B.A., Establecimiento tipográfico de Moreno y Núñez, 1886.

SILVERIO DOMÍNGUEZ, *Palomas y gavilanes*, ed. F. Lajouane, B.A., Libraire Générale, 1886.

PEDRO ECHAGÜE, *Cuatro noches en el mar, o sea Amalia y Amelia*, San Juan, Tipografía de la Unión, 1886.

EDUARDO GUTIÉRREZ, *Carlo Lanza*, B.A., Imprenta de P. Buffet, 1886.

EDUARDO GUTIÉRREZ, *Lanza el gran banquero—continuación de Carlo Lanza*, B.A., N. Tommasi, c. 1886.

EDUARDO GUTIÉRREZ, *El Chacho—Dramas militares*, B.A., N. Tommasi, 1886.

EDUARDO GUTIÉRREZ, *Los montoneros—Dramas militares*, B.A., N. Tommasi, c. 1886.

EDUARDO GUTIÉRREZ, *El rastreador—Dramas militares*, B.A., N. Tommasi, c. 1886.

EDUARDO GUTIÉRREZ, *La muerte de un héroe—Dramas militares*, B.A., c. 1886.

EDUARDO GUTIÉRREZ, *Los hermanos Barrientos*, B.A., N. Tommasi, 1886.

EDUARDO GUTIÉRREZ, *Ignacio Monges*, ed. N. Tommasi, B.A., Imprenta de El Orden, 1886.

EDUARDO GUTIÉRREZ, *Pastor Luna*, B.A., N. Tommasi, 1886.

KARL LEHARDY, *Clelia*, ed. F. Lajouane, B.A., Libraire Générale—51-53 Calle Perú, 1886.

LUIS A. MOHR, *Verdad y ficción*, B.A., Imprenta de El Censor, 1886.

ENRIQUE ORTEGA, *Una hora menguada*, B.A., Imprenta de J. Peuser, 1886.

ENRIQUE ORTEGA, *Vida porteña—Un drama íntimo y La familia H,*
B.A., La Plata, Imprenta de J. Peuser, 1886.

SEGUNDO I. VILLAFAÑE, *Don Lino Velázquez,* ed. F. Lajouane, B.A.,
Libraire Générale, 1886.

ESTANISLAO S. ZEBALLOS, *Painé y la dinastía de los zorros,* B.A., La
Plata, Imprenta de J. Peuser, 1886.

VENTURA AGUILAR, *Otilia—episodio de la guerra de Cuba,* ed. Emilio
de Mársico, B.A., 1887.

EUGENIO M. AUZÓN, *Severina,* B.A., Imprenta de M. Biedma, 1887.

ANTONIO BABUGLIA, *Nenna,* ed. Emilio de Mársico, B.A., 1887.

JOSÉ VICTORIANO CABRAL, *Amelia de Floriani, o el castillo del diablo,*
B.A., Imprenta de M. Biedma, 1887.

EUGENIO CAMBACERES, *En la sangre,* in *Sud-América,* September 12 to
November 14, 1887.

PASTOR M. CARBALLIDO, *Días sombríos,* ed. Llambías y Pardo, B.A., 1887.

ROBERTO J. PAYRÓ, *Scripta,* B.A., La Plata, Imprenta de J. Peuser, 1887.

ESTANISLAO S. ZEBALLOS, *Relmu, reina de los Pinares,* B.A., Imprenta
de J. Peuser, 1887.

VENTURA AGUILAR, *Noche penal,* B.A., Imprenta de Buffet y Bosch,
1888.

ANTONIO BABUGLIA, *Wanda,* ed. Emilio de Mársico, B.A., 1888.

MIGUEL BROWNE, *La primera conquista de Ésther,* B.A., 1888.

JUANA MANUELA GORRITI, *Oasis en la vida,* ed. F. Lajouane, B.A., 1888.

EDUARDO GUTIÉRREZ, *La mazorca,* B.A., N. Tommasi, 1888.

EDUARDO GUTIÉRREZ, *El puñal del terror,* B.A., N. Tommasi, 1888.

EDUARDO GUTIÉRREZ, *Una tragedia de doce años,* B.A., N. Tommasi, c.
1888.

LOLA LARROSA DE ANSALDO, *Hija mía,* B.A., Imprenta de Juan A. Alsina, 1888.

ANTONIO B. MASSIOTI, *Tierra y cielo—estudio social bonaerense,* ed. F.
Lajouane, B.A., Imprenta de M. Biedma, 1888.

CARLOS MARÍA OCANTOS, *León Zaldívar,* Madrid, Imprenta de Fortanet,
1888.

ROBERTO J. PAYRÓ, *Novelas y fantasías—segunda serie de Scripta,* B.A.,
La Plata, Imprenta de J. Peuser, 1888.

SEGUNDO I. VILLAFAÑE, *Emilio Love,* ed. F. Lajouane, B.A., Imprenta
de Mackern y McLean, 1888.

VENTURA AGUILAR, *Castruccio—episodio novelesco de actualidad,* B.A.,
Imprenta de Buffet y Bosch, 1889.

LOLA LARROSA DE ANSALDO, *El lujo,* B.A., Imprenta de Juan A. Alsina,
1889.

ENRIQUE ORTEGA, *Los casamientos del diablo,* Paris, Librería Española
de Garnier Hermanos, 1889.

ENRIQUE ORTEGA, *Justos y pecadores,* Paris, Librería de Garnier Hermanos, 1889.

MANUEL T. PODESTÁ, *Irresponsable,* B.A., Imprenta de La Tribuna Nacional, 1889.

MARCOS F. ARREDONDO, *Carmen, o batallas de la vida,* B.A., Imprenta
Rápida, 1890.

EUGENIO M. AUZÓN, *Conflicto entre dos amores,* B.A., Imprenta Sud-
América, 1890.

MANUEL BAHAMONDE, *Abismos,* ed. F. Lajouane, B.A., Imprenta de M.
Biedma, 1890.

MANUEL BAHAMONDE, *Buenos Aires novelesco,* B.A., 1890.

MANUEL BAHAMONDE, *El último Dobaiba*, ed. A. Barreiro y Ramos, Montevideo, B.A., Imprenta de M. Biedma, 1890.

TEODORO Y. MARQUES, *Tragedia de la vida*, La Plata, Imprenta Americana de M. Cerdeña del Río y Cía, 1890.

FABIO MONROY, *El ángel de la virtud*, B.A., Imprenta Rápida, 1890.

ALBERTO DEL SOLAR, *Rastaquouère*, ed. F. Lajouane, B.A., 1890.

C. M. BLANCO, *Salvaje*, B.A., Barcelona, Casa editora Franco-Española, 1891.

CARLOS BLOMBERG, *El doctor Jacobo*, ed. Ignacio Mosquera, B.A., 1891.

JOSÉ MARÍA MIRÓ, *La bolsa*, B.A., Imprenta de la Nación, 1891.

CARLOS MARÍA OCANTOS, *Quilito*, Paris, Librería Española de Garnier Hermanos, 1891.

SEGUNDO I. VILLAFAÑE, *Horas de fiebre*, B.A., Imprenta de Juan A. Alsina, 1891.

MANUEL BAHAMONDE, *Mareos*, ed. B. Valdettaro, B.A., 1892.

CARLOS MARÍA OCANTOS, *Entre dos luces*, B.A., La Plata, and Rosario, Imprenta de J. Peuser, 1892.

FILIBERTO DE OLIVEIRA CÉZAR, *Los amores de una india—viaje al país de los Tobas*, B.A., La Plata, Imprenta de J. Peuser, 1892.

MANUEL T. PODESTÁ, *Alma de niña*, B.A., Imprenta de P. Coni e hijos, 1892.

GERVASIO MARQUES, *La liga*, B.A., Imprenta de la Nación, 1893.

CARLOS MARÍA OCANTOS, *El candidato—segunda parte de Entre dos luces*, B.A., La Plata, and Rosario, Imprenta de J. Peuser, 1893.

FILIBERTO DE OLIVEIRA CÉZAR, *El cacique blanco—costumbres de los araucanos en la pampa*, B.A., Casa editora de J. Peuser, 1893.

CARLOS MARÍA OCANTOS, *La Ginesa*, B.A., Imprenta de Pablo E. Coni e hijos, 1894.

FRANCISCO A. SICARDI, *Libro extraño*, B.A., 1894-1902.

ALBERTO DEL SOLAR, *Contra la marea*, ed. F. Lajouane, B.A., 1894.

UN ANTIGUO COMISARIO DE POLICÍA (sic), *El descuartizador—historia íntima de un asesino*, B.A., 1894.

CARLOS OCTAVIO BUNGE, *Mi amigo Luis*, B.A., Imprenta Elzeviriana, 1895.

LOLA LARROSA DE ANSALDO, *Los esposos*, B.A., Compañía Sud-Americana de Billetes de Banco, 1895.

ENRIQUE E. RIVAROLA, *Mandinga*, ed. Leopoldo López, B.A., 1895.

FRANCISCO GRANDMONTAGNE, *Teodoro Foronda—evoluciones de la sociedad argentina*, B.A., Tipografía La Vasconia, 1896, 2 vols.

EDUARDO L. HOLMBERG, *La bolsa de huesos*, B.A., Compañía Sud-Americana de Billetes de Banco, 1896.

EDUARDO L. HOLMBERG, *La casa endiablada*, B.A., Compañía Sud-Americana de Billetes de Banco, 1896.

EDUARDO L. HOLMBERG, *Nelly*, B.A., Compañía Sud-Americana de Billetes de Banco, 1896.

VICENTE FIDEL LÓPEZ, *La loca de la guardia*, ed. Carlos Casavalle, B.A., Imprenta de Mayo, 1896.

GERVASIO MARQUES, *En la sierra*, ed. Ángel Estrada y Cía, B.A., Imprenta de Juan A. Alsina, 1896.

PEDRO G. MORANTE, *Grandezas*, ed. F. Lajouane, B.A., 1896.

CARLOS MARÍA OCANTOS, *Tobi*, Madrid, Imprenta del sucursal de J. Cruzado, a cargo de Felipe Márquez, 1896.

ISAAC R. PEARSON, *Patria*, B.A., Imprenta La Revista, 1896.

ADOLFO SALDÍAS, *Bianchetto—la patria del trabajo*, ed. F. Lajouane, B.A., 1896.

GUILLERMO STOCK, *El valor de la vida*, B.A., 1896.
JOSÉ VICTORIANO CABRAL, *La campana de San Telmo y la conspiración de 1839 contra el dictador Rosas*, B.A., Imprenta de M. Biedma e hijo, 1897.
CARLOS MARÍA OCANTOS, *Promisión*, Madrid, Establecimiento tipográfico de I. Moreno, 1897.
FRANCISCO GRANDMONTAGNE, *La maldonada*, B.A., Imprenta Artística, 1898.
CARLOS MARÍA OCANTOS, *Misia Jeromita*, Madrid, Establecimiento tipográfico de I. Moreno, 1898.
JOSÉ MARÍA VÉLEZ, *La casta*, Córdoba, Tipografía La Minerva de Alfonso Aveta, 1898.
JOSÉ LUIS CANTILO, *Quimera*, B.A., Librería Bredahl, 1899.
EDUARDO GUTIÉRREZ, *Una demanda curiosa*, Obras Inéditas, B.A., Schurer-Stolle, 1899.
EDUARDO GUTIÉRREZ, *Un viaje infernal*, Obras Inéditas, B.A., 1899.
ISAAC R. PEARSON, *El triunfo del siglo*, B.A., Imprenta La Revista, 1899.
AMARANTO T. RIVERO, *Guantes blancos y conciencias negras*, ed. Ángel S. Maranta, B.A., 1899.

Inasmuch as the novels of Carlos María Ocantos, whom we consider at length in our study, reach into the twentieth century, it is well to list the remaining works of this author.

Pequeñas miserias, Madrid, 1900.
Don Perfecto, Barcelona, Montaner y Simón, 1902.
Nebulosa, Madrid, Establecimiento tipográfico de I. Moreno, 1904.
El peligro, Madrid, Imprenta de Valentín Tordesillas, 1911.
Riquez—memorias de un viejo verde, Madrid, Imprenta de Valentín Tordesillas, 1914.
Fru Jenny—seis novelas danesas, Paris, B.A., Casa Editorial Hispano-Americana, 1915.
El camión—seis novelas españolas, Madrid, Tipografía de la Revista de Archivos, Bibliotecas, y Museos, 1922.
Victoria, Madrid, Imprenta de la Revista de Archivos, ... , 1922.
La cola de paja, Madrid, Tipografía de la Revista de Archivos, . . . , 1923.
La ola, Madrid, Tipografía de la Revista de Archivos, ... , 1925.
El secreto del doctor Barbado, Madrid, Imprenta de G. Hernández y Galo Sáez, 1926.
Tulia, Madrid, Imprenta G. Hernández y Galo Sáez, 1927.
El emboscado, Madrid, Imprenta G. Hernández y Galo Sáez, 1928.
Fray Judas, Madrid, Imprenta G. Hernández y Galo Sáez, 1929.

II. Bibliographies, Book Catalogues, Library Catalogues, Bulletins, Bibliographical Yearbooks, Biographical Dictionaries, and Similar Sources of Reference for a Study of the Argentine Novel.

Academia Literaria del Plata. *Catálogo de la Biblioteca.* B.A., Casa Editora Alfa y Omega, 1912.
Asociación Bernardino Rivadavia. *Catálogo de la Biblioteca Popular del Municipio.* B.A., 1926.
Asociación Biblioteca Sarmiento. *Catálogo de la Biblioteca Pública Tucumán*, 1909. Tucumán, La Velocidad, 1910.

Besterman, Theodore. *A World Bibliography of Bibliographies and of Bibliographical Catalogues, Calendars, Abstracts, Digests, Indexes, and the like.* London, Privately published by the author, 25 Park Crescent, 1947.

Biblioteca y Museo Popular de San Fernando. *Catálogo de los libros, mapas, cuadros, bustos, y demás objetos que contiene.* B.A., Taller tipográfico de la Penitenciaria, 1890.

Biedma, José Juan and Pillado, José Antonio. *Diccionario biográfico argentino.* B.A., Imprenta de M. Biedma e hijo, 1897. Unfinished; work includes only letters "A-Abra."

Binayán, Narciso. "Bibliografía de bibliografías argentinas," *La Revista de la Universidad de Buenos Aires,* año XVI, B.A., 1919.

Boletín bibliográfico sudamericano de la imprenta y librería Mayo de Carlos Casavalle. B.A., Imprenta de Mayo, 1870.

Briseño, Ramón. *Estadística bibliográfica de la literatura chilena.* Santiago de Chile, Imprenta Chilena, 1862, 2 vols.

Cabot, Acisclo M. (son). *Bibliografía de 1866.* B.A., Imprenta Española, 1867.

Casavalle, Carlos. *Boletín bibliográfico sud-americano, y extracto del catálogo.* B.A., 1870.

Casavalle, Carlos. *Catálogo de los libros argentinos editados y expuestos por Carlos Casavalle, con explicaciones y juicios críticos acerca de ellos.* B.A., Imprenta de Mayo, 1882.

Catálogo de la Biblioteca del Club del Progreso. B.A., Imprenta de Antonio Molinari, 1913.

Catálogo de la Biblioteca de Jockey Club. B.A. Talleres gráficos argentinos de L. J. Rosso, 1919.

Catálogo de la Biblioteca de La Prensa. B.A., Imprenta de G. Kraft, 1916.

Catálogo de la Biblioteca Sarmiento Popular. Tucumán, Imprenta de El Orden, 1888.

Catálogo de libros argentinos (y algunos de otros países de América), en el que figuran numerosos libros raros y colecciones agotados. B.A., J. Lajouane y Cía, 1936.

Catálogo general de la Librería Española e Hispanoamericana, años 1901-1930. Cámaras Oficiales del Libro de Madrid y de Barcelona, Vols. I-IV, Letters A-Q.

Catálogo metódico de la Biblioteca Nacional, seguido de una tabla alfabética de autores. B.A., Taller tipográfico de la Biblioteca Nacional, 1911, Tomo III, Literatura.

Coester, Alfred Lester. *A Tentative Bibliography of the Belles-lettres of the Argentine Republic.* Cambridge, Mass., Harvard University Press, 1933.

Cortés, José Domingo. *Diccionario biográfico americano.* Paris, Tipografía Lahure, 1875.

Echevarrieta, A. Marcelo. *Diccionario biográfico de la República Argentina.* B.A., 1940.

Estrada, Dardo. *Historia y bibliografía de la imprenta en Montevideo, 1810-1865.* Montevideo, Librería Cervantes, 1912.

Extracto del catálogo de la librería de Mayo de Carlos Casavalle, B.A., Imprenta de Mayo, n.d.

Figueroa, Pedro P. *Miscelánea biográfica americana.* Santiago de Chile, Imprenta de la Unión, 1888.

García, Perfecto. *Bibliografía americana. Especialidad en obras de autores argentinos, repertorio alfabético, con un apéndice por orden cronológico de algunos libros y folletos raros, 1796-1853.* B.A., 1916.

216 MYRON I. LICHTBLAU

Grismer, Raymond L.; Lepine, Joseph E.; and Olmsted, Richard H. *A Bibliography of Articles on Spanish Literature.* Minneapolis, Burgess Publishing Co., 1933.

Grismer, Raymond L. *A New Bibliography of the Literatures of Spain and Spanish America.* Minneapolis, Taylor-made Perine Book Co. 1941.

Grismer, Raymond L. *A Reference Index to Twelve Thousand Spanish American Authors.* N. Y., The H. W. Wilson Co., 1939.

Grosvenor Library, Catalogue of Books on Latin America. Buffalo, The Grosvenor Library, 1901.

Gutiérrez, Juan María. *Bibliografía de la primera imprenta de Buenos Aires. Revista de Buenos Aires,* B.A., 1866, Vols. VIII, IX, X.

Jones, Cecil Knight. *Argentine Books Presented to the George Washington University Library. Modern Language Journal,* N. Y., 1927, XII, 42-44.

Jones, Cecil Knight. "Hispano-Americana in the Library of Congress." *Hispanic American Historical Review,* 1919, II, 96-104.

Lamas, Andrés. *Colección de obras, documentos y noticias inéditas, o poco conocidas, para servir a la historia física, política, y literaria del Río de la Plata.* B.A., Imprenta Popular, 1873.

Leavitt, Sturgis E. *Argentine Literature; a Bibliography of Literary Criticism, Biography and Literary Controversy.* University of North Carolina Studies in Language and Literature, I, Chapel Hill, 1924.

Libros argentinos—catálogo de la librería de Mayo del Sr. D. Carlos Casavalle. B.A., 1880-1885.

Lovell y Sainz de Aja, Alfredo. *Seudónimos, anagramas, criptónimos, alónimos, títulos nobiliarios, etc., usados por escritores.* Rosario, Argentina, 1950.

Luquiens, Frederick Bliss. *Spanish American Literature in the Yale University Library.* New Haven, Yale University Press, 1939.

Malariño, Joaquín E. *Diccionario parlamentario del Congreso.* B.A., 1890.

Martínez, Benigno T. *Diccionario biográfico-bibliográfico de escritores antiguos y modernos nacidos en los países del habla castellana.* B.A., 1866. Only introduction was published.

Medina, José Toribio. *Diccionario de anónimos y seudónimos hispano-americanos.* Publicaciones del Instituto de Investigaciones Históricas, XXVI, B.A., Imprenta de la Universidad, 1925, Vols. I and II.

Memoria de la secretaría y tesorería del Colegio Nacional de la Capital, año 1884. B.A., Taller tipográfico de la Penitenciaria, 1885.

Mendilaharzu, Fortunato. *Bibliografía general argentina.* B.A., Talleres gráficos argentinos de L. J. Rosso, 1929.

Molina Arrotea, Carlos; et al. *Diccionario biográfico nacional.* Nos. 1 and 2, B.A., Imprenta Rivadavia de Manuel Sánchez y Cía, 1877; Nos. 3 and 4, B.A., Imprenta de M. Biedma, 1879, 1881.

Muzzio, Julio A. *Diccionario histórico biográfico de la República Argentina.* Librería La Facultad de J. Roldán, 1920.

Navarro Viola, Alberto. *Anuario bibliográfico de la República Argentina, 1879-1887.* B.A., Imprenta del Mercurio, 1880-1887, 8 vols. From 1885 to 1887 Enrique Navarro Viola edited the work.

Scotto, José Arturo. *Notas biográficas publicadas en la sección "Efemérides americanas" de la Nación, en los años 1907-1909.* B.A., L. J. Rosso y Cía, 1910.

Torres Caicedo, José M. *Ensayos biográficos y de crítica literaria sobre los principales poetas y literatos hispanoamericanos.* 1st series, Paris, Librería de Guillaumin y Cía, 1863; 2nd series, Paris, Librería Europea, 1868.

Udaondo, Enrique. *Diccionario biográfico argentino.* B.A., Imprenta y Casa editora Coni, 1938.

Victorica, Ricardo. *Errores y omisiones del "Diccionario de anónimos y seudónimos hispanoamericanos de J. T. Medina."* B.A., 1928.

Victorica, Ricardo. *Nueva Epanortosis al "Diccionario de anónimos y seudónimos" de J. T. Medina.* B.A., 1929.

Yaben, Jacinto R. *Biografías argentinas y sudamericanas.* B.A., Editorial Metrópolis, 1938, 5 vols.

Zinny, Antonio. *Catálogo general razonado de las obras adquiridas en las Provincias Argentinas, a las que agregan muchas otras más o menos raras.* B.A., 1887.

III. Books and Articles on Individual Authors and Individual Novels (list is arranged chronologically according to author treated).

Ventura Aguilar

Ventura Aguilar. *Otros horizontes.* Montevideo, Imprenta La Colonia Española, 1886. The work contains autobiographical material.

Juan Bautista Alberdi

Anon. "Peregrinación de Luz del Día." *La Nación,* June 24, 1875.

José Manuel Estrada. "Examen crítico de Peregrinación de Luz del Día." *Revista del Río de la Plata,* B.A., 1876, XI, 86-139.

Martín García Merou. "Peregrinación de Luz del Día." Prologue to novel in edition of La Cultura Argentina, B.A., 1916.

Ricardo Rojas. "Luz del Día en América." Prologue to novel in Biblioteca Argentina, B.A., 1916.

José María Rosa. "Peregrinación de Luz del Día." Prologue to novel in Editorial Choele-Choel, B.A., n.d.

Juan Antonio Argerich

Anon. "Inocentes o culpables." *La Patria Argentina,* June 22, 1884, p. 4.

Anon. "Inocentes o culpables." *La Ilustración Argentina,* July 10, 1884, p. 150.

Juan Santos. "La Novela en El Plata—Inocentes o culpables." *La Prensa,* March 1, 1885, p. 3.

Anon. "Juan Antonio Argerich." *La Prensa,* August 22, 1924, p. 8.

Eugenio M. Auzón

Remember (sic). "Severina." *Sud-América,* June 16, 1887, p. 4.

Santiago Vaca Guzmán. "Severina." Prologue to work, B.A., Imprenta de M. Biedma, 1887. This article also appeared in *La Patria,* June 16, 1887, p. 4.

Anon. "Eugenio M. Auzón." *El Hogar,* B.A., September 9, 1927, p. 5.

Anon. "Eugenio M. Auzón." *La Prensa,* August 19, 1936, p. 6.

Antonio Babuglia

Félix Leo. "Nenna." *La Patria,* May 28, 1887, p. 2.

Manuel Bahamonde

María Bahamonde de Sánchez Caballero. "Datos biográficos de Manuel Bahamonde." Prologue to *Al pie de la castilla* by Manuel Bahamonde, B.A., Imprenta López, 1936, p. 5.

Ángel Julio Blanco

Ángel Julio Blanco. Letter to Rufino Varela revealing autobiographical data. *La Tribuna,* March 2, 1859, p. 2.

Álbano Honores. "Ángel Julio Blanco." *El Tiempo,* April 9, 1898, p. 3.

Carlos Octavio Bunge

Anon. "Carlos Octavio Bunge." *La Prensa,* May 23, 1918, p. 8.

José Victoriano Cabral

Anon. "Lina Montalván, de José V. Cabral." *El Nacional,* April 15, 1880, p. 3.

Anon. "José V. Cabral." *La Nación,* January 10, 1915, p. 5.

Eugenio Cambaceres

Anon. "Pot-pourri—silbidos de un vago." *La Nueva Revista de Buenos Aires,* año II, B.A., 1882, V, 569-572.

Sam Weller, "Música sentimental." *El Diario,* September 28, 1884, p. 4.

Miguel Cané. "Música sentimental." *Sud-América,* September 30, 1884, p. 2.

Anon. "Noticia sobre Sin rumbo." *Sud-América,* October 29, 1885, p. 2.

Arturo Giménez Pastor. "Música sentimental." Introduction to novel in Editorial Minerva, 1924.

Carlos Alberto Leumann. "Eugenio Cambaceres—en el centenario de su nacimiento." *La Prensa,* August 8, 1943, Sec. II, p. 1.

Roberto F. Giusti. "Un escritor porteño: Eugenio Cambaceres." *La Prensa,* November 29, 1943, supplement, Sec. II, p. 1.

Miguel Cané (father)

Anon. "La familia de Sconner." *La Tribuna,* September 4, 1858, p. 2.

Vicente Fidel López. "Ésther." A letter to Miguel Cané in Biblioteca Americana, B.A., November, 1858, IV, 268-271.

C. M. de Viel Castel. "Ésther." *La Tribuna,* December 6, 1858, p. 3.

Manuel Mujica Láinez. *Miguel Cané (padre), un romántico porteño.* B.A., Ediciones C.E.P.A., 1942.

José Luis Cantilo

Anon. "José Luis Cantilo." *La Prensa,* October 12, 1944, p. 6.

José María Cantilo

Anon. "José María Cantilo." *La Patria,* June 8, 1877, p. 2.

Anon. "José María Cantilo." *La Nación,* March 15, 1949, p. 4.

Bernabé Demaría

Josefina Pelliza de Sagasta. "Revelaciones de un manuscrito, de Bernabé Demaría." Letter to Demaría, signed January 12, 1871, included in the 1906 edition of the novel, B.A., Imprenta Europea de M. A. Rosas, 1906.

Silverio Domínguez

Ceferino de la Costa. "Una carta a Ceferino de la Calle." *Sud-América,* October 7, 1886, p. 4.

Legajo #8941. Facultad de Ciencias Médicas de la Universidad de Buenos Aires, n.d. This document gives biographical information concerning the author.

Pedro Echagüe

Alfredo Monla Figueroa. "La Rinconada y La Chapanay." Part of appendix to the 1924 edition of *La Rinconada,* B.A., Imprenta Coni, 1924.

Margarita Mugnos de Escudero. "Dos novelas regionales—La Rinconada y La Chapanay." Prologue to the volume that includes both novels, B.A., El Ateneo, 1931.

Santiago Estrada

C. (sic). "El hogar en la pampa." *El Correo del Domingo,* July 29, 1866, pp. 34-35.

L. D. Desteffanis. "El hogar en la pampa." *El Correo del Domingo,* August 19, 1866, pp. 85-86.

Martín García Merou
A. A. "Ley social." *La Patria,* December 21, 1885, p. 4.
Eugenio Cambaceres. "Ley social." *Sud-América,* December 28, 1885, p. 2.
Adolfo Mitre. "Ley social." A letter to author of novel, in *Sud-América,* December 30, 1885, p. 2.

Juana Manuela Gorriti
Rafael Obligado. "La señora doña M. Gorriti y sus obras." *La Revista Literaria,* B.A., April 1, 1875, pp. 114-117.
Francisco Sosa. "Juana Manuela Gorriti." *Revista Nacional,* B.A., 1892, XVI, 351-360.
Santiago Estrada. "Juana Manuela Gorriti." *Revista Nacional,* B.A., 1892, XVI, 361-367.
Walter G. Weyland. "Juana Manuela Gorriti." Prologue to *Narraciones,* Vol. XX of Clásicos Argentinos, B.A., Ediciones Estrada, 1946.

Francisco Grandmontagne
Anon. "Teodoro Foronda." Announcement of coming publication of novel, in *La Nación,* October 14, 1896, p. 4.
Anon. "Francisco Grandmontagne." *La Prensa,* June 2, 1936, p. 11.

Paul Groussac
Anon. "Fruto vedado." *La Patria Argentina,* October 8, 1884, p. 3.
Sam Weller. "Fruto vedado." *El Diario,* October 10, 1884, p. 4.
Tito (sic). "Fruto vedado." *La Prensa,* October 10, 1884, p. 3.
Juan Santos. "La novela en el Plata—Fruto vedado," *Sud-América,* March 3, 1885, p. 4.
Anon. "Paul Groussac." *La Prensa,* June 28, 1929, p. 15.
Alfonso de la Ferrere. "Paul Groussac." *Nosotros,* B.A., July, 1929, LXV, 9-15.
Juan B. González. "Groussac, novelista." Nosotros, B.A., July, 1929, LXV, 132-147.
Juan Canter. "Fruto vedado." *Nosotros,* B.A., June, 1930, LXVIII, 359-379.

Rosa Guerra
Anon. "Lucía Miranda, de Rosa Guerra." A letter to author of novel, in *La Tribuna,* June 26, 1860, p. 3.
Juan F. Segui. "Lucía Miranda, de Rosa Guerra." *La Tribuna,* August 12, 1860, p. 4.

Eduardo Gutiérrez
Pilar Lusarreta. "Un novelista malogrado—Eduardo Gutiérrez." *La Nación,* December 7, 1941, Sec. II, p. 2.

Eduardo L. Holmberg
J. C. "Viaje maravilloso del Sr. Nic-Nac al planeta Marte." *El Plata Literario,* May 15, 1876, pp. 21-26.
Joaquín V. González. "Nelly." *La Prensa,* January 26, 1896, p. 4.
Miguel Escalada. "Nelly." *La Nación,* October 6, 1896, p. 2.
Anon. "Eduardo L. Holmberg." *La Prensa,* November 5, 1937, p. 12.

Pedro S. Lamas
Pedro S. Lamas. "Silvia." A letter from Paris to Dr. Ignacio Gutiérrez Ponce, in *El Nacional,* May 2, 1885, p. 4, containing information about the author and his work.
Eduarda Mansilla de García. "Silvia, de Pedro S. Lamas." *El País,* June 14, 1902, p. 5. Article originally dated May 29, 1885.
Anon. "Pedro S. Lamas." *La Nación,* January 4, 1922, p. 5.

Laurindo Lapuente

Hermilio. "Virtud y amor hasta la tumba." *La Espada de Lavalle*, B.A., July 22, 1858, p. 4.

Anon. "Laurindo Lapuente." *La República*, B.A., November 17, 1870, p. 2.

Manuel Argerich. "Laurindo Lapuente." A discourse reproduced in *La República*, B.A., November 18, 1870, p. 2.

Pedro Goyena. "Laurindo Lapuente." *La Revista Argentina*, B.A., 1871, X, 169-179.

Nicanor Larrain

Anon. "Nicanor Larrain." *La Nación*, January 9, 1940, p. 5.

Anon. "Nicanor Larrain." *La Prensa*, January 12, 1940, p. 16.

Lola Larrosa de Ansaldo

Federico Tobal. "Hija mía, de Lola Larrosa de Ansaldo." Part of prologue to her novel *Los esposos*, B.A., 1893.

Anon. "Dos palabras sobre la autora—Lola Larrosa de Ansaldo." Part of prologue to her novel *Los esposos*, B.A., 1893 .

Karl Lehardy

Anon. "Clelia, de Lehardy." *La Patria*, August 5, 1886, p. 3.

Julio Llanos

Anon. "Julio Llanos." *La Nación*, March 27, 1933, p. 5.

Anon. "Julio Llanos." *La Prensa*, March 28, 1933, p. 12.

Lucio Vicente López

Anon. "La gran aldea." *Sud-América*, July 21, 1884, p. 4.

Sam Weller. "La gran aldea." *El Diario*, August 5, 1884, p. 3.

Juan Santos. "La gran aldea." *La Prensa*, May 9, 1885, p. 2.

Vicente Fidel López

Miguel Cané. "La novia del hereje." An article dated December 11, 1855, appearing in *La Revista de Buenos Aires*, año I, No. 8, B.A., 1863, II, 624-632.

Francisco López Torres

Anon. "Francisco López Torres." *La Nación*, March 23, 1871, p. 4.

Tomás Moncayo. *Discurso en la tumba del Dr. Francisco López Torres*. B.A., Imprenta Calle Garantías, número 212, 1871.

Juan Lussich

Anon. "Juan Lussich." *La Prensa*, November 18, 1885, p. 3.

Eduarda Mansilla de García

Rafael Pombo. "Eduarda Mansilla de García." Preface to novel *El médico de San Luis*, B.A., 1860.

Lucio V. Mansilla. "Más sobre la historia de la novela en La América del Sud—Eduarda Mansilla de García." *Revista de Buenos Aires*, año I, No. 2, B.A., 1863, I, 297-301.

Juan María Gutiérrez. "El médico de San Luis." *Revista de Ciencias y Letras del Círculo Literario de Buenos Aires*, B.A., 1864, I, No. I, 69-79.

Ventura de la Vega. "El médico de San Luis." *Revista de Ciencias y Letras del Círculo Literario de Buenos Aires*, B.A., 1864, I, No. I, 79-87.

Juana Manso de Noronha

Cora Oliva. "Conversaciones literarias—la novela." *La Ondina del Plata*, B.A., July 8, 1877, pp. 311-314.

José Mármol

José Mármol. "Amalia." Notice to public, in *El Paraná*, B.A., October 25, 1852, p. 2.

Mariano A. Pelliza. "Amalia." *La Ilustración Argentina,* B.A., November 30, 1883, pp. 385-386.
Adolfo Mitre. "Amalia." Prologue to novel, edition of Clásicos Argentinos, XIV, B.A., Ediciones Estrada, 1944.

Gervasio Marques

Segundo I. Villafañe. "Gervasio Marques." *La Nación,* March 6, 1893, p. 2.

José María Miró

Alberto del Solar. "Un bello libro—La bolsa." *La Nación,* November 9, 1891, p. 2.
Ernesto Quesada. *Dos novelas sociológicas—La bolsa y Quilito.* B.A., La Plata and Rosario, Imprenta de J. Peuser, 1892.
Adolfo Mitre. "La bolsa." Prologue to novel, edition of Clásicos Argentinos, XXI, B.A., Ediciones Estrada, 1946.

Bartolomé Mitre

Antonio Pagés Larraya. "Las ediciones de Soledad." *Logos,* Revista de la Facultad de Filosofía y Letras de la Universidad de Buenos Aires, año II, No. 3, B.A., 1943, pp. 110-114.

Luis A. Mohr

Anon. "Luis A. Mohr." *La Nación,* June 25, 1929, p. 8.

Carlos María Ocantos

Calixto Oyuela. "La cruz de la falta." *Revista Científica y Literaria,* B.A., 1883, I, 62-64.
Anon. "La cruz de la falta." *La Nueva Revista de Buenos Aires,* B.A., 1883, VIII, 659-668.
J. A. A. "León Zaldívar." *Sud-América,* March 6, 1886, p. 4.
J. Ortega Munilla. "León Zaldívar." A letter from Madrid to the editor of *La Nación,* in *La Nación,* May 11, 1888, p. 3.
Ready (sic). "Entre dos luces." *La Prensa,* December 9, 1892, p. 3.
Anon. "Tobi." *La Prensa,* March 11, 1896, p. 4.
Theodore Andersson. *Carlos María Ocantos—Argentine Novelist.* New Haven, Yale University Press, 1934.

Margarita Rufina Ochagavia

Francisco Bilbao. "Un ángel o un demonio, por M. Rufina Ochagavia." *La Revista del Nuevo Mundo,* Nos. 1 and 2, B.A., July 11, 1857, pp. 331-336.
Anon. "Un ángel o un demonio." *La Prensa,* November 18, 1857, p. 2.

Filiberto de Oliveira Cézar

Anon. "Filiberto de Oliveira Cézar." *La Nación,* November 26, 1910, p. 13.

Enrique Ortega

L. B. "Enrique Ortega." *Sud-América,* January 12, 1887, p. 4.
Anon. "Enrique Ortega." *La Nación,* October 17, 1912, p. 11.
Anon. "Enrique Ortega." *La Prensa,* October 17, 1912, p. 12.

Isaac R. Pearson

————. *Patria, novela argentina por Isaac R. Pearson—juicios favorables y adversos.* B.A., Tipografía La Revista, 1896.
Francisco Durá. "El triunfo del siglo, de Isaac R. Pearson." Prologue to novel, B.A., Imprenta de la Revista, 1899.
Anon. "Isaac R. Pearson." *La Nación,* August 24, 1945, p. 6.
Anon. "Isaac R. Pearson." *La Prensa,* August 24, 1945, p. 16.

Josefina Pelliza de Sagasta

José Francisco López. "Margarita, por Josefina Pelliza de Sagasta." *El Tribuno,* March 5, 1876, p. 3.

Manuel T. Podestá

Carlos Palma. "Impresiones literarias—Irresponsable." *La Patria,* January 27, 1890, p. 4.

Eduardo Saenz. "Irresponsable." A letter to the author of the novel, in *La Prensa,* February 1, 1890, p. 2.

N. Piñero. "Irresponsable." A letter to the author of the novel, in *La Nación,* February 25, 1890, p. 2.

Tirabeque. "Irresponsable." *La Prensa,* April 6, 1890 and April 12, 1890, p. 3.

Julián Martel. "Manuel T. Podestá—Alma de niña." *La Nación,* October 9, 1892, p. 3.

Anon. "Manuel T. Podestá." *La Nación,* August 10, 1920, p. 6.

Anon. "Manuel T. Podestá." *La Prensa,* August 10, 1920, p. 7.

Enrique Rivarola

A. A. "Enrique Rivarola." *La Ilustración Argentina,* B.A. August 10, 1883, pp. 253-255.

Julio Llanos. "Amar al vuelo." *La Prensa,* April 22, 1885, p. 3.

Juan A. Piaggio. "Amar al vuelo." *La Nación,* November 5, 1886, p. 3.

Anon. "Enrique Rivarola." *La Nación,* October 28, 1931, p. 7.

Anon. "Enrique Rivarola." *La Prensa,* October 28, 1931, p. 9.

José V. Rocha

Anon. "Un drama de la vida." *El Nacional,* January 14, 1858, p. 2.

Francisco A. Sicardi

Luis Berisso. "Un libro extraño." *La Nación,* June 11, 1898, p. 4.

Emma Napolitano. *Francisco A. Sicardi.* Instituto de Literatura Argentina, Facultad de Filosofía y Letras de la Universidad de Buenos Aires, Sección Crítica, B.A., Imprenta de la Universidad, 1942.

Alberto del Solar

Juan Cancio. "Rastaquouère." *La Nación,* October 29, 1890, p. 4.

Rafael Obligado. "Contra la marea." *La Nación,* November 7, 1894, p. 3.

Anon. "Alberto del Solar." *La Nación,* August 10, 1921, p. 5.

Anon. "Alberto del Solar." *La Prensa,* August 10, 1921, p. 11.

Guillermo Stock

Juan Julián Lastra. *Un escritor de éstos y de otros tiempos—Guillermo Stock.* B.A., 1940.

Anon. "Guillermo Stock." *La Nación,* November 19, 1944, p. 9.

———. *Guillermo Stock—recordado en el primer aniversario de su fallecimiento, por amigos, colegas y ex-alumnos.* B.A., 1945.

Héctor F. Varela

El Lápiz (sic). *Elisa Lynch, por Orion.* B.A., Imprenta de la Discusión, 1870.

Luis V. Varela

Juan Carlos Gómez. "La huella del crimen." A letter to the author, included in novel, B.A., Imprenta de Mayo, 1877, pp. I-VIII.

Aditardo Heredia. "La huella del crimen." Part of introduction to novel, B.A., Imprenta de Mayo, 1877, pp. IX-XV.

José María Vélez

Anon. "José María Vélez." *Caras y Caretas,* B.A., November 20, 1915, p. 49.

Segundo I. Villafañe

Carlos Palma. "Libros y autores—Emilio Love, por Segundo I. Villafañe." *La Patria,* October 15, 1888, p. 4.

Anon. "Segundo I. Villafañe." *La Ilustración Sudamericana,* B.A., November 15, 1901, p. 325.

Anon. "Segundo I. Villafañe." *La Nación,* May 26, 1937, p. 16.
                         Estanislao S. Zeballos
Anon. "Estanislao S. Zeballos." *La Nación,* October 5, 1923, p. 5.

IV. Books and Articles on the Argentine Novel and Argentine Literature
     in General.

AITA, ANTONIO. "Algunos aspectos de la novela argentina." *Nosotros,*
     B.A., April, 1929, LXIV, 5-21.
ARGERICH, ANTONIO. *Naturalismo*—disertación leída en Politeama,
     con motivo de la velada literaria a beneficio de Gervasio Méndez.
     B.A., Imprenta de Ostwald, 1882.
BARREDA, RAFAEL. "La novela en Buenos Aires." *La Patria Argentina,*
     July 31, 1884, p. 3.
BUCICH ESCOBAR, ISMAEL. *Otros tiempos, otros hombres.* B.A., 1932.
DARNET DE FERREYRA, ANA JULIA. *Historia de la literatura americana
     y argentina.* B.A., Ángel Estrada y Cía, 1938.
DUPRAT, LUIS. "La novela." *Artes y Letras,* B.A., February 26, 1893,
     pp. 193-195.
DUPRAT, LUIS. "Nuestra guerra a Zolá." *Artes y Letras,* B.A., July 9,
     1893, pp. 356-357.
ESTRELLA GUTIÉRREZ, FERMÍN. *Panorama sintético de la literatura
     argentina.* Santiago de Chile, Ediciones Ercilla, 1938.
GÁLVEZ, MANUEL. *Amigos y maestros de mi juventud—recuerdos de
     la vida literaria, 1900-1910.* B.A., Editorial Kraft, 1944.
GAMABEL, DR. "La obra y el fin de Zolá." *Artes y Letras,* B.A., July 1,
     1893, pp. 345-348.
GARCÍA, GERMÁN. *La novela argentina.* B.A., Editorial Sudamericana,
     1952.
GARCÍA MEROU, MARTÍN. *Confidencias literarias.* B.A., Imprenta y
     casa editora Argos, 1893.
GARCÍA MEROU, MARTÍN. *Libros y autores; La novela en la Plata; De
     todo un poco; Bosquejos históricos.* B.A., Libraire Générale, 1886.
GARCÍA MEROU, MARTÍN. *Recuerdos literarios.* B.A., La Cultura Ar-
     gentina, 1915.
GARCÍA VELLOSO, ENRIQUE. *Historia de la literatura argentina.* B.A.,
     Ángel Estrada y Cía, 1914.
MACHALI CAZÓN, RAMÓN. *Ensayos críticos y literarios.* Paris, Librería
     Española de Garnier Hermanos, 1889.
MARTÍNEZ, FELIPE. *La literatura argentina desde la conquista hasta
     nuestros días.* B.A., 1905.
MARTÍNEZ, GUSTAVO A. *El naturalismo y Zolá.* Santa Fe, Imprenta de
     J. Benaprés, 1902.
MORALES, ERNESTO. *Literatura argentina.* Editorial Atlántida, 1944.
MOYA, ISMAEL. *Orígenes del teatro y de la novela argentinos,* B.A., 1925.
OBSERVADOR. "Literatos y literaturas—observaciones caprichosas." *Sud-
     América,* August 25, 1886, p. 4.
PAGÉS LARRAYA, ANTONIO. "Buenos Aires en la novela." *Revista de la
     Universidad de Buenos Aires,* B.A., January, 1946, pp. 253-275.
PAGÉS LARRAYA, ANTONIO. "La crisis del noventa en nuestra novela—
     el ciclo de la 'Bolsa.'" *La Nación,* May 4, 1947, Sec. 2, pp. 1-2.

PAGÉS LARRAYA, ANTONIO. "Nuestra crisis de madurez y la novela."
La Nación, March 4, 1945, Sec. 2, p. 1.
PERA, CELESTINO L. "Zolá contra Zolá." *Artes y Letras.* B.A., January
22, 1893, pp. 113-115.
PINTO, JUAN. *Panorama de la literatura argentina contemporánea.* B.A.,
Editorial Mundi, 1941.
QUESADA, ERNESTO. *Reseñas y críticas.* B.A., F. Lajouane, 1893.
RHODE, JORGE MAX. *Las ideas estéticas en la literatura argentina.* B.A.,
Coni, 1921-1926, 4 vols.
ROJAS, RICARDO. *Historia de la literatura argentina.* B.A., Editorial Lo-
sada, 1948, 8 vols.

V. General Reference Works on Argentine History and Culture

BALESTRA, JUAN. *El noventa: una evolución política argentina.* B.A.,
Editorial La Facultad de J. Roldán y Cía, 1935.
COBOS DARACT, JULIO. *Historia argentina.* B.A., *Editorial Virtus,* 1920.
CORBIERE, EMILIO P. *El gaucho, desde su origen hasta nuestros días.*
B.A., L. J. Rosso, 1929.
DÁVALOS, JUAN CARLOS. *Los gauchos.* B.A., Editorial La Facultad de
J. Roldán y Cía, 1928.
GARCÍA MEROU, MARTÍN. *Historia de la República Argentina, 1800-
1870.* B.A., A. Estrada y Cía, 1899, 2 vols.
LEVENE, RICARDO. *Historia de las ideas sociales argentinas,* B.A., Espasa-
Calpe Argentina, 1947.
LEVENE, RICARDO. *Lecciones de historia argentina.* B.A., J. Lajouane
y Cía, 1937, 2 vols.
MENDÍA, JOSÉ M. and NAÓN, L. O. *La revolución del '90.* B.A., Edito-
rial Artes y Letras, 1927.
PELLIZA, MARIANO A. *Historia argentina desde su origen hasta la orga-
nización nacional.* B.A., Lajouane y Cía, 1910.
RIVERO ASTENGO, AGUSTÍN P. *Juárez Celmán: estudio histórico y do-
cumental de una época argentina.* B.A., Kraft, 1944.
ROSSI, VICENTE. *El gaucho: su origen y evolución.* Río de la Plata, Im-
prenta Argentina, 1921.
SOLA, ALFONSO DE. *Un estadista argentino—Nicolás Avellaneda.* Ma-
drid, C. Santos González, 1915.
SOMMI, LUIS V. *La revolución del '90.* B.A., Editorial Monteagudo, 1948.
VEDIA Y MITRE, MARIANO DE. *Roca.* Paris, Cabaut y Cía, 1928.
WALTHER, JUAN CARLOS. *La conquista del desierto: síntesis histórica
de los principales sucesos ocurridos y operaciones militares realizadas
en la Pampa y Patagonia, contra los indios, años 1527-1885.* B.A.,
Biblioteca del Oficial, 1947-1948.

VI. Hispanic-American Literature in General

BARBAGELATA, HUGO D. *La novela y el cuento en Hispanoamérica.*
Montevideo, Librería El Mundo Editorial, 1947.
BERISSO, LUIS. *El pensamiento de América.* B.A., 1898.

BLANCO-FOMBONA, RUFINO. *Grandes escritores de América—siglo XIX.* Madrid, Renacimiento, 1917.

CENTO, I. *La novela hispano-americana.* Santiago de Chile, Editorial Nascimiento, 1934.

COESTER, ALFRED. *The Literary History of Spanish America.* N. Y., The Macmillan Co., 1928.

HENRÍQUEZ-UREÑA, PEDRO. "Apuntaciones sobre la novela en América." *Humanidades,* Publicación de la Facultad de Humanidades y Ciencias de la Educación, Universidad Nacional de la Plata, XV, La Plata, 1927, pp. 133-146.

HENRÍQUEZ-UREÑA, PEDRO. *Literary Currents in Hispanic America.* Cambridge, Mass., Harvard University Press, 1945.

LEGUIZAMÓN, JULIO A. *Historia de la literatura hispanoamericana.* B.A., Editoriales Reunidas, 1945.

LEONARD, IRVING A. *Books of the Brave.* Cambridge, Mass., Harvard University Press, 1949.

SÁNCHEZ, LUIS ALBERTO. *América: novela sin novelistas.* Santiago de Chile, Ediciones Ercilla, 1940.

SÁNCHEZ, LUIS ALBERTO. *Historia de la literatura americana—desde los orígenes hasta nuestros días.* Santiago de Chile, Ediciones Ercilla, 1940.

SAZ, AGUSTÍN DEL. *Resumen de historia de la novela hispanoamericana.* Barcelona, Editorial Atlántida, 1949.

SPELL, JEFFERSON REA. *Contemporary Spanish-American Fiction.* Chapel Hill, University of N. Carolina Press, 1944.

TORRES-RÍOSECO, ARTURO. *La novela en la América Hispana.* University of California Publications in Modern Philology, Vol. 21, No. 2, Berkeley, California, 1941, pp. 159-256.